The Second World War
Tank Crisis

The Second World War Tank Crisis

The Fall and Rise of British Armour, 1919–1945

Dick Taylor

Pen & Sword
MILITARY

First published in Great Britain in 2021 by
Pen & Sword Military
An imprint of
Pen & Sword Books Ltd
Yorkshire – Philadelphia

ISBN 978 1 39900 352 0

Typeset by Mac Style
Printed and bound by CPI Group (UK) Ltd, Croydon CR0 4YY

Pen & Sword Books Limited incorporates the imprints of Atlas,
Archaeology, Aviation, Discovery, Family History, Fiction, History,
Maritime, Military, Military Classics, Politics, Select, Transport,
True Crime, Air World, Frontline Publishing, Leo Cooper, Remember
When, Seaforth Publishing, The Praetorian Press, Wharncliffe
Local History, Wharncliffe Transport, Wharncliffe True Crime
and White Owl.

For a complete list of Pen & Sword titles please contact

PEN & SWORD BOOKS LIMITED
47 Church Street, Barnsley, South Yorkshire, S70 2AS, England
E-mail: enquiries@pen-and-sword.co.uk
Website: www.pen-and-sword.co.uk

Or

PEN AND SWORD BOOKS
1950 Lawrence Rd, Havertown, PA 19083, USA
E-mail: Uspen-and-sword@casematepublishers.com
Website: www.penandswordbooks.com

Contents

Foreword		vi
Introduction		viii
Chapter 1	What is a Tank for?	1
Chapter 2	A Peculiar Genius – Tank Design and Development in Britain 1919–1936	16
Chapter 3	Learning to Crawl: Rearmament and Reorganisation	29
Chapter 4	British Tanks Between the Wars	75
Chapter 5	Fourth Best? The Crisis of the Early War Years	103
Chapter 6	The Tanks of the Early War Years	129
Chapter 7	Playing Catch-up 1942–1943	150
Chapter 8	The Late War Tanks	175
Chapter 9	Lessons Finally Learned? 1944–1945	190
Conclusion		208
Appendix		213
Abbreviations		218
Notes		220
Bibliography		234
Index		240

Foreword

One of the benefits of working in an archive, such as the Tank Museum's, is the enjoyment of coming across material and photographs which have rarely or never seen the light of day. But however much I enjoy that moment, the real pride for me is in knowing when we have assisted a historian or researcher with finding that crucial link, a little bit of information that helps them publish or further their research. That is why assisting historians like Dick Taylor with research into archive material to use in his latest book is always a joy, as he is able to contextualise it, make it relevant, and of course accessible to a far wider audience than it has sitting safely cared for in a dusty box down here in Bovington.

The Archive has certainly expanded since 2000 when I started as an enthusiastic, albeit naive, volunteer while studying War Studies at King's College. The days of using paperclips attached to catalogue cards on the documents thankfully are long gone, but the ethos of the Archive hasn't changed: we are here to catalogue and care for the collection, to accept relevant donations, and, most importantly, to allow users access to this collection.

And what a collection it is. Put simply, the Tank Museum houses the largest collection of material related to the development of British armoured warfare in the world, as well as material relating to many other nations. It encompasses material relevant to the Royal Tank Regiment and its predecessors, as well as the wider Royal Armoured Corps, and contains material from War Diaries and operational reports to the individual diaries and accounts of veterans. It holds technical data from repair and user manuals and illustrated spare parts lists, to Second World War Contract Cards listing the numbers of AFVs built, when and by whom, and even 900,000 microfiche aperture cards containing all the postwar FV drawings for British AFVs.

New material arrives regularly, be it a photo album on the building of the one-off Contentious project, or a whole series of documents released by the MoD on the development of British armour from the 1970s to 1990. To this end, a lot of the Archive's staff resources are focused purely on the accurate cataloguing of this material for use in the Museum's Collections database, because if you don't know what you have in your collection, or where it is, then you can't make it accessible to future historians and researchers.

But it is important for the reader to realise that this is not a one-way street. An archive can act as a catalyst to kick-start your research. To get the most out of this or indeed any other archive or collection, it's important that the researcher can give the archivist as much information and insight into what they are looking to research as they can. If you can explain your research topic and what it is you are specifically looking for to a knowledgeable archivist, then they can help able identify other areas of the collection which may be relevant to your study which may not have been apparent in your initial enquiry. Remember: you know your topic of study; the archivist should know what they have in their collection, and where you may find that hidden fact or quote which may make your day. Dick Taylor made best use of the archive here in researching this book, and we are delighted to have helped him in his task. We can now see the product of many hours of diligent research come to fruition in the form of a key study into an under-researched area of armoured history that will take its rightful place as part of our archive.

Stuart Wheeler
Archive Manager
Bovington Tank Museum

Introduction

'Our own tanks were unequal to the job because they were not good enough. There may be various ways of dodging this plain truth but anyone who wishes to do so will find himself arguing with the crews... one can only hope that sooner or later the scandal of British tank manufacture will come out.'
Alan Moorehead *Desert Trilogy*

'British tanks until late in the war were mechanical abortions.'
Corelli Barnett *The Audit of War*

'Tank crews were murdered because they were sent into battle so ill-prepared.'
Peter Beale *Death by Design*

Strong words. The history and performance of British tanks in the Second World War has brought forth accusations that remind one of the allegations of incompetence and sheer bloody murder often raised against some generals of the First World War. Indeed, it is difficult to bring to mind any other aspect of British weapon performance during the Second World War that excites such levels of emotion and sense of failure. Unfortunately, many of the accusations appear at first sight to be true: British tanks were in many ways a disgrace as they were almost always technologically behind the larger and more powerful tanks produced by the Germans. This was particularly true in the critical period from 1940 until 1944, when the Germans were able to produce tanks that were both better armed and armoured. It is therefore difficult to avoid the conclusion that many of the British army failures in the desert campaign or indeed in Italy and Normandy were directly due to inferior tanks. However, behind the facts are causes, and history is about disassembling the reasons and choices and decisions, and not just the presentation of facts. This work is not an apology for the manifest failings of Britain to produce workmanlike tanks for its crews during the Second World War; rather, it seeks to examine the reasons why Great Britain, the country that invented the tank, was consistently unable to field fighting tanks in either quality or quantity throughout the Second World War. It will concentrate on one specific aspect of the failure, that of production, which of course is linked to the design and development aspects of such projects, but in passing of course other topics will need to be commented on. These include finance, doctrine, organisation, and technological advances, not to mention the changing needs of the users.

An enormous amount of literature has already been published alleging that during the Second World War there was what amounted to a 'Great British Tank Scandal', a provocative title deliberately chosen for his examination of the subject by Britain's foremost armour historian, David Fletcher. That British tanks were often less capable in many respects than their usual opponents, the Germans, is eminently provable, but there is also little doubt that this has been taken to extremes at times. The received wisdom currently is that all aspects of British tank doctrine, design, production, development and use throughout the whole of the war years were equally faulty, often with fatal consequences for the crews who were sent to fight and to be 'murdered' in appalling tanks that amounted to nothing less than 'mechanical abortions'. One commentator has asked that the 'guilty men' be named, implying that not only were the failures avoidable, but also that those responsible were criminally negligent. The topic has thus taken on the status of a myth, and like all myths should not be taken at face value but should be questioned and analysed. Unfortunately, although much has been written about the performance of British tanks in the field, with an increasing body of work looking at allied topics such as doctrine, training and organisation, very little has been published about their design and development, and less still about the companies which built them. This lack of material is particularly noticeable when compared to the production of RAF aircraft, the story of which is told in depth in many volumes.

Four main factors contributed to the success – or otherwise – of British tanks. These were, firstly, the organisation and doctrine (both governmental and military) behind the specification and use of tanks. Next was the human element, which includes such topics as the selection of crews, low-level tactics, training and morale, and performance in battle. This second factor will not be mentioned here other than to discuss some of the maintenance aspects related to the way in which the tanks were designed and built, but the former will require comment as it is necessary to explain how many decisions were driven by overarching government or military policy, often dating back to the end of the First World War or the 1920s. The third factor is the dichotomy of quality versus quantity – not only of the equipment itself, but also whether these subjects were given the correct relative priority. This is a major thrust of this work. The last factor is one which was outside the control of the designers, generals, and politicians – the strength of the opposition. Although they could not control this factor, they could certainly take it into account, and whether or not this happened will need to be investigated.

As accusations alleging it abound, how should we define 'failure'? Some comparisons and benchmarking with other production experiences will be necessary; in order to do this, two areas will be examined. The German experience will be assessed, particularly in terms of technological comparisons. Secondly it will be pertinent to look at how aircraft were built for the RAF, as there was a great deal of competition for scarce resources within the UK and the RAF had a lot of support and momentum on its side – in some ways this became more of an enemy to British tank production than anything the Germans were doing, and certainly was more important than, for example, the effects of the Blitz. Historical study demands comparisons to be made, and the choice of Germany for a comparison of production experiences (rather than the usual comparison with the USA) is valid for three reasons. Firstly, we can look at the German tanks that the British tanks fought against and investigate whether the German tanks were really of a better quality as is so often alleged. Secondly, were their tank production methods similar to those used in Britain, and did Germany suffer from any similar deficiencies in the approach to mass production? Lastly, of course, the timescales of rearmament were similar. Across the Atlantic, the US determination to massively increase their neglected armoured force was in many ways akin to Britain's experience, in that in the minds of the senior generals tanks went almost overnight from being viewed as a 'pretty mechanical toy' to *the* land weapon of decision. The US tanks, the M4 Sherman in particular, also built up a reputation for reliability that has been much discussed in other works, as it was this reputation that all British-made tanks were judged against. As will be seen, this reputation was not entirely well-founded, and certainly when the Cromwell was eventually fielded in 1944 it had the beating of just about every other tank in western Europe in terms of mechanical reliability, including the Sherman – nor did it readily catch fire, a major failing of the US tank. The only other nation whose tank-building programme was comparable in the period in terms of scale was the Soviet Union, and for a number of reasons the USSR will not be included here. Among these are: the direct attacks on Russian tank building facilities from both ground and air; the large-scale relocation of Soviet tank factories to the east; the fact that all Soviet tanks were made in state-owned facilities; and the entirely different labour situation.

Contrasts and comparisons will be made with the production of aircraft for the RAF. This approach will allow us to largely remove those differences caused by national characteristics and economic conditions, workers' attitudes and skills, and by such wartime events as the Blitz, and will highlight the completely different attitude to aircraft rearmament that prevailed in the 1930s, as well as the access to scarce raw materials, manufacturing firms, component makers, machine tools, designers, and of course skilled labour. Finally, we should also seek to identify any apparently missed opportunities, whether these were considered and discounted at the time – and also therefore why this happened – as well as those that are more apparent only with the benefit of hindsight.

It is refreshing to be able to report that the true extent of alleged tactical and operational failings has already begun to be questioned and revised, including by John Buckley in his excellent work *British Armour in the Normandy Campaign 1944*, in which he argues that while certain aspects of British tank use were poor, particularly in the area of inadequate main armament, in many other respects the 'tank gap' was less obvious. He argues that by late 1944 the British tanks were in many ways superior to the German and US equivalents, and that the much-trumpeted German technical superiority was in itself something of a myth. Montgomery was famously able to posit that had 'von Rundstedt had been equipped with British armour when he attacked in the Ardennes on 16th December 1944, he would have reached the Meuse in thirty-six hours' – but alternatively, had Britain been equipped with German Tigers and Panthers, the breakout from Normandy could not have happened.[1]

This work will therefore continue the revisionist theme by concentrating on the two related subjects of British tank design and development, and more particularly, it will unashamedly focus on the under-researched theme of tank production, in order to identify those areas which contributed to any failure, and explain why this happened. It will not be possible to look at the more esoteric projects, variants, trials, cancelled experimental tanks and the like, but will concentrate solely on the story of the mainstream gun tanks that went into service and which all too often let their crews down. The related but often opposing issues of quantity versus quality will thus be a constant thread throughout.

It may surprise many to discover that until the middle of 1940 British tanks were in many respects at least the equal of anything that the Germans were producing; that the barren period was from late 1940 until summer 1944; and that by the last year of the war British designs were once more in the ascendancy, finally producing one of the most balanced and reliable tank designs to see active service during the war (the Comet), and then the best main battle tank anywhere in the world for the next two decades (the Centurion). This work therefore will question the true extent of the apparent 'failure', as well as attempting to explain the reasons for it. It is an explanation, not an apology.

Chapter 1

What is a Tank for?

The difficulty about the tank has really been to make up our minds exactly what we want.

Admiral Sir Harold Brown,
Director General Munitions Production, 1939

These were the years when ideas were two a penny [but] when no-one had enough experience to make up his mind as to the possibilities of this weapon…
Brigadier G. Macleod Ross

The role of the tank

It is important to understand the methods and terms employed in Britain to classify the different types of tanks, otherwise many of the documents used, and indeed the decisions made, will remain unclear. The name 'tank' was originally coined as a cover-name to preserve the secrecy of a new weapon and became the accepted terminology in most nations of the world. When, in 1918, the British introduced a faster and lighter machine than the previous types then in service, it was designated as a Medium Tank, the existing designs becoming Heavy Tanks by default. It should be noted that such terms referred purely to the weight of the tank and were not in any way descriptive of the role it was expected to perform. In the early 1920s the use of the term Light Tank came into vogue, and referred to tanks of around 10 tons and under, with Medium Tanks being those above 10 tons.[1] In the absence of any other direction the Medium Tank of the 1920s and 1930s was considered to be what these days would be called a Battle Tank, designed to fulfill the two main purposes of a tank: supporting one's own infantry and the destruction of enemy armour. Light Tanks were to be used for reconnaissance and scouting, and also played an important role in training.[2]

By 1934 the army had decided that it needed three different types of tanks, each with distinct roles, and for the first time a classification system attempted to define the role, rather than just the weight, of the equipment.

The Light Tank was useful for policing the Empire, where its small size and relatively weak armour and armament would not prevent it from intimidating recalcitrant tribesmen. From around 1937 the Light Tank also became the equipment of the newly mechanised cavalry regiments, allowing them (on paper at least) to conduct something similar to their traditional roles of scouting and reconnaissance. They were never meant to come into direct contact with enemy tanks or indeed anti-tank weapons; they were to rely on speed and concealment to avoid confrontation. How this was to be guaranteed was never clarified, because it was impossible to do so. Light Tanks had two great benefits for politicians; they were cheap to build, and therefore they could be produced in sufficient numbers to perpetuate the myth that Britain was maintaining a substantial tank force, and the country could trumpet both in parliament and in the press that it possessed hundreds of tanks. For the first and by no means the last time, quantity would out-trump quality.

The term 'tankette' was coined to describe a particular sub-division of such machines. Smaller even than Light Tanks, tankettes were low and small and could carry a machine-gun within a lightly armoured shell. Generally, they had a two or even a one-man crew, and were designed to be used by the infantry. Martel, the Assistant Director of Mechanisation, was involved on a personal level with Light Tank and tankette design from the 1920s onwards and alleged that such small machines could be made for £500, whereas a Medium typically cost £8,000. His claim was later proved false, but the assertion stuck.[3] When in the mid-1930s it became clear that a new tank was urgently required to replace the outdated Medium IIs: 'the task of Brough [Director of Mechanisation] and Hobart [Inspector of the Royal Tank Corps] was doubly hampered by continuing the Coalition government's financial stringency and in addition by the appeal of cheapness inherent in the tankette.'[4] Tankettes never saw action, as they were never seriously considered for mass production when army rearmament started seriously in the late 1930s. However, they were useful for some development work, both technical and doctrinal, and, most importantly, led to the development of the infantry tracked carriers used in the Second World War, the Bren, Scout, and Universal carriers and their many derivatives.

From about 1927 the term 'Infantry Tank' had started to be used in Britain to describe the 'smallest cheapest and most compact machine which will transport one man over almost any ground and provide protection...'[5] The key word was *cheapest*, a word which would bedevil and hinder development for at least the next ten years. The quotation also indicates an attitude which was quite common, that small vehicles, manned by one or two men, were the future. This philosophy of cheapness and compactness was to lead to the later development of the first purpose-built infantry tank, the well-armoured but woefully under-gunned A11. In this sense, the term really meant 'a tank for the infantry', rather than 'a tank to support the infantry'. This was about to change.

By 1934 the term Infantry Tank (or I-Tank) was being used to describe the armoured weapon of break-in, a true tank designed for one task – to support the infantry and to allow them to break-in (as opposed to breakout) of a defended position. Its origins were buried deep in the experiences of the First World War. The I-Tank concept appealed to the more reactionary elements in the army; not only was it cheap, but it was there simply to support the infantry, who remained the arm of decision. It did not appear to contain any of the scary undertones of a desire to form an armoured army that would threaten the existence of the two traditional fighting arms, the infantry and the cavalry, as well as to some degree the artillery. For those whose ideas about the next conflict were rooted in the previous one, the idea of such a design had an appeal, and this was to be reinforced during the so-called Phoney War of 1939–40, when it appeared that trench warfare might once again be a real possibility. The attributes of an Infantry Tank were: thick armour, to make it impervious to attack by anti-tank guns/rifles or field artillery; slow speed, as all it had to do was accompany the infantry at a (at most) slow running pace; and to carry a weapon capable of providing fire support – to many this meant the machine-gun, making the I-Tank little more than a mobile MG pillbox. And if this was the limit of its role, then cheap and unsophisticated would surely suffice?

The final category, which appeared around 1934, was the Cruiser Tank, the term replacing the ambiguous Medium Tank, which was to be the weapon of exploitation. It was meant to equip the regiments in the newly created 'Mobile' Division, later to be renamed the Armoured Division. Once the infantry, supported by the I-Tanks, had penetrated the enemy main defensive line, the Cruisers would charge through the gap or preferably, avoid the enemy main defensive positions and move around the flanks, destroying enemy reserves and headquarters and pursuing the demoralised and retreating enemy until they surrendered. Therefore, the Cruiser did not require thick armour, as it would only be confronting the enemy where it was already weak. Initially the armour requirement was a paltry 14mm, and the subsequent and ever-increasing requirement for more armour was to prove to be awkward, as more armour added weight, reducing speed and range, and putting additional stress on the engine and suspension. The Cruiser did require a high turn of speed and a reasonable range, rather like the naval ships that it took its name from. Tragically, no one took this naval analogy to its logical conclusion by asking the question: 'What will happen if the Cruiser encounters the tank equivalent of a battleship, better armoured and better gunned?' This is exactly what happened. Even as the first Cruisers were being designed, the Germans were building well-armoured and armed tanks which were roughly the same standard as the British equivalents, but crucially were able to be both up-armoured and up-gunned with little difficulty, enabling a qualitative lead to be gained and then maintained.[6] They were also committing to equipping their infantry with a small anti-tank gun. Only 37mm in calibre, it could nevertheless easily penetrate 14mm and more.

In the course of the war, the British would slowly come to the realisation that this doctrine was badly flawed, and a single general-purpose tank capable of fulfilling all battlefield tasks was required. They did not manage this until 1945, when the Universal (sometimes referred to as the Capital) tank was fielded in the shape of the Centurion, and even then, it was initially thought of as a heavy cruiser. It is worthy of note that Britain was the only nation in the world that defined tank roles and thus designs in this way, and this policy was adhered to despite many indications of its flaws, only being grudgingly abandoned in 1944.

The British system of tank classification

When a specification was issued by the General Staff for development of a new tank, a serial number prefixed by the letter 'A' was issued; for example, the Crusader Cruiser tank began life as GS specification A15. Occasionally a suffix was added to the designation for clarity; for example, the A27L was the Liberty-engined Centaur, whereas the A27M was the similar but Meteor-engined Cromwell. Tanks designed privately, for example the Vickers Valentine, received no 'A' number, even when subsequently accepted into service.[7] When production tanks were developed into a significantly different model, a new 'Mark' number was issued; during the period we are concerned with, this was always designated using Roman numerals – e.g. Churchill Mk VII. The mark system is an important indication of technological development, as it generally gives a good overall sense of the improvements made to each type of tank. During their life, some tanks ran to many marks; the Crusader only had three, whereas the Cromwell went to eight, and the Valentine to eleven. Although designed to add clarity, the changing of production contracts from one mark to another, sometimes in mid-run, is a cause of much confusion for the researcher, as will be explored later.

British tanks were never officially named before the Second World War. Some nicknames had been used, but never in an official capacity; rather, they were allocated a soulless designation, such as Cruiser Tank Mk 1. The use of the name Matilda for the Infantry Tanks A11 and A12 was initially unofficial, but from around October 1941 with the introduction of the Churchill, and at the insistence of the Prime Minister who gave his name to the tank, it became commonplace to officially name tanks, with cruisers always starting with C, and in the process creating a tradition that lasts to this day.[8] As an example, the tank designated initially as the A13 Mk III could also be known as the Cruiser Tank Mk V, or by its name, Covenanter. It ran to five marks; thus, we can find a designation such as: A13 Mk III Cruiser Tank Mk V Covenanter Mk IV! Any given tank could thus have multiple designations, and primary source files often take a degree of deciphering to clarify exactly which tank is being discussed. It is clear that this confusion existed even during the war, as some contemporary documents often make no sense due to misunderstanding on the part of the authors. For example, the Infantry Tank Mk IV Churchill was erroneously listed by some as a heavy cruiser, a terrible designation that confused weight and role, and the confusion caused by the outwardly similar Cavalier, Centaur and Cromwell types was legendary. In some cases, particularly with the Valentine, I-Tanks used as cruisers (due to lack of the latter) were accounted for as cruisers, not as infantry tanks, which causes difficulties when trying to put an accurate figure on tank production. And added to that could be post-production modifications: re-engined Centaurs might or might not be renamed Cromwells, and a huge programme of updating and reworking played havoc with the Churchill fleet, some tanks being up-marked twice and then converted into a specialised role. Although the production cards for the vast majority of tanks and other Armoured Fighting Vehicles (AFVs) exist in the archive of the Bovington Tank Museum, they have been subject to many confusing manuscript amendments making the task of interpretation very difficult. The result must always be therefore in the eyes of the researcher. Every effort has been made to resolve one question that still remains unanswered: how many tanks, of which type – and mark – did Britain produce immediately before and during the Second World War? Feel free to disagree – but only after you have conducted your own primary research!

The three primary characteristics

It must be understood that to design a tank a balance needs to be struck between three primary characteristics: firepower, mobility and armoured protection. No tank can achieve perfection in all three areas, so the design is always a compromise, and reflects the relative importance of each of the components. Thus, the specification for a new tank is critical, and should be a clear guide for the designer. The specification must be written in such a way that the designer understands the constraints – the things the machine must do – placed upon him. Thus, the specification can help or hinder the designer. It is necessary to understand these three prime characteristics in some detail, as this knowledge will be necessary when assessing certain decisions taken.

Firepower

The supremacy that the machine-gun gained during the First World War was embedded deeply in the military mind, and there was a body of opinion that suggested that tanks should either be armed only with machine-guns, or at least should have a large number of the weapons in addition to the main cannon.[9] It was considered that as the tank was primarily an infantry support weapon it would not usually be required to fight enemy tanks and therefore this combination of weapons would suffice. Experimental designs between the wars fairly bristled with machine-guns pointing out in all directions. This feature was endorsed by both Charles Broad and George Lindsay, two of the leading RTC modernisers in the 1920s, and who, as successive Chief Instructors at the Tank Corps Central Schools in Bovington, were partly responsible for developing the tactics and techniques required by the Corps, particularly regarding gunnery. Their opinions and decisions would have a large impact on the future purpose and thus design of tanks. They confirmed the (later proved to be erroneous) convictions that firing on the move was the most important technique, and that machine-guns alone could deal with the new and growing menace of anti-tank guns.[10] Broad wrote that machine-guns were to be mounted 'primarily for keeping down hostile anti-tank fire, and enabling tanks to close with the least loss.'[11] During the First World War, the majority of tanks had been destroyed by normal German artillery guns firing at static tanks at relatively short ranges, and which had experienced great difficulty in hitting even very slow-moving tanks. Between the wars, as armour carried by tanks was still relatively thin, many nations chose to build their anti-tank defence policy based on this method, backed up with purpose-built but small calibre anti-tank rifles carried by the infantry. The introduction of small anti-tank guns for use by the infantry only really started to come into vogue following the Spanish Civil War that started in 1936, and therefore was still a relatively new concept when the Second World War broke out.

If a gun was to be fitted to a tank, then it was believed that rather than going to the expense and trouble of building a bespoke model just for use on tanks, as artillery pieces were capable of destroying tanks, it should be based on or preferably identical to an existing design; in the British system, all gun design was the responsibility of the Royal Artillery (RA). The 57mm 6-pounder guns used on the Male tanks in the First World War were never officially supplied by the army and were taken from surplus naval stocks, so beginning a practice of using what could be made available on tanks rather than what was required. The RA experimented with specialised anti-tank rifles and guns of small calibre during the 1920s, the calibre required being determined by the size of the armour plate likely to be faced, which it was believed would never exceed 20mm; many vehicles of the time used just 8mm. Budgetary considerations restricted what could be achieved. The Vickers medium tanks which were the standard RTC equipment of the 1920s and 1930s mounted a low-velocity dual-purpose 3-pounder gun, capable of firing both HE (high explosive) and solid-shot AP. Just prior to the outbreak of hostilities a new 2-pounder gun became the main weapon mounted in both Cruiser and Infantry tanks, the same weapon also coming into service as the first British wheeled anti-tank gun built specifically for that purpose. The lack of an HE shell for the 2-pounder created a critical capability shortfall that was not realised at the time, but which would later lead to the deaths of many tank crews, unable to deal with well-emplaced German anti-tank guns.

Armour protection

A tank is a tank largely because it is armoured, and the amount of armour to be carried and the method of joining the plates became serious issues in Britain from the rearmament period onwards. This requires some explanation. Until late in the 1930s, the prime reason for armouring tanks was mainly to provide protection from machine-gun bullets, shell fragments, and from anti-tank rifle bullets, and *not* from high-velocity anti-tank gun shells. The experience of the First World War had shown that a tank could be easily knocked out by normal artillery guns achieving a direct hit with an HE shell, and until both tank mobility and armour protection were improved massively, this method remained sufficient. It was not until the late 1930s that the new threat of specialist anti-tank guns of 20mm to 40mm calibre became a reality. This meant that the type and quality of armour and also the quantity – thickness – required would both become important issues, as well as how best to use this armour to construct the vehicle.

As already noted, in the early interwar period armour was relatively thin. For example, the Mk V, the tank that the British ended the First World War with, used a maximum of 12mm of armour, while the Medium II of a decade later had less, a paltry 8mm. The very successful German Panzer Mk IV started life in 1935 with only 30mm and its stablemate, the Panzer Mk III, had the same amount on the front only, with as little as 20mm at the rear and only 16mm covering the engine decks and the belly. The more numerous light Panzer II only mounted between 5mm and 15mm of armour, and the many Skoda tanks that the Germans had captured following the occupation of Czechoslovakia again used 30mm as a standard. The French alone tended to mount thick armour as a matter of course, in some cases as much as 60mm, as they considered tanks to be purely for infantry support and therefore requiring good protection – akin to the policy adopted with the British Infantry tank.[12]

As soon as it became clear that the power of anti-tank weapons was on the increase – the race between offensive firepower and defensive armament is a constant theme in the evolution of the tank even to this day – it became equally obvious that unless tanks could mount more armour, they could quickly become irrelevant. Indeed, some influential generals thought they already were: General Hugh Elles had led the embryonic tank units in the First World War with great effect, but by the time of his appointment in 1934 as Master General of the Ordnance (MGO), and so responsible for weapon design, he believed the increasing power of the anti-tank gun had rendered the tank obsolete.[13] British doctrine on the amount of armour carried by tanks had to change, as Hancock noted:

> The 8mm of armoured protection which had been accepted in the interwar period was abandoned: 14mm was regarded as essential as early as 1935; soon 30mm was a minimum standard for Cruisers and 60mm for Infantry tanks. These steps… produced immediate dilemmas in speed and manouverability. By 1938 it was reported that the Germans were maintaining these qualities as primary in AFVs, the French had concentrated on defensive armour [and] 'all their machines can be classed as infantry tanks.[14]

The different strategical assessments made by Germany and France can be seen by this prioritisation, whereas the British way just represented muddled thinking. In any case, a League of Nations convention limited tank weight to 16 tons and the then-current Royal Engineers bridging equipment had an even lower maximum weight.[15] Armour weight did later become an issue when calls came to speed I-Tanks up, once the realisation had dawned that walking pace was too slow, preventing them being used in other roles and making them easy targets. Bigger engines were needed.

Mobility – engines

Probably the greatest failing of foresight in the area of tank mobility was the lack of realisation that tanks would, as they became heavier, require purpose-built engines. This was to handicap performance until 1943 and only then was the situation improved by the adoption of a modified aero engine. While tanks remained light in weight, with only rudimentary suspensions, and only needing to travel at a few miles per hour, the lack of power was not much of an issue. But as they became heavier, and efficient suspensions were developed, demands for greater speed and manoeuverability were voiced. It was widely assumed that modified commercial engines would always be able to be adapted to power tanks, but this proved to be a fallacy.

In many cases, the engines used lacked raw power or were unnecessarily complicated, or both. In 1941 the *minimum* acceptable power to weight ratio was set as 15bhp per ton, but this was often not achieved, and certainly not before 1943.[16] In order to keep costs down, the engine used on the A11 Infantry tank Mk I was a commercial Ford of 70hp; although this was a simple engine to maintain and parts were readily available, the power to weight ratio was a mere 6bhp per ton. The larger A12 Matilda II Infantry tank was powered by a pair of engines linked by a complicated gear arrangement, which was the only way to get sufficient horsepower into the limited space in the engine compartment. Power to weight ratio was still only in the area of 7bhp per ton. The design was a complete compromise, and this showed in the performance and the difficult maintenance – the only positive aspect was that if one engine failed, the tank might just be able to limp back to safety on the other.[17] Fitting engines of limited power incapable of further development was frequent – the old and notoriously unreliable 340bhp Liberty aero-engine chosen for the A15 Crusader only produced 17bhp per ton for a tank that was meant to derive protection from a high top speed, and which hindered attempts at up-gunning and up-armouring.[18] The Liberty also featured a horrendous design feature as it used exposed valves which were wrecked by desert sand, the environment in which most British tank battles were fought from June 1940 until May 1943.

Worse could happen, including choosing inappropriate engine makers. When the A22 Churchill was specified, the Tank Board:

> gave the overall dimensions of the space into which the new engine could be accommodated with the order to design a petrol engine to develop at least 350 bhp at 4200 rpm. Unbelievably, the contract was given to a firm who had [never] produced an engine larger than 27bhp.[19]

Often, the reasons for such decisions were to be found at the earliest stages of design. For one thing, costs had to be kept down and no one would sanction spending money on research and development of such an engine, which would only be used in, at most, a few hundred or at best a few thousand machines. Martel, very much a cruiser tank enthusiast, wrote privately to Basil Liddell Hart in July 1937 to complain, and put his finger on part of the problem:

> We are in a proper mess. Six years ago, we had the best medium tank in the world – the 16 tonner... but General Brough [Director of Mechanisation] swung the policy round to small commercial engines and cheaper medium tanks. As a result, we got all duds... we have to go into production now on an indifferent machine...[20]

He was referring to the A9. However, in most cases the GS specifications issued by the War Office would tell the designer which engine to use, his hands were tied, and blame cannot be attached to a design team which simply did what it was told to do. And almost without exception, the engine selected for the specification was already at its limit in terms of power-to-weight ratio for the projected total weight of the tank. As a design matured, both in development and in service, additional weight was invariably added, in terms of more armour, additional equipment, extra ammunition, fuel and so on, and this only made the situation worse. A clear-headed review would have indicated that the only efficient way to build engines for tanks was to build tank engines, but the option was never taken.

To some – probably many – officers the real purpose of the engine was to make the tank able to move faster, and in the pre-war period, as potential speeds increased, there developed something of an obsession with speed. But, as Wavell noted: 'Speed is, unfortunately, a most expensive commodity: alike in battleships, motor cars, racehorses and women; any comparatively small increase may double the price of the article.'[21] He was right, and the obsession with top speed was to surface particularly with the concept of the Cruiser tank. What should have been specified was good overall cross-country mobility, including rapid acceleration; this was the one attribute that would most assist a tank crew getting out of a tight spot, but this was not realised until well after the war.

Mobility – suspension and tracks

As noted, mobility in a tank is more than just the top speed and the size of engine. As speeds increased, the crews tended to be thrown about, which was both tiring for them and also potentially injurious. They required a more comfortable ride, and as RTC doctrine taught that firing was to be done on the move, a stable platform was necessary. This led to the need for efficient suspension systems, able to absorb the typical shocks suffered when the tank was moving cross-country at 'battle' speed. The majority of such systems comprised externally mounted units bearing one or more road wheels, with some form of springing. The great advantage of externally mounted units was that they could be easily changed in the field if they became damaged. Many of the suspension systems used in the Infantry tanks, as well as in the A9 and A10 Cruisers, were off-the-shelf designs either from the talented hand of Sir John Carden at Vickers-Armstrong, or from the specialist Slow-Motion Company, but these were not well suited to a fast and comfortable ride that allowed guns to be fired accurately on the move; at speed the A9 bounced like 'a rubber ball'. There was a pressing need to find a better system for use on the cruiser family, and this will be explored later.

Secondary characteristics

Beyond the three primary attributes of firepower, protection and mobility, there are also other secondary characteristics of tanks, which are of great importance to the builder and even more so to the user, but to which scant attention was often paid during the war. These include:

• Produceability: designing the tank and its sub-systems for rapid mass-production using available materials, plant and manpower,[22] and also building in the ability to make specification changes and improvements during the run without affecting production.

- Reliability: the ability of the tank to keep going under genuine service conditions when maintenance would be limited or nil for long periods.
- Maintainability: the ease of maintenance for the crew in the field and maintenance fitters in forward workshops, which if neglected impacts upon reliability.
- Longevity: having a reasonable service life before requiring major repair or becoming obsolete, and incorporating the stretch potential for mounting improved weapons, armour or automotive systems, including the ability to be updated in the field.
- Ergonomics: how well the machine is designed with the user in mind and which allows it to be efficiently operated. This much-neglected aspect leads to tired crews who perform badly in battle and make poor decisions. As well as comfort, ergonomics include well-designed controls, safety features, low noise levels and adequate ventilation and heating or cooling.

The recipe for a perfectly balanced tank will blend all these factors in an efficient way in order to produce a tank that meets the specification, is made quickly and cheaply, is loved by its crews because it protects them and always starts first time, and is able to deliver the effects desired upon the enemy. As soon as one or more of these elements starts to go out of kilter, the tank will become less efficient, and if too many fail, the tank will be ineffective. Unfortunately, that is exactly what happened to some degree with almost every British tank produced between 1934 and 1943. Even pre-war these failings were well known and identified by the professionals – it did not take a war to reveal them. Colonel Tilly was a senior officer in the RTC and pronounced on the debut of the brand-new A9 Cruiser and following its early trials at the hands of real tank crewmen: 'It's a dud. Too small for cross-country work, the crew are too cramped to work their weapons or wireless; it bounces like a rubber ball; the tracks come off.'[23]

Other design considerations

Beyond these characteristics, there is another area that must be investigated in order to understand the constraints that designers worked within, and which was to become a huge handicap to the development of battleworthy tanks. That was the railway loading gauge.

It was an article of faith that all British tanks had to be able to be transported on railway wagons, or flats, throughout the UK rail network. When the network had been built in the nineteenth century, thousands of tunnels, cuttings and the like had been built, and a method was needed in order to allow the safe passage of trains and wagons without any danger of hitting them, as well as when passing other trains on double lines. To allow the safe loading of wagons, a rail loading gauge diagram was produced which specified the maximum dimensions of the cargo – which included tanks loaded onto flats. The British gauge has been labelled as the most restrictive in the world, as many of the tunnels were built before standardisation could be agreed, and therefore the gauge reflects the narrowest of the tunnels – even though they may be in places where tanks are unlikely ever to be transported. However, the inclusion of the most restrictive gauge became an *auto da fe* of the War Office, and it was included in almost all GS specifications for new equipment, including all tanks.[24] The application of the gauge is quite complicated, but in broad terms this meant a space envelope of about 9ft wide by just over 10ft high.

The effect of this was to impose a maximum width limit on the design of tanks, which could not, under any circumstances, be exceeded. This had two negative effects. Firstly, there is a relationship between the width of a tracked vehicle and the length of the track on the ground. This is known as the L/C ratio, where L is the length of track on the ground, and C the distance between the track centres. Ideally, this should be about 1.6 (length) to 1 (width). If the ratio is exceeded in either direction, problems with steering will follow. Therefore, if the ratio is less than the ideal – e.g. the tank takes on a squarish form – the tank will want to continue in a straight line and will be difficult to turn. If, however, it is too long, the tank will want to continually steer itself and the driver will have to make constant adjustments, meaning precision steering will be extremely difficult. The length of track on the ground also determines the overall length of the vehicle, which ideally should not be more than about half as much again as the L figure. Thus it can be seen that, by imposing a maximum width on the tank designers, other dimensions are also fixed or at least controlled. The size of British tanks was thus fixed to a maximum. This, combined with the amounts of armour specified to be carried and frequently the engine type noted in the specification document, made British tanks small and cramped, not good for ergonomic reasons. However, there was a bigger problem than this.

By limiting the width of the tank, the diameter of the turret ring in which the turret revolved was also limited to a maximum. Because British tanks were almost invariably designed with the hull as a simple box structure, and did not project sideways over the tracks, the overall diameter of the turret ring was thus made smaller than it might have been. Had either the loading gauge been disregarded (meaning that routing tanks around the country would take a little more effort in order to avoid the smallest of the tunnels), and/or the hull designed in such a way as to increase the size of the turret ring (see for example the design of the Russian T34, the M4 Sherman or the German Panzer IV and Panther), then a larger turret could have been used, good not only for the crew space and ergonomics, but much more importantly, to allow a bigger main gun to be fitted.[25]

The maximum size of the main armament is inextricably linked to the diameter of the turret ring: in broad terms, the larger the diameter of the ring, the larger the gun that can be mounted. This is because the turret has to remain balanced in order to allow easy traverse, whether by hand or power; additionally, the turret and hull design must allow for the full length of recoil thorough all angles of elevation and depression, plus it must include sufficient space to load the ammunition, again through all angles. If the designer can build in a bigger turret ring than is strictly necessary, then the tank will have what today is known as stretch potential and can be more easily upgraded. But by designing a tank the other way around, such as by making the turret ring diameter only just large enough for the specified gun, trying to fit a larger gun (and ammunition) subsequently will prove to be very difficult if not impossible. This was exactly what happened with the War Office insistence, in the early years of the war, in specifying the 2-pounder gun as the main armament on almost all British tanks, allowing the designers to build the tank around that gun. Therefore, when the larger 6-pounder became available, many of the British tanks, even the newest (rather than most modern – the term is used advisedly!) models could either not mount the gun at all (A9, A10, A13, Covenanter), or only with difficulty, and then generally by sacrificing the third turret crew member, meaning that the tank commander had to load the guns in addition to all his other responsibilities. This applied to the Valentine and the Crusader. When the 17-pounder design was approved in 1943, it proved to be impossible to mount this outstanding tank-killing gun onto any British tanks at all; eventually it was shoe-horned into the larger Sherman turret, not without much difficulty, to become the Firefly. Even the Comet of 1945 could not mount it because its hull design was based upon the Cromwell, and had to resort to using what was in effect a bespoke, smaller version of the gun, known as the 77mm. The 17-pounder ended up being mounted onto stop-gap designs such as the Valentine Archer SPG, on which it had to face over the rear of the vehicle, or the horribly awkward A30 Challenger design.

Even the forty-ton Churchill could not mount it and had to be injected with steroids to produce the so-called Super Churchill, aka 'Black Prince' design capable of carrying it, which was abandoned after the war. Only the Centurion, designed *ab initio* in 1943, could take the 17-pounder, and this tank proved its worth over the next decade because the engineering team did not have to design the tank around the railway loading gauge, and had also deliberately built in stretch potential. It was later up-gunned twice, to mount the 20-pounder and then the famous 105mm L7 gun of the late 1950s.

Overall widths and turret ring dimensions of selected tanks

Tank	Width over tracks	Turret ring diameter	Remarks
Matilda II	8ft 6in	54⅓in	Designed around 2-pounder gun. Incapable of mounting 6-pounder.
Valentine	8ft 7½in	57½in	Designed around 2-pounder gun. Capable of mounting 6-pounder and 75mm with new two-man turret design.
A13 Mk II	8ft 4in	54in	Designed around 2-pounder gun. Incapable of mounting 6-pounder.
Crusader	9ft 1in	55½in	Designed around 2-pounder gun. Capable of mounting 6-pounder with new two-man turret design.
Churchill	10ft 8in (including air inlets)	54¼in	Designed around 2-pounder gun. Capable of mounting 6-pounder and 75mm with new turret design.
Cromwell	10ft	57in	Designed around 6-pounder gun. Capable of mounting 75mm and 95mm.
Comet	9ft 11in	64in	Designed around 77mm gun. Incapable of mounting 17-pounder.
Centurion	11ft 0in	74in	Designed around 17-pounder gun, with stretch potential built in.
M4 Sherman (USA)	8ft 7in min to 9ft 10in max	69in	Designed around 75mm medium-velocity gun. Capable of mounting 105mm howitzer, and 76mm gun with new turret design.
Panzer IV (Germany)	9ft 5in	64in	Designed around 75mm low-velocity gun, later upgraded to take 75mm high-velocity gun with no major turret redesign.
Panther (Germany)	10ft 9in	66in	Designed around 75mm high-velocity gun. Incapable of mounting 88mm.
Tiger I (Germany)	11ft 8in	73in	Designed around 88mm gun.

Chapter 2

A Peculiar Genius – Tank Design and Development in Britain 1919–1936

The necessities of war created it in a night, but the economics of peace have caused it to wither in a day.

Brigadier Ross *The Business of Tanks*

British tank design was probably better than any other in the world at the time but the shortage of orders and money, and the lack of a clear decision on requirements, never gave tank production a chance.

Major General N.W. Duncan
British Armoured Fighting Vehicles 1919–1940

Such is the peculiar genius of the British people, and their political organizations, that they have set out as major protagonists in two world wars within a quarter of a century of each other, without having their army even moderately prepared on either occasion.

WO 277/31

The role of government and the war office

In the years after the First World War was concluded, the Tank Corps soldiered on initially with a handful of the tired and obsolete tanks left over from the war, the majority having been broken up for scrap. The only significant re-equipment for the corps (elevated to become the Royal Tank Corps or RTC in 1923) was the provision of around 200 Vickers Medium Tanks Mk I and II starting in 1923 and being completed in 1930.[1] These tanks featured a fully rotating turret and a coaxial machine gun for the first time on a British service tank, but otherwise were mainly notable for the fact that they remained in service until the outbreak of the Second World War, becoming increasingly tired in the process as the crews got the most out of them each and every training season. A number of modifications and improvements were made over the years, most notably the equipping of them with radio sets capable of both receiving and transmitting and allowing the first steps to be taken to develop a genuine system of radio control. Other than these Mediums, from the late 1920s some units of the RTC were equipped with cheap and cheerless Light Tanks (including many of the so-called Tankettes) and, for imperial policing in India and elsewhere in the Empire, eleven armoured car companies were operated.

Responsibility for the provision of almost all weapons for the army rested with the Master General of the Ordnance (MGO), a member of the Army Council and thus a senior and very influential voice at the War Office. Until 1936 he was the officer ultimately responsible for weapons design, development and production. Under him came the directors of specialist boards dealing with specified vehicles, weapons and equipment. The main ones of these were responsible for artillery, ordnance services, the Royal Ordnance Factories,[2] and, from 1928, mechanisation.[3] The MGO was assisted by the CIGS's Specification Committee, which decided on the specification of new equipment. This committee met to consider the need for and then develop the draft specifications, the issue of which was the responsibility of the individual board concerned – in the case of AFVs, this was the Director of Mechanization. The final version of the draft was known as the General Staff (GS) specification, which gave the designers the start point for designing each new tank; often it was more than this, and tied the designers' hands in terms of which engine they were to use and the like. If the designer for the project was official, the specification was passed to the design department of the Department of Tank Design (DTD), that organisation residing at Woolwich.[4] If however a private firm was given the contract, generally meaning Vickers-Armstrong, the DTD was bypassed, and had no say on how the specification was translated into a tank design, the communication being between the Director and the company.

It is reasonable to question whether the General Staff were sufficiently technically competent to issue such an important document; the answer is a resounding no. It has to be remembered that for the majority of the 1930s, despite his title and his responsibility for tank development, the Director of Mechanization had no trained and qualified tank designers within his department; the specifications were written by a small group of over-worked and relatively junior general staff officers, whose individual experience (and personal views) could be important factors in the development of the specification. The Director of Artillery, the very competent and technically educated Campbell Clarke, argued that:

The [current] General Staff… is necessarily incompetent, by lack of experience and basic education in elementary technology to initiate or decide policy on new weapons… a modern General Staff should have a strong technically trained element.

The provision of guns and cannons and their associated ammunition and fire control systems, including those used on tanks, were the responsibility of the Director of Artillery. From 1928 when the new post of Director of Mechanization was created, both Directors worked for the MGO, but the opportunity was not taken to pass responsibility for tank weapons to the latter.[5] Postan summed up the situation prior to rearmament:

The relationship between development and production prior to 1936 ensured the autonomy of each. The evolution of new weapons was a responsibility of the technical branches of the War Office; though occasionally outside firms designed, it was [nearly] always to a War Office specification, and often in competition with an official design… During rearmament this distinction gradually blurred…[6]

The realisation by the army in 1934 that Germany was Britain's most immediate potential enemy led to pressure on the politicians to accept that a continental (meaning European) commitment was necessary, something that successive British governments had avoided for centuries. In many ways this was self-seeking on the part of the senior generals, as only recognition of such a commitment would allow the army to begin to rearm to the levels that it thought necessary, bearing in mind that the Royal Navy and in particular the Royal Air Force were starting to see money become available for rearmament and expansion. In 1934 the army hesitatingly created the first Army Tank Brigade, a formation designed for close support of the infantry – this at the time when German ambitions were looking at creating a number of armoured divisions designed for rapid strike operations. Forming the brigade from existing units was quite straightforward – equipping it with suitable tanks for the role it was expected to undertake was to take much longer. In the same financial year, 1934, the total amount of money available for the whole of the army portion of the defence budget was only around 10% of the total, a meagre £2 million, which was just enough to pay for four new infantry divisions (which were very much cheaper to operate than cavalry or armour).[7] While this financial situation remained the existing structure could cope, but as rearmament gathered pace, rather than reinforce the existing departments, the decision was made to completely reorganise.

In 1936 the post of Director General of Munitions Production was created, and many of the functions of the MGO were transferred to that office, including crucially that for tank production. This organisational situation was to change again only two years later, in 1938. During the 1930s, as far as official designs went, the Royal Ordnance Factory in Woolwich was the production facility responsible for turning the DTD design into a working tank, by building it – quite literally – by hand. Due to financial constraints this was not a frequent demand, and ROF Woolwich was only involved in rare forays into actual tank construction, often only being called upon to build one tank per year. These culminated in the experimental DTD-designed A7 series of three tanks, which when the A7E3 model was built in 1937 was far ahead of its time in many ways and was also notable as the very last totally government-designed and manufactured tank to appear until the Centurion of 1945. The A7 and its military design lineage were to be the cause of some embarrassment later, when a number of civilian firms were struggling to design and build battle-worthy tanks. In April 1938 the Tank Design Section at Woolwich was officially forbidden by the Mechanization Board to mention the success of the A7E3 design – it was clearly being referred to by Woolwich in an 'I told you so' manner.[8] Ross estimated that pre-war the Tank Design Section employed thirty experienced designers; he did not record what happened to them, although it can be surmised that a few of them would have remained in the emasculated section, and those that did were subsequently restricted to commenting on, and suggesting improvements to, civilian companies' designs.[9] This was a clear waste of scarce talent, but the fateful decision had been made by the government that certain types of existing heavy industry would be capable of both designing and building tanks. After all, the logic went, tanks were:

> essentially comparable to other heavy engineering projects, [and] it was this which prevented much fundamental research being undertaken and which saw the tank designers under the Superintendent of Tank Design gradually dwindle in numbers and importance...[10]

In the mid-1930s there was only one company in Britain capable of the task. In fact, it was the world leader, Vickers-Armstrongs (V-A), referred to as Vickers for short.

The role of private industry

The sole private company in Britain involved in the design, development and production of tanks was Vickers-Armstrongs Ltd.[11] Of the industrial companies that had been involved in tank building during the First World War – Fosters, Fowlers, Metropolitan, Beardmores, Marshalls – none could see a commercial future for tanks and thus they reverted to civilian production; in any case they were tank builders, not designers. As Kenneth Macksey commented, in the climate of the times, the 'opportunities for private venture in the armaments business were few and far between.'[12] Vickers was the only game in town, and Postan described the company as:

> Vickers-Armstrongs Ltd, without whose solitary and pioneering efforts the country would have possessed no facilities for the design and development of armoured vehicles.[13]

This was no exaggeration, but Vickers was not doing business for the sake of altruism nor with the benefit of some extraordinary prescience. As any commercial undertaking would be, the firm was concerned with producing products that would sell, if not to the British army, then certainly to the increasing number of buyer countries worldwide. It was not prepared to spend a lot of money on what in modern terms would be called research and development on the off-chance that the British government might decide to rearm at some indefinite point in the future. Therefore, Vickers and all its sub-companies only allocated around £20,000 per annum for its own experimental tank work, with the emphasis on making export models.[14] A saying that was current in the army at the time reflected the reliance that the War Office nevertheless placed on the company, for all means of warlike materiel: 'Leave it to Vickers'.

In terms of designing and building experimental models of tanks specifically for the British army, in the late 1920s Vickers had produced three notable prototypes based on GS specifications issued as related earlier: these were the heavy A1E1 Independent, the Medium Mk III, and the A6. The Independent was a large and complex 30-ton tank, of which a solitary and enormously expensive example was built in the mid-1920s.[15] Designed by Sir George Buckham of Vickers, one author thought that it 'was the first machine anywhere in the world that deserved to be called a battle tank'[16] and that 'in every other respect Independent was years ahead of its time.'[17] The Independent bristled with small MG turrets pointing in every direction, and featured the first tentative efforts at giving the commander effective control of all of the crew members in his tank.

The A6 or Sixteen-Tonner was a smaller tank but again in many ways an advanced design that borrowed heavily on the A1 experience. It was considered to be a potential replacement for the in-service Mediums, but only three were ever built for trials; it seems that there might well have been an order for a number of service tanks had the Wall Street Crash not happened.[18] Subsequently three Medium Mk IIIs were built, the idea being to build a tank similar to the A6 and for much the same purpose but at much reduced outlay, but again it was not brought into service, more on the grounds of cost than for technical reasons.[19] Each A6 cost around £16,000 – the sum of £1,000 per ton became the generally accepted price for a medium tank throughout the 1930s, despite the advantages of mass production not being factored in – the figure really related to hand-built tanks only. But it was important that the notion of what constituted 'cheap' when building tanks now had a yardstick to use as a measure.[20]

A notable feature of all of these designs was the inclusion of multiple machine-gun armed sub-turrets, the Independent having no fewer than four. As well as making the tanks expensive and complex, they required large crews and were hugely difficult to control, but most crucially, revealed the fallacious and enduring belief that the machine-gun was the weapon of choice for the suppression of enemy infantry and anti-tank guns, rather than the HE shell. This decision would have serious repercussions in the conflict to come.

Where Vickers could make money, keeping its tank design department busy and allowing at least some form of British expertise in the field to continue, was in building large numbers of relatively unsophisticated light tanks and small general-purpose tracked armoured vehicles that came to be known as carriers. The chief designer of these vehicles for Vickers was the brilliant and innovative Sir John Carden, without doubt the finest AFV designer Britain had, who was tragically killed in a (suspicious) air crash in 1935, denying Britain the services of one of the few men who could possibly have prevented many of the design disasters of the next decade from occurring; he was certainly the most experienced, bar none. His obituary of December 1935 in *The Times* was extremely prescient, written at a time when the possibility of re-equipping the RTC with new tanks was a distant dream and few people believed that another war was really approaching:

The death of Sir John Carden is a heavy blow to the progress of mechanisation in the British Army, and it comes at a particularly unfortunate time... For a number of years past the progress of tank design in this country has largely depended on the mechanical genius of Sir John Carden.[21]

Smithers also considered Carden a genius and labelled those left to carry on Carden's work within Vickers as 'no more than good journeymen',[22] although that is slightly unfair on Leslie Little, who replaced him as chief designer. Carden had worked closely with Giffard Martel, a gifted and imaginative if amateur light tank builder who built small tanks in his own time and at his own expense in his garage while simultaneously working as a staff college instructor. Carden also collaborated with Vivian Loyd, a former army officer, to produce the Carden-Loyd series of light tracked vehicles, but it seems clear that despite Loyd's undoubted engineering expertise, the true brilliance was supplied by Carden, whose loss was on the scale of the aircraft industry being denied R.J. Mitchell, Barnes Wallis and Sydney Camm at one stroke. The critical point here is that despite having no government-sponsored tank design branch and very little funding, probably until 1934 if not a little later, Britain could still claim to lead the world in the field of designing tanks.[23]

Among the many small tanks that Vickers produced commercially in the inter-war period was the so-called Six-Ton Tank, trialled and rejected by the British army but widely sold abroad, including to Finland, Poland and Russia.[24] The US government also borrowed an example, and the Six-Tonner provided the start point in many of these countries for their own independent tank design, giving them a head start as the tank was in fact an extremely advanced design. Directly from the design came the Russian T26 and the American 'Combat Cars'; these would eventually lead to the T34 and the Sherman.

Not everyone was content with this monopoly of 'Leaving it to Vickers'.[25] On 30 October 1936, the MGO Sir Hugh Elles told a War Office meeting that competition with Vickers was absolutely necessary – this was almost certainly not due to objections to the monopoly *per se*, but rather to his realisation that Vickers would not be able to cope with the scale of design and production required should war come. This led directly to other companies being brought into the tank business, the first of these being Vulcan Foundry, a failing locomotive builder, and Nuffield Mechanization & Aero, a firm created specifically to develop Cruiser tanks with the Christie chassis.[26] The story of these and other firms is told in another chapter.

The retention of existing industrial production within Britain was important to the government as a response to the world financial crisis and to prevent large-scale unemployment, as well as for possible rearmament. In 1936 the Sub-Committee on War Office Production Report stated: 'There is a very limited production capacity in this country which cannot be extended merely by increasing demand.'[27] It was noted that:

> The most economical method of keeping alive machinery specifically required for munitions, and of encouraging the setting up of reserve plant for emergency production, is to place contracts in peace which will give a reasonable return to the firms concerned... firms must have peacetime experience if the skilled labour is to be available [in wartime].[28]

So it was that a number of failing companies, with no experience of building tanks let alone designing them, became responsible for both functions in the Second World War. Despite the total inexperience of these newly-introduced private companies, in many ways the greatest single brake on Britain's ability to produce war-winning tank designs in this period was caused by one massive systemic failing: the unwillingness of the senior leadership of the British army to continue the armoured revolution glimpsed during the First World War, and to develop a fully mechanised, modern army, capable of fighting the next war, rather than refighting the previous one. We must, therefore, briefly examine Britain's ambivalent attitude to armoured forces in the inter-war period.

Over-egging the pudding: the fight to mechanise

Most senior British officers acknowledged only two combat arms – the infantry and the cavalry. There were two supporting arms, the Royal Artillery and the Royal Engineers, who were also the army's technicians, and one service for the provision of logistics, the Army Service Corps. It is galling to discover that many of the same officers who believed that First World War conditions were a singular aberration then used their experiences from that conflict when preparing their troops for the next war. One result of this was the abiding preference for slow but relatively well armoured tanks, the sole purpose of which was to enable the infantry to advance on foot in order to close with and defeat the enemy.

In 1919 the messiah of armoured warfare Boney Fuller had circulated a memorandum called 'Reorganization of the Tank Corps'. In it he proposed replacing all of the twenty-eight regular cavalry regiments with tank battalions, replacing one of the four infantry companies in each infantry battalion with a tank company, and replacing all horse-drawn transport with motorised tractors. Naturally, all the troops manning these vehicles were to come from the Tank Corps, and the cavalry, who clearly (to his mind at least) lacked the technical bent necessary to adapt to the internal combustion engine and modern warfare, should be disbanded lock, stock and barrel. Over 1,300 new tanks would be needed to equip the force he envisioned, at a cost estimated to be in excess of £9 million for the capital expenditure alone.[29] Nothing could be more guaranteed to arouse suspicion and antagonism throughout the army than this sort of proposal. It was nothing less than a takeover attempt by an upstart unit which was not even certain of escaping disbandment once the mud had settled. It was to poison the relationship between the Tank Corps and much of the rest of the army for the next two decades, just when the new force needed all the friends it could muster.[30]

When Field Marshal Sir George Milne – Uncle George to all – became the Chief of the Imperial General Staff (CIGS) in March 1926, a new era began in the War Office. Generally depicted as the embodiment of an old-school reactionary, Milne's reputation was tarnished by the deliberate mud-slinging of Fuller and Liddell Hart, who used the press to claim that he was opposed to any form of change. The truth is rather different. The mechanisation of the army, which had stalled after the amazing progress made during the First World War, was to be reinvigorated, albeit at a 'carefully considered' – which translates as slow – pace, and only as and when budgetary considerations would allow. He intended to introduce what he called 'mechanicalisation' to the army, with his biggest constraint being lack of funds. It was Milne who authorised the Experimental Mechanized Force exercises of 1927–1929, but he was aware that even as CIGS he needed to bring the other members of the Army Council with him, and thus was determined to proceed only at a reasonable pace in order to avoid scaring the horses.

Unfortunately, Milne seems to have lacked the necessary drive or authority required to impose his decisions on the other members of the Army Council. He also realised that unless he could persuade the Indian Army to mechanise, it would be more difficult to force the issue at home. And the Indian Army (IA), which was not under his command, was reluctant to do so, believing that armoured cars, not tanks, were the only types of AFV suitable. This was to act as another brake on progress:

> The opinions of senior officers in the forces engaged in imperial policing were given very great weight; [for example] the views of the Commander in Chief India could [and did] consequently delay the substitution of HE shell for shrapnel despite a consensus of technical opinion at the War Office.[31]

Although trials had suggested that medium tanks were unsuitable for service in India whereas the light tanks had surprised many by performing well in trials there, the RTC could expect little help and rather some hindrance from the senior officers in the extremely reactionary IA hierarchy: 'A major war was long regarded as a distant contingency and, accordingly the opinion of the Commander in Chief India, [this] was of direct relevance in reaching decisions on new weapons'.[32]

Milne, despite being a moderniser, also appears to have harboured some nagging fears of an 'RTC take-over', and even if this threat was not quite as realistic as some may have liked to believe, the mere idea was 'a real stumbling block to progress.'[33] Luckily for the traditionalists, Milne was replaced as CIGS in February 1933 by General Montgomery-Massingberd, a true reactionary and believer in the primacy of the cavalry, infantry and artillery. He was a gunner by trade and the only sort of tank he could conceive of was an infantry support tank, with the emphasis on the word support. And from April 1936 the next CIGS, General Sir Cyril Deverell, was another conservative who made no bones about the fact that he disliked tanks.[34] Men like these derailed the tentative progress made under Milne and made decisions that were to have fateful consequences in the next conflict. Thus, the slow moves towards mechanisation that Milne had started to attempt were to be greatly handicapped, if not quite reversed. Sometimes this was in ways that the RTC had no right to expect. On his appointment as MGO in 1934 Major General Sir Hugh Elles would have appeared to the members of the RTC to be the ideal man to support the cause of mechanisation and to recommend RTC expansion, as he had commanded the Tank Corps in France in the First World War where his reputation was impeccable. He was initially seen as 'the man whom everybody expected to take the whole tank business firmly by the scruff', but once in post he 'seemed incapable of making up his mind what the army needed, or of pressing hard enough for any serviceable tank at all'.[35] Elles still thought mainly of tank operations along First World War lines, and tended to decry the concept of fast-moving armoured brigades; he believed that the new anti-tank guns coming into service would decimate the thin-skinned Cruisers being proposed. In some ways, of course, he was to be proved right. The root of the problem was that he remained wedded to the slow-moving infantry battle and therefore prioritised the extremely limited amounts of support for AFVs toward the procurement of infantry tanks rather than cruisers, and made no attempt at all to investigate the development of a single medium tank that was capable of fulfilling all roles, the direction that the A6 and A7 tanks had been groping towards.[36] He somewhat reluctantly ordered production of the insipid Matilda I infantry tank because of its thick defensive armour, which he knew was capable of resisting the anti-tank guns then in service, but was less convinced by the argument for cruiser tanks with their more expansive role. Additionally, he was under immense political and military pressure to build up the Royal Artillery-operated anti-aircraft forces that were being rapidly expanded for the defence of the UK, and these were to remain the absolute priority for scarce army funding throughout the second half of the 1930s. It was a relief to many when the Secretary of State for War Leslie Hore-Belisha replaced him at the end of 1937, at the same time suspending the office of MGO and transferring the responsibilities to the Director General of Munitions Production – which in itself caused problems as the Army Council lost its established weapons and equipment supremo, with his staff and all their experience.

Doctrine? What doctrine?

Politicians are responsible for deciding where the threats to national defence and security lie, and how they might be countered through diplomacy, economic measures, or the application of military force. If the latter is required, the military staff must have prepared robust plans that will allow a successful outcome, and these plans can only be formed on the basis of clearly defined doctrinal principles. A current definition of doctrine is: 'the fundamental principles by which military forces guide their actions in support of military objectives.' Another definition stated that doctrine is simply 'what an army thinks.'[37] Doctrine can serve a number of purposes.

It gives guidance to military staff, their advisers and academics, as well as to the civilian companies providing equipment, all of whom are involved in the area of ultimate concern to the soldiers themselves: how good is the equipment they will be expected to fight their next conflict with? To put it very simply, which kit should the army be equipped with, and how much of it is necessary? It is in this area that the inter-war army doctrine must be examined, as there is a definite link between the doctrine advocated by the army and the equipment that it procured to allow that doctrine to be applied.

One of the first tank doctrine publications printed after the First World War was the Charles Broad and George Lindsay authored 'Provisional Instructions for Tanks and Armoured Cars' published in 1927. It was not a War Office-funded pamphlet and had to be purchased by interested officers from HMSO for ninepence. It cannot therefore be considered as doctrine and it concentrated as much on low-level tactics as on the philosophical element and overarching doctrinal principles. In fact, many official and demi-official military pamphlets of this era were remarkable for their tendency to give general guidance or points for attention, rather than detailing exact methods or procedures. The British army has never liked being told from above how to run its own affairs, even by its own chain of command, and this was still true in the 1930s. Doctrine between the wars was thus often at best semi-official. Much written doctrine was in the form of privately-published monographs, which had to be paid for by the interested individual – many of these were devoured and adopted by the armoured aficionados in other countries, including Germany and the USSR. This lack of doctrinal framework was a handicap; had the higher echelons of the army been more doctrinally focused, they would have realised that experimentation in modern methods of warfare was critical. The much more staff- and doctrine-focused German army did exactly the opposite, committing a large part of their limited resources during the early 1930s to trials, and as a result developing the concept of *Blitzkrieg* which drove the designs of armoured vehicles they required to fight the next war.

In 1929 the British General Staff were sufficiently muddled about the whole concept of mechanisation as to believe that the army possessed two types of unit, combat and mobile, as if the two were somehow incompatible.[38] The 1934 Staff Duties Directorate stated that 'The British Army, small in size, must at least be highly scientific, and a clear duty which falls to the War Office is to keep abreast or ahead of modern developments in every department of war materiel.'[39] This aspiration was not reflected in the 1937 version of *Infantry Training*, the 'bible' aimed at educating the main fighting arm of the army – many of whom had never even seen a tank – which carried no more than a few paragraphs suggesting how cooperation with tanks might proceed; it was more suited in approach to the previous war than to the future.[40] As Field Marshal Michael Carver pointed out:

Tanks had practically never fought other tanks. Experience of tanks [in the First World War] was of no help... In default of experience, the army had to rely on theory or, as most commanders did, on what they regarded as pragmatic common sense or even happy-go-lucky intuition.[41] The lack of coherent doctrine led inevitably to muddled and contradictory thinking, and it is hardly surprising that the manufacturers were confused about what was required, or that the War Office was unable to notice the potential faults and problems being stored up for later.

Chapter 3

Learning to Crawl:
Rearmament and Reorganisation

From the tent, the armourers, accomplishing the knights,
with busy hammers closing rivets up, give dreadful note of preparation.
Shakespeare Henry V

The task of the Treasury, and the defence departments, would have been much
simpler if it had been known that war would break out in September 1939.
George Peden

The authorities believed that faults could be ironed out with the two pilot
models and any modifications incorporated into production tanks. They were
wrong.
David Fletcher Crusader and Covenanter Cruiser Tanks

The mechanical failings of British tanks were largely the fault of commercial
firms incompetent at design, development and manufacture.
Corelli Barnett The Audit of War

Financing Rearmament

The tentative decision to begin rearmament was taken within government much earlier than many people realise; the end of the Ten-Year Rule in 1932 allowed the potential, if not the reality, of some rearmament to begin. It was only begun in earnest in 1935, and slowly, oh-so-slowly, gathered pace. There were many reasons for this lack of speed, by no means all down to governmental intransigence, and the word slow is used advisedly. Before pointing fingers, it is necessary to understand the limiting factors that severely affected not only the pace of the rearmament programme, but also the priorities that became necessary, and which had such a major impact on the production of an armoured force. Even once the decision was finally taken to start rearmament, the capability of Britain to rearm was limited by a number of factors. Most obvious was the financial aspect, but also critical was the ability of industry to provide new equipment, which itself was a function of the availability of plant, skilled manpower, raw materials, and time.

Probably the biggest political constraint to any form of rearmament in Britain in the 1920s and into the early 1930s was the Ten-Year Rule. First applied in August 1919, this was a general rule that stated that Britain would not expect to fight a major war for the next ten years, i.e. not before August 1929. This clearly would have major implications for the army (and the other services), as it was not used to give the forces a ten-year long breathing space in which to assess the lessons from the war, reorganise and re-equip, and thus end the period ready for the next challenge. Rather, it was used as a means of strangling the services of funding, causing reductions in size, and preventing any meaningful research and development. In July 1928, as the rule was nearing the end of its life, the Chancellor, one Winston Churchill, amended the meaning of the rule to read:

> It should now be laid down as a standing assumption that at any given date there will be no major war for ten years from that date.[1]

This much more specific version was in effect a rolling rule applied on a daily basis that meant that until someone rescinded the rule, the next ten years could be considered to be safe. This was applied, as most decisions by chancellors are, for purely budgetary reasons. Until the rule was cancelled there could be no serious rearmament for any of the services. It was to remain in place, despite the frequent and vigorous objections of the service chiefs, until 23 March 1932; ironically, it was fear of Japanese actions in the Far East rather than German aggression in Europe that finally caused it to be rescinded, Hitler not yet being in power.[2] In the nearly fourteen years of its application the rule did incalculable harm, and Churchill's 'lone voice in the wilderness' warnings in the 1930s must always be weighed against the damage he did to the services by his amendment to the rule in the previous decade. As a history of Churchill noted:

> It is difficult to estimate the damage caused by the Ten-Years (sic) rule. All three services were affected. The Army was hit hardest of all... The greatest danger of the rule lay in its assumptions: that Britain's decision

makers of the future would be able to identify any potential threat in good time and that the transformation from a process of disarmament to one of rearmament would be swift... the policies to which the rule gave rise brought about the atrophy of frameworks for military development and production.[3]

The rule was all about saving money as the war had wrecked Britain's finances and seriously challenged her position as the world's leading financial centre. Financial orthodoxy dictated that an adverse balance of payments situation was to be avoided at all costs, and this, more than any other financial factor, severely limited the amount of money available to the government, let alone for rearmament purposes. Strong arguments were constructed and successfully fielded by the Treasury, pointing out that excessive sums spent on rearmament would not only lead to Britain being accused of militarism, but would also inexorably lead to financial ruin; and that rearmament could only take place at a pace dictated by what was affordable – which meant next to nothing. The resistance to using government loans to fund any form of defence was very strong, despite arguments that defence spending would act as a welcome stimulus to dormant sections of British industry, ironically a concept deployed by Hitler once he became Chancellor in 1933. Only in 1937, and for the first time in peacetime, was a British government loan taken out to finance rearmament. This was a huge moment in the rearmament process, particularly considering the fragile financial state and the widespread objection to 'militarism' in all its forms:

Within the country as a whole military expenditure in peace-time was regretted... No better illustration of this can be found than the almost total absence of any examination by General Staff or technical experts among the general public of the equipment lessons of the 1914–18 war... Experience of the 1914–18 war had been very ill-digested at the War Office, and small efforts were made in the 1920s to master its lessons.[4]

Each year, after a round of bargaining, the Treasury allocated a sum to each service, in effect forcing each service to cut its coat according to the cloth made available – meaning it had to prioritise its programmes very carefully, as there was hardly enough money allocated for maintenance, let alone any form of improvement or expansion, including, once again, research and development. Each year, the bargaining would begin with the three services submitting their initial bids for the next financial year, known as the estimates. After months of to-ing and fro-ing, the final sum to be made available for the next financial year was decided by the Treasury, with the War Office having no right of appeal once the decision had been made. Importantly, money thus allocated could not be carried over into future years, nor indeed passed into another budgetary area or 'vote' designed for another purpose, so any unspent sum was lost. The army had the greatest difficulty in spending its paltry sums, in part as the small equipment contracts it could afford to fund were commercially unattractive but also, and increasingly from 1932 on, the Royal Navy and especially the RAF had identified the best of the industrial companies Britain had, and were dealing with them exclusively, leaving the army out in the cold. The army thus had no choice but to look around for firms that were available, rather than those that were at the top of the game.

Britain, after years of decline and mass unemployment, lacked capacity and confidence. As Christopher Price noted: 'Lost productive capacity is [in effect] lost forever. New capacity can be created only when new capital mobilises resources...'[5] In the years since the armistice, Britain had systematically and deliberately dismantled its armaments industry, leaving Vickers-Armstrongs as the sole tank-producing company and very few others interested in building other types of military vehicles. The inability to spend the yearly allocation started to become an acute problem for the army. For instance, in 1937 £34 million allocated to its rearmament programmes remained unspent, as there was insufficient plant within the industrial base; in rough terms, this could have built around 1,500 medium tanks.[6] Additionally, the funds had been allocated for *direct* military expenditure, and it does not appear that there was any suggestion or attempt to allocate the unapportioned millions to investment in plant or training. This would have been seen by the Treasury as offering unfair competitive advantage to the companies involved, and this would not be tolerated, however great the emergency. As even the limited amounts available could not be spent fast enough, by late 1937, with the financial year well into its second half, it was reported that although £81 million had been made available for the so-called deficiency programmes – i.e. those that needed the most urgent attention (and which did not yet include tanks) – only £35 million pounds (28%) of contracts had actually been placed with industry. The official reason given was that to spend the full amount would have interfered with normal (i.e. civilian) industrial production:

> The Director-General of Munitions Production had, therefore, placed only a limited amount of orders in accordance with the Government's policy that industry should not be interfered with...[7]

In February 1937 Sir Thomas Inskip, occupying the newly-created office of Minister for the Co-ordination of Defence, submitted his 'Final Report on Defence Expenditure in Future Years'; in it he recommended that rather than simply allocate funds to programmes deemed to be a priority in terms of foreign policy or military objectives, those programmes which, as well as producing equipment, would also result in an increase in British manufacturing capacity over the next two years must be fully funded, and that spending therefore must be related to maximum production in the future. In effect he was arguing that the bulk of the money that would be allocated anyway over the coming five years should be spent within the next two. This was a far-sighted policy designed to provide the maximum enhancement to Britain's military strength and thus support appeasement efforts, but which also meant that those programmes that could not demonstrate an increase in production would struggle for inclusion.[8] By 1937 industry generally was enjoying something of a boom, and many firms that a couple of years before had struggled were now fully occupied. When finally, belatedly, attention at the War Office switched to the inadequacies of Britain's small and ageing tank fleet, only a handful of close-to-failing companies were available for the new task of not only building, but also designing, the new tanks required.

> The North British Locomotive Co, for example, registered losses for every year between 1921 and 1937... this firm, along with others like Fowler and the Vulcan Foundry Co, was probably saved from extinction by tank orders.[9]

It was a recipe for disaster.

The future maintenance of the enhanced forces now being created was also of great concern to the Treasury. As early as May 1937 Richard Hopkins of the Treasury noted that 'there is a grave danger that at the end of the rearmament period we have built up our armed forces to a level that is beyond our capacity to maintain.'[10] The figures allocated in defence budgets were only for the reconstruction and/or modernisation of the forces, and it was estimated in January 1939 that the *maintenance* figure, once the agreed rearmament programmes were complete, could be over £300 million per year.[11] By June 1939 that figure had risen to £450 million.[12] The lack of attention paid to the maintenance, particularly the provision of spare parts, was to bedevil Britain's armoured soldiers for years to come.

The inability to spend the monies being allocated remained a constant problem in the battle to develop a new range of modern tanks:

From May 1936 to May 1939 the financial requirement of the War Office tank programme multiplied threefold; this was based on the steady increase in the number of new divisions authorised, [but] was not actually expended.[13]

The sums requested by the army for AFV development were as follows:[14, 15]

Date	Request	Allocation	Percentage
May 1936	£12m	Nil	0
Nov 1936	£23.7m	Nil	0
May 1937	£29.7m	£3.5m	12%
May 1938	£22.7m	£5.5m	24%
May 1939	£36m	£10m	28%

The increases asked for were primarily intended to fund the infantry tank programme only and had much less to do with Cruiser tank development, which was not to come into the spotlight until after Dunkirk. It remains one of the great tragedies that when money did become available for building tanks, including playing catch-up in the neglected research and development field, it was unable to be spent. As the design facilities in the country were so limited there was no one able or available to design experimental models to allow experience to be gained and new concepts to be tested, and this lack of capacity was to prove costly in subsequent years. Not only could new components and sub-systems have been designed and tested, particularly although not exclusively engines, but this knowledge could then have been passed on to the inexperienced companies who were being pressed into the tank design business. As an indicator of how far behind Britain had fallen in terms of quantity, the following table is instructive:

World tank state in 1936

	Light	Medium	Approximate total
USSR	2,000	4,000	6,000
Germany	1,600	300–400	2,000
Italy	600–800	700	1,400
France	500–600	180	750
Japan	450	150–200	600
UK	209^	166#	375
USA	135	19	154

Notes:
^ – two-thirds obsolete
# – 164 obsolete, meaning the Medium I/II tanks. The other two were two Medium IIIs.
Source: Hancock, Design, p309.

As a result of Italian aggression and posturing that threated British possessions and interests in the Mediterranean, in 1937 the sum allocated to AFV development was set at £3.5 million, a figure unheard of since 1918. The following year this rose by another £2 million and in 1939 it was set at £10 million. In 1940, with the war underway and all the financial shackles finally off, the sum allocated was a staggering £200 million.[16]

The realisation that another European war was inevitable came late, not only to a large section of the British public but also to their government; it finally occurred in spring 1939, after Hitler had annexed the rump of Czechoslovakia. Until this mental transition had been made, peacetime practices would continue, industry would see the commercial imperative as their overriding concern, and the attitude of the government remained hopeful that their stated aim of avoiding war through deterrence and diplomacy might still prevail. There were undoubtedly memories of late summer 1914 in some politicians' minds: the orthodoxy was that the arms race and militarism prevalent then had contributed massively to the outbreak of the First World War. The July 1939 Economic Advisory Council's Committee on Economic Information report to the government concluded that 'our defence programme has nothing to lose and everything to gain by the adoption of remedies less drastic than those required in war, but appropriate to a time which we dare not regard as peace.'[17]

The cost of building a tank in the 1930s was generally accepted to be around £1,000 per ton, although this was inflated by the need to build development models by hand, which was not necessarily indicative of bulk production; nonetheless, the figure was widely used.[18] During the years 1927 to 1936 the sums available annually for all forms of tank development varied between £22,500 and £93,750 – scarcely liberal when the manufacture of a single experimental medium tank might cost anything up to £30,000.[19] By the mid-1930s one source indicates an annual total expenditure of only £400,000 for all the army's armoured vehicles, including spares.[20] Most of this would be spent on building light tanks, armoured cars and carriers, not genuine battle tanks. Using car prices for comparison, in 1925 a Crossley Manchester saloon car cost £925,[21] while a top-of-the-range 1926 Sunbeam 30hp cost around £1,295.[22] J.D. Scott summarised the inter-war pre-rearmament tank development policy nicely:

> Since the finance allocated for development in the inter-war years did not allow the production of more than about one pilot model per annum, the possibility of a highly experimental tank proving a complete failure was an exceedingly grave risk. Everything was against the genuine research project. It was a system which provided some very fine pieces of mechanical engineering, but it did not provide... any considerable body of theoretical knowledge about the tank as a weapon. The system, indeed, was associated with the tendency to regard the tank as a composite of gun and vehicle, and not as a unique entity with complex engineering qualities of its own.[23]

This inability to see the tank as a unique weapon of war, requiring specialist, nay expert, skills, was to cause great problems in the years to come. And we can conclude this part by returning to the overriding problem of finance: Colonel Justice Tilly, the Chief Instructor at the RTC depot in Bovington, had a revealing conversation with a War Office financier in 1936 who said that he was 'quite willing to find whatever money the tank people needed if only the General Staff could make up their minds what they wanted.'[24] If only both halves of that statement had been true...

The Cinderella service, or rearmament as a competition

> The period of rearmament [for the Army was] marked by a growing tension between the demands for new designs and up-to-date models on the one hand, and on the other the desperate urgency to obtain supplies of any equipment at all.[25]

From the point at which the Ten-Year Rule was rescinded in early 1932, the three services began to battle even harder with each other for the still limited funds being made available. From the outset, the army was handicapped. Memories of the First World War were fresh and uppermost in everyone's minds, and the overall attitude was 'never again'. The newly-formed Royal Air Force made much of its modernity, and claimed that it could reduce casualties by controlling land from the air; small-scale police actions in the Empire were cited as proof of this, and the doctrine of 'air control' was attractive to politicians. The new theories of airpower espoused by Giulio Douhet, Italian air actions in Abyssinia, and the murderous air raids on civilian targets during the Spanish Civil War seemed to reinforce this view. On 10 November 1932 Stanley Baldwin made his famous remark that 'The bomber will always get through'. So just at the point when the first tentative steps were about to be taken to rearm in some modest way, airpower and civilian air defence were at the front of most politicians' minds. In a letter to his sisters in February 1936, Chamberlain (then the Chancellor) had confided that he feared that the next war would be like the last, and that the country's resources would be 'more profitably employed in the air and on the sea [rather] than in building up great armies'.[26]

The services were in direct competition with each other not only for larger slices of the defence budget, but also for the available production facilities. Many components that went together to make up systems on ships, vehicles and in aircraft were required by all three services – optics, radios, engines, instruments and the like. Once a particular service had arranged a contract with a specific firm, the relationship was likely to continue, often to the exclusion of the other services. The role of the Principal Supply Officers' Committee (PSOC), a sub-committee of the Committee for Imperial Defence or CID, was to sort out these frictions, but it does not appear to have been overly successful. When the Ministry of Supply (MoS) was belatedly formed in 1939, it was in effect immediately in competition with the established supply officers from the Admiralty and the Air Ministry, and competition rather than cooperation was often the order of the day. It is a fact of life that within military specialties, most specialists consider their own area of expertise to be the single most important, to the exclusion of all others; this attitude certainly prevailed throughout the war years, with the Ministry of Aircraft Production in particular never being afraid to handicap the army in order to achieve its own ends.[27]

Despite being the favoured service, even the RAF often found it increasingly difficult to improve production and it fell behind its own ambitious schedule. This led to a number of attempts by Lord Swinton, the Air Minister from 1935 until May 1938, to force compulsory labour mobilisation upon the government, a policy that was both politically and socially unacceptable in peacetime, and which was consistently refused.[28] Swinton's rationale was not necessarily to increase the number of firms producing for the RAF, but rather to allow the creation of a second shift within existing facilities. Without compulsion, the production of aircraft continued to fall behind the schedule and reflected the realities of too many companies trying to expand by competing for a limited amount of skilled manpower. This was important for the army over the next few years, as had Swinton's proposal been accepted, the Air Ministry would have achieved an even greater hegemony over Britain's production than it actually managed. In monetary terms the RAF also managed to increase its percentage share of actual expenditure faster year on year, as well as increasing its overall share of the money available, from under 16 percent in 1934 to 36 percent in 1939; this meant that more and more commercial firms became in effect part of the Air Ministry procurement system, and could not be approached by the other services. In comparison, the army share went down from nearly 35 percent to 30 percent in the same timeframe – and what made this worse still for the majority of the army was that from November 1937 a large part of the army's increased funds could only be used for its contribution to ADGB, the Air Defence of Great Britain.

UK Armed Services expenditure 1934–1939 (£ millions)

	RN	% of Total	Army	% of Total	RAF	% of Total
1934	56.6	49.7	39.7	34.85	17.6	15.45
1935	64.8	47.3	44.7	32.6	27.5	20.1
1936	81.1	43.6	54.9	29.5	50.1	26.9
1937	78	39.5	63	31.9	56.3	28.6
1938	96	37.6	86.7	33.9	72.8	28.5
1939	98	33.6	88.3	30.2	105.7	36.2

Source: Gibbs *Rearmament* p532.

NB: Figures for 1937 and 1938 exclude additional sums from Defence Loans

The army also needed to decide where its priorities lay. The Defence Requirements Committee in November 1935 had suggested three priorities of tasks for the army:

- Imperial defence.
- Home defence including the anti-aircraft artillery element of ADGB.
- Reinforcements and/or a field force in time of war with adequate equipment and reserves[29]

This order of priority was subsequently endorsed and adopted, and everyone knew what it meant: although more money would be forthcoming for all three services, within the army there would not be sufficient for the third priority area to receive any. Gibbs labelled the whole period between 1936 and 1938 as one of 'limited liability' for the army, with no appetite for a continental commitment or even recognition by many politicians that the army might, once more, have to deploy in force to Europe. Despite the many and frequent protestations by the army chiefs that the government must recognise the centuries-old traditional British strategy of defending Britain by maintaining the balance of power within Europe, and if that failed, to fight on the Continent in support of allies, the government continued to resist. Chancellor of the Exchequer Chamberlain wrote to Liddell Hart in March 1937: 'We shall never again send to the continent an Army on the scale of that which we put into the field in the Great War.'

The reasons for this stance were as much emotional as political. After the experiences of the First World War, the man on the Clapham omnibus (and on the Edinburgh, Cardiff and Belfast equivalents) was simply not prepared to consider a repetition – unless and until there was no other option left. To offer overt support to France was not a wise political position in the mid-1930s; it had too many resonances, particularly as the received wisdom at that time was that inflexible alliance systems had been one of the major causes of the war. It was not until the spring of 1939 that the government finally realised that it could procrastinate no longer and began to plan in earnest for a continental commitment involving primarily the army. Only then could army rearmament begin in earnest – four years after the RAF expansion had begun. The lead established by the RAF, their control of key parts of industry (including engine manufacture), and their constant claim for top priority were to bedevil production in support of the army throughout the war, even after air superiority had been won.

Gibbs noted that: 'From [May 1937] onwards, for the next twelve months, the whole problem of the role, size, organisation and cost of the army became involved in the comprehensive review of defence expenditure'.[30] This review was to be carried out by Sir John Simon, the Chancellor. This review then led directly to a further recommendation in December 1937 by Inskip, the Minister for the Co-ordination of Defence, concluding that it was now essential to review *all* defence programmes to determine which should have first priority, and which should be cancelled or postponed. Critically, the report was of the opinion that the need for a field force had been over-stated, even opining that France:

> no longer looks to us... to supply an expeditionary force... it seems reasonable to assume that the operations involved are unlikely to be waged with the sustained intensity or on the scale to be expected in the case of operations on the continent.[31]

A hammer-blow for the supporters of tank warfare fell when he went on to state 'it should be possible to effect a very substantial reduction... in the provision of tanks, especially of the heavier kind.' Inskip, conscious of the enormity of getting the decision wrong, finished rather pathetically by warning his colleagues 'of the possible consequences of this proposal in order that they may share my responsibility'.[32] Collective responsibility indeed! Inskip's proposals did not completely kill off the idea of a modernised field force, but he did continue to insist that such a commitment was the lowest priority, and that if the force was to be funded, it must be scaled down, in order to save £14 million. One mobile (armoured) division continued to feature on the proposed Order of Battle; the problem was obtaining sufficient priority to begin the task of equipping it with real tanks. It was estimated that an armoured division cost two and a half times as much as its infantry equivalent.[33]

During this period of uncertainty other decisions were being made that further handicapped the development of armoured forces. At a ministerial meeting on 8 November 1937, a decision was taken to 'instruct the War Office that the provision of anti-aircraft defences is to have absolute priority over all other forms of war material.'[34] In February 1938 the Chiefs of Staff Committee listing of critical deficiencies included the estimate that by April 1939, the army would be deficient by 35 percent of the required quantity of heavy AA guns, whereas tanks would be 45 percent deficient, and tank and

A/T guns 60 percent deficient.[35] Because of the 1937 policy decision the anti-aircraft gun shortfall would thus be the priority for rectification; the tank gun shortfall would continue well into 1940 and result in tanks deploying to France without their armament. Hore-Belisha was greatly concerned that the demands of ADGB for guns would impact on the other types of guns required by the army; these included not only tank and anti-tank guns, but also field artillery.[36] The existing gun production capacity was only capable of dealing with the two highest priority types: AA and naval guns; the other types would only be made once these two requirements had been completed. This would take another two years.

The effect of the priority given to air defence within the army cannot be understated. In 1938, the energetic Minister for War, Leslie Hore-Belisha, complained that the army had to move £37 million from other areas within its already overstretched budget to use for AA defence in order to comply with the government's priority of home defence. This had the effect of removing about 43 percent of that year's budget that otherwise could have been used on other areas. What these areas are is not stated, so we cannot be certain that tanks were directly affected; it is, however, indicative of the strains within the system, and is another example of a type of rationing.[37] Another result was that 'AA development absorbed an immense amount of the research and design resources available.'[38]

The German Anschluss with Austria in March 1938 did not cause the government to revise its position with regard to the field force; instead, on the 24th, Chamberlain merely spoke of further increasing the requirements of the RAF and AA defences.[39] It was not until after the Czechoslovakia crisis in March 1939 that the required sea-change in policy with regard to the field force and a European commitment happened:

> That change amounted to an acceptance of the view... that ability to take part in a Continental war must be regarded as a major commitment of the army and that such a commitment would involve very much larger land forces than had been previously contemplated... the wheel, so far as the army was concerned, had turned full circle back to 1918... The new policy... represented the most radical change in Britain's strategic plans... but the change took six or seven months to develop.[40]

The way was now open to build up a much larger deployable army, which would include one (later increased to two) Armoured Division, plus a number of independent Army Tank Brigades. The problem was that it was simply impossible to produce the weapons needed quickly enough, for two reasons. Firstly, because the previous 'no continental commitment' policy had precluded any preparatory planning, and secondly, because the spare industrial capacity simply did not exist.

The problems of industry

The desperate effort to rearm without recreating an armaments industry... meant employing capacity for production which, unlike Vickers, totally lacked the know-how of armaments work... Repeated instructions from the Principal Supply Officers [were] embodied in most GS specifications that designs should be 'easy to manufacture' and contain 'no scarce raw materials'. 'Ease of manufacture' meant one thing to a specialist firm like Vickers; quite another thing to the engineering concerns new to armaments work which were now called on... [41]

There was no tank production equivalent of the Ministry of Aircraft Production (MAP) funded 'Shadow Scheme'. This scheme was designed to assist the large-scale provision of aircraft for the RAF:

whereby the leading motor manufacturers were called upon to make plans to expand, in an emergency, the production of aero engines and aircraft... [Proposed in 1936] its object was to provide means whereby the output of the regular aircraft manufacturing firms could be supplemented if emergency arose, but not unless it arose... the motor manufacturers, with their experience of production in quantity, were requested to supervise the erection and equipping, and subsequently the management, of factories capable of making components for engines or the assembly of aircraft. The actual products were to be of designs emanating from the regular aircraft industry. [42]

This foresight paid huge dividends for the MAP. Indeed, without it, Beaverbrook's miracle of aircraft production in 1940 would not have been possible. Unfortunately, a similar scheme was never employed – or even contemplated – for the building of tanks. In part this was understandable, as all the surplus capacity that could have been used to build tanks was already committed to the production of aircraft. The closest tank manufacture came to the scheme was the allocation of 'parents' to consortia of firms building a particular type of tank, in which the parent supervised the building of their designs by other firms. In this context, the closing sentence of the quotation above is critical. The 'Shadow' production companies were never expected to design their own aircraft; this was left to the parents, seen as the experts. In the field of tank production, the parent companies were also expected to design the tanks that were to be built, but there was only one firm that was close to being expert, and that of course was Vickers, which was much too busy itself to be able to assist the others, which in any case remained commercial competitors, war or not. Interestingly, only one of the companies that had built the First World War tank fleet played a large part in the Second World War organisation, in the shape of Metro-Cammell. Tank design was thus left in the hands of entirely unsuitable organisations. Kenneth Macksey missed the point slightly when he wrote of: 'the inability of British industry to adapt itself overnight to making tanks of quality in large numbers… [this] was now a major stumbling block…'. This was not the fault of industry, but rather of the politicians who had failed to set up the tank equivalent of the Shadow Scheme, restricting themselves to the pale shadow of the parenting system.[43] The official history of production commented that:

> Production reasons [were] behind the system of 'design parentage', which was characteristic of tank evolution during the war. It was assumed that a firm allocated to tank production would make a better job of its own designs and could be expected to educate other members of the production group into the new manufacturing problems involved. That in the straitened circumstances of 1941 this was a wise attitude can hardly be disputed. Once quality considerations came to the fore again it was to be more questionable.[44]

There were actually two types of tank parent companies. The Vehicle Design Parent was the company solely responsible to the MoS for the correct functioning of the completed vehicle in all respects from both the mechanical and operational points of view, meaning it did fulfill the specification. The Component or Sub-Assembly Design Parent was the company responsible to the Vehicle Design Parent for the correct functioning of a specific component insofar as it was applicable to the particular vehicle concerned. In some instances these companies were to alter the design or specification of a sub-component without informing the design parent of the change, with results that might be imagined.[45] An unfortunate side-effect of this parenting system was that as many of the sub-contractors were unable to assemble complete tanks and were restricted to merely building sub-assemblies, often large, these then often had to be moved around the country to places that could assemble them. This was obviously terribly inefficient as it included the largest items, such as hulls, turrets, and engines. In an extreme example, some Valentine components were manufactured in the USA before being shipped to Britain.[46]

In Britain, one of the effects of relying on private companies was that even after war had been declared many of those companies continued to use their normal peacetime methods and mentalities, despite the changed circumstances. The clearest manifestation of this was the impact of Lord Nuffield, the founder of Morris Motors and the head of the newly-created armaments firm of Nuffield Mechanization and Aero, (NMA, 1936) which had Mr E.S. Luyks as managing director and chief designer.[47] This company was to become notorious for going its own way, and the government felt unable or unwilling to take a stronger line. In many cases this led to confrontation and problems, but in one clear instance it had a positive impact. This was regarding the production of the Crusader, a cruiser tank based on their existing A13 design. NMA had been asked to build the existing London Midland and Scottish Railway (LMSR) designed Covenanter, an utterly awful tank, but preferred instead to build its own Cruiser design, the A15, subsequently called the Crusader. Although badly flawed in many areas, the latter was at least battleworthy and in the absence of anything better was to become a mainstay of the tank battles in North Africa in early 1942. However, the same attitude prevailed when NMA was asked to design a Crusader replacement, the A24 Cavalier. Their insistence on retaining outmoded A13 and A15 features, in order to ease production, led to that tank being an abject failure. Indeed, Lord Nuffield even suggested to the MoS in early 1943 that his group should build even more of the discredited Cavalier, rather than the better Centaur, quoting a number of staggeringly disingenuous reasons for this, again simply to make it easier for the company. Luckily the deceit was seen through and Cavalier production remained capped at 500 all-but-useless vehicles, with the much-better Centaur and then Cromwell tanks taking their place, luckily for the crews who had to operate them in action.[48] David Fletcher correctly identified that:

[Any] contractor's ability to build the ideal vehicle depended on the quality and range of his machine tools and the quality of his workforce... the only firms with production capacity to spare were unlikely to get their share [of a booming market]... It was largely their adherence to traditional practices that got them in this position in the first place. They lacked modern plant, the skills required to develop new techniques, and the resources to acquire those skills... their plant and skilled workforce were all geared to traditional riveting techniques... It hardly suits mass production; nor did it augur well for the interchangeability of parts...[49]

Fletcher had put his finger on one of the key reasons for the problems of tank production: the outdated British craftsman tradition. He noted that most firms were proud exponents of the great British art of craftsmanship, which might be defined as: 'the ability to fit together two things that do not fit.' This tradition was based around practices that slowed down production as well as causing great problems for the tank crews and needs to be examined in detail.

Building tanks by hand: the curse of the craftsman

Craftsmanship is the enemy of mass production.
Maurice Otley

In many ways using the term 'production' to describe how British tanks were made in the period is a misnomer. Production to the modern mind implies efficiency and using minimum resources to maximum effect. Although wartime propaganda films loved to show apparently huge factory floors where happy workers crawled over dozens of shiny new tanks nearing completion, in most cases this was far from the truth. Workplaces were often inadequately designed and ill-equipped with specialist machine tools, relying instead on general tools which could be used for various tasks, but which required skilled and often expert operators. Components were put together literally by hand and eye and 'involved much hand-fitting and finishing'.[50] The British tradition of hand-finishing which was such a bonus in the production of high-quality but low-volume consumer goods would prove to be a massive handicap when trying to turn out the weapons of war. The companies lacked modern production-line machines, methods, and most importantly mentality, partly in fact *because* of the reliance on their skilled workers: 'The benefits of a skill-rich labour force, however, were not free. By virtue of their reliance on skilled craftsmen British employers relinquished much of their authority over the production methods employed in their works'.[51]

In one way the army itself had contributed to the problem. In the early 1920s the Chief Inspector of Armaments at Woolwich had insisted on the very highest build standard for the Vickers Mediums being produced; as only a couple of hundred were made, spread out over a few years, this was a wholly sound method to ensure value for money, but one which created a mind-set entirely at odds with the needs for rapid production.[52] Hancock reflected that 'Even in the period of greatest stringency [i.e. during the period of the Great Tank Crisis from 1940 until 1941] designs were still marked by great finish and the 'Rolls-Royce' appearance of weapons was sometimes adversely criticised…'.[53] The criticism came from astute warriors who realised that the perfect was definitely the enemy of the good – or good enough. Things had to change, but this would not be simple: 'Only radical reorganization and massive investment could see these problems overcome, even in wartime.'[54] Hancock's point about the unhelpfulness of the craftsmanship tradition is critical here; under the so-called 'English System', each workstation was equipped with a vice, files and grinding tools, in order to fit together the 'things that do not fit'. Many photographs of the period demonstrate this clearly, and stand in comparison with the assembly lines of the US factories using the Ford-inspired 'American System' or assembly line, where components were designed and built to much more exacting standards, any part that did not fit being rejected rather than modified.

A tragedy is that this much more efficient method was actually nothing new, having been first employed to some degree during the US Civil War to make rifles, and Oldsmobile cars had been built in this way from 1901. Indeed, a type of assembly line devised by Isambard Kingdom Brunel's father had been in use in Royal Navy dockyards in the early nineteenth century. Most US workers were therefore assemblers of parts rather than skilled craftsmen (and increasingly, women), the key factors making them efficient being the high standardised quality of the individual components, plus the fact that each worker had no more than a few closely related tasks to perform at a single location from which he scarcely moved. Components were delivered to him rather than having to leave the place of work to find the items needed. In Britain it was common for one skilled workman to be required to do a multitude of operations, from grinding and lathe work, to making bolts and screws and other even more complex components by hand. He would frequently move around the factory in order to collect parts, and rarely performed the same operation repetitively which would have led to a greater competency and thus increased output. Ross noted with exasperation that: '[The British] pursued [their] love affair with craftsmanship... There was no place for craftsmanship in an American production plant, even the presence of a vise [sic] or bench in such factories was regarded as a sign of incompetence. Accuracy was invariably the enemy of craftsmanship'.[55] Ross also gave an excellent description of the US method in 1942, and as a tank soldier himself must have been greatly angered that Britain could not match this efficiency:

> The assembly line comprises an under-floor moving cableway to which the 'dollies' supporting the ever growing tank are attached. They are thus moved forward, along the assembly line from station to the next at pre-determined intervals of time. At each station a definite operation is completed; it may be the installation of the engine, or of the mounting of the gun... whatever the operation it has to be done within the stationary period of the line, after which the whole line advances to the next station. This means too, that at every movement forward a completed tank moves off the line and is driven away for testing. To supply each station with the assemblies to be incorporated, a bank is set up at each station; the bank being replenished as necessary, usually by overhead trolley from the stores. The bank is kept as small as possible to save valuable floor space... inspection takes place continuously during assembly...[56]

Compare this with this description of the Vauxhall Churchill factory in Luton at around the same time. Initially Vauxhall only made trucks on the site, but in May 1940 the MoS asked them to construct an extension to that factory capable of building fifty tank engines per week:

> Fortunately, there was a piece of vacant land adjacent to [the works] ...work commenced on the building fourteen days after receiving instructions to produce the tank engine. At this juncture it should be mentioned that questions regarding the possibility of this building being used for tank assembly were answered with an emphatic 'No'. The erection of the building therefore proceeded with [just] sufficient headroom to accommodate standard lifting tackle...

Shortly after the extension was completed, the MoS changed its mind:

> the consternation that followed the instruction that tanks themselves
> *were* to be built in this new building can well be imagined... the low
> headroom precluded the installing of standard type overhead traveling
> cranes. This meant that special low headroom cranes had to be made
> for slinging from the roof trusses and the latter had to be strengthened
> for the purpose... A large fleet of lorries was necessary to take the
> precise number of inspected parts to the various assembly plants...The
> actual method of assembling the vehicles differed to some extent in
> each plant owing to the different facilities available... the hull [was]
> supported on cast iron stands to enable the operator to work underneath
> the hull... [after wheels were fitted] it was then connected to the hull
> in front of it by chains... the whole line was towed forward one station
> [by] the completed vehicle at the end of the line...[57]

This ad hoc method would have been laughable to US engineers. Imagine
the strain on the engine and transmission of the single just-completed tank,
dragging the *whole* of the rest of the line forward, possibly as many as ten
partially completed tanks at a time; no wonder so many Churchills were
found to have serious mechanical faults on arrival in units.[58]

The companies were invariably unable to keep pace with their own (overly
optimistic) production forecasts, and were thrown into confusion when
forced to implement design changes in mid-run, all the more so if asked
to switch to a new model entirely, which the American system made much
easier to implement without seriously damaging output. In the 1930s there
were very few true car plants in Britain, with Daimler and Humber being
the only noteworthy examples, and which used the latest American methods
to maximise production. Such methods were not used by the locomotive and
ship-building companies, or foundries, that were suddenly called upon to
start producing tanks from a standing start from 1936 onwards.[59] In 1939
Arnold Toynbee, commenting on the plight of the British car industry, was
in fact speaking more generally of British industry when he said that 'the
country that gave birth to the Industrial System of production is a by-word
for its technological conservatism...'.[60]

Of course, another of the problems of a skills-based system is that
it requires skilled personnel to make it work, and such personnel were
hard to come by in wartime, following the huge expansion of all types of

manufacturing industries as rearmament gathered momentum. For example, the total numbers of personnel of both sexes employed in the munitions industries in June 1939 was 3.13 million. By August 1941 this had risen to 5 million, an increase of 60 percent. This put an additional burden on the skilled and semi-skilled worker, as well as management, as they had to find the time and resources to train the extra workers while doing their own jobs as well.[61] Of course, the tank industry was only a percentage of this total, and specific figures are difficult to find. However, in December 1942 the workforce employed on tank production was estimated at 190,000, which then decreased as production was throttled back, with 160,000 employed in June 1945.[62]

As an example of how efficiencies could be made by employing new production methods, the Rootes factory in Coventry discovered that by using jigs rather than hand production, they were able to reduce the time to machine one particular component from the original 40 minutes to just four and a half.[63] This is not to say that jigs were always the answer. A calculation conducted for the aircraft industry suggested that for many component parts, particularly those with production runs of 500 or under, it was actually more economical to make the items by hand than to go to the time and expense of creating jigs. It was found that only for runs of over 1,000 components was jigging and tooling always the most economical method.[64] But however efficient firms might become, the system adopted often conspired to hinder the development of all sorts of army weapons, and tanks in particular:

> The provision of equipment for the Army was more directly conditioned by terrain than was the case with services which were essentially not tied to the land...There was another reason why [Army equipment was affected] more than the other services – the highly specialised nature of most of the modern soldier's weapons...This weakness was aggravated not only because Army equipment ceased, by and large, to be manufactured by specialist firms...[65]

Royal Navy warships were designed to operate worldwide, in a huge variety of conditions, but always on the sea. RAF aircraft required some modifications to operate in extreme environments, but these were usually of a minor nature, and the air itself was reasonably consistent and forgiving. But army vehicles, including tanks, needed a much clearer statement of their likely operating terrain. Thick mud, dust, sand, extremes of heat and cold, high humidity, rocks and beaches, steep hills, urban areas: all of these and more required specific provision by the designers. Therefore, strategic doctrine impacted hugely on the performance of the vehicle – a vehicle built solely with service in the fields of northern Europe in mind would struggle in the jungle or the desert, or when landed on a pebble beach. Additionally, both of the other services could draw huge amounts of useful information not only from their own operations, but also from the civilian equivalents. Tanks had no such civil equivalents, as Professor Hay noted:

> The tank… proved to be distinctly unlike the products of all the British heavy engineering firms (except the one armaments firm, Vickers-Armstrongs); the motor industry, though it might appear suited to tank development and production, was in fact highly unsuited for either, and the unsuitability increased as tanks grew bigger and heavier.[66]

It is clear that this was not fully appreciated at the time. Indeed, the assumption was widely made that the tank was simply a large vehicle, and therefore companies used to designing lorries, tractors or even locomotives would be able to make the transition to tank design easily. This assumption was to prove woefully incorrect.

Designing tanks from scratch: the curse of the draughtsman

> *Search through a catalogue of aircraft and you will find that [its name] is inextricably linked with that of its manufacturer, or at least the parent design company. Compare this with the tanks.*
>
> David Fletcher[67]

Over the period, it is clear that industry suffered as much from problems associated with poor design as from manufacturing difficulties:

> The case of the Crusader was outstanding… Nuffield Mechanization were given a free hand in meeting the specification, and did not consult the Department of Tank Design, who had no say until they saw the prototype. The DTD report on [the prototype], made in the autumn of 1940, was unfavourable, but was little regarded, and the Crusader was [as late as 1942] practically unaltered in the points in which it had been criticized. It was only very gradually that the Department of Tank

Design was able to emerge from this humiliating position... In due course, however, the firms themselves began to seek its advice... Thus by the middle of the war the DTD and a number of firms [but by no means all] were all capable of design work.[68]

It was thus not just in the field of production that British industry struggled; it was just as handicapped by the lack of skilled designers and draughtsmen. This applied mainly to the newer and smaller firms, but even Vickers suffered, and the problem went further than just the production of designs and blueprints:

As soon as large orders were involved which exceeded Vickers' productive capacity, the whole question of ease of manufacture became an integral problem of tank design. Vickers' designs were frequently of a kind which involved industrial skills and techniques not possessed by the engineering firms who were now to make tanks. There were thus two problems: how to obtain new design resources, and how to ensure that designs should be readily manufactured by it... If design were put into the hands of the firm which was to manufacture, would not the difficulty sort itself out? Design resources would be provided voluntarily by firms who were assured of later production orders, and they would naturally develop models compatible with their [own, often very limited] manufacturing experience and plant... The orders which began to flow from 1936 onwards went, on the whole, to firms with idle capacity, and it is hardly surprising therefore that the design resources of firms which found it difficult to survive the economic stresses of the early 1930s were often fairly tenuous. In November 1936 Vulcan Foundry were given the job of preparing designs for Matilda II, with some assistance from the Tank Design Section at Woolwich.[69] From then until May 1937 they employed only two draughtsmen on this complicated and entirely unfamiliar work; six months later the number had only risen to eight. When in 1937 the firm was asked to design a new medium tank, their representative replied that only after design on Matilda was completed would the firm have 'a small party of skilled designers' and he added that 'it was almost impossible to obtain more designing staff under present conditions'. In November 1939 Harland and Wolff were given the design of the projected Infantry Tank A20 on the grounds that they were 'the only possible firm with half-a-million pounds worth of suitable machinery not being used.' The firm was able to employ only 'three or four draughtsmen'. One organisation, it is true, was created intentionally to supply another specialist armaments firm: Nuffield Mechanizations and Aero Ltd. But the new firm suffered severely from its origin in the light engineering of the motor industry, a type of enterprise which was notoriously poor in genuine design resources.[70]

Hancock summarised it thus: 'It is easier to build a factory than to gather a design team'.[71] This situation was at the very heart of the later difficulties. There was also a missed opportunity to use the know-how of Vickers' experienced design team, as they were best placed to design and develop really top-class tanks; indeed, they were the *only* organisation which was well-placed to succeed. In other words, the MoS could have used them to fill the gap caused by the lack of an official organisation tasked with designing tanks, tasking them to turn official specifications into tanks designed for battle, rather than tanks designed for ease of production using existing facilities and skillsets. The production of the tanks to those designs could then be undertaken by any of the motor vehicle and heavy engineering firms, who would become simply manufacturers, or in some cases just assemblers, of the chosen designs, supervised by Vickers in a kind of grand tank shadow scheme. This would completely remove the requirement for inexperienced design teams to try to initiate a complex project from scratch, reduce the number of different models being built and allow much easier – and faster – introduction of modifications without affecting overall production capacity. In this way, one company at a time could temporarily suspend production to rejig and retool for modifications or even completely new models, without affecting overall output too much. Smaller firms brought into the overall scheme could use their particular area of expertise to make the most appropriate components, leaving assembly of the complete tanks to those companies who were best suited to the task. So, the heavy engineering firms could build the large components including armour and suspensions, and the light engineering firms the large numbers of smaller components required. Vickers' could also provide the overall quality assurance mechanism.

However, this option was not taken, for two main reasons. One was that creating 'shadow' firms capable of building large tanks would require a large amount of government assistance to obtain the necessary floorspace, machinery and retraining to allow them to operate on the Vickers' model using Vickers' techniques – in many cases this would require brand new everything. In fact, this objection never had to be faced, as the second reason had already killed the possibility dead. All the companies involved were private ventures, with shareholders and boards of directors. Their profit-motive remained throughout the war. The government simply would not consider compelling these firms to become in effect 'hostilities-only' satellites of Vickers, doomed to be surplus and therefore uncommercial once the war ended. And so the effort was dissipated among a number of firms totally inexperienced in both design and production of tanks, but which were available and willing to give tank-building a go. It was something of a wonder that they managed to produce tanks at all. That they did was tribute to the assistance provided by members of the Mechanization Board; neither the relatively small firm of Vulcan Foundry (locomotive builders) nor the much larger Harland & Wolff (shipbuilding) would have known where to start in the late 1930s had the Board not been involved from the outset. But the Board could only advise and assist; in the final analysis they could not design the tanks in detail, which meant that the designs suffered not only from the inexperience of the designers, but also from company prejudices and the practice of designing the tank around a firm's existing manufacturing machinery and preferences, not to say the capabilities – or otherwise – of the workforce.

Another option of course would have been simply to revitalise and enhance the emasculated Department of Tank Design. On 22 December 1939, an unnamed author penned this response to the CIGS and MGO who had commented on a proposal to 'hand over tank design to civilian firms who.. have little technical experience of this kind of work and *none* of the military requirements':

It is for consideration whether the present design staff at Woolwich and the MEE,[72] suitably augmented, could not produce much better results... An organisation of this sort would enable a much closer contact to be established between the users and the designers. There would be greater control over the progress of designs and a greater economy would result.[73]

Clearly this proposal fell on stony ground. Hancock though noted a trend of improvement, albeit gradual, but agreed that the lack of an official design bureau was a serious weakness throughout the war:

However tentative and hesitant the AFV designs of the years 1935–1940 may appear, they represent a great intensification of effort compared with the preceding decade. The multiplication of design work nevertheless coincided… with the closing down of the official design department for AFVs under the Superintendent of Design which, in effect, meant the restriction of the Superintendent of Design's participation in tank design to the 'fighting portion of the machine' rather than the chassis.[74]

It is worth asking whether this experience was unique to the fledgling tank industry. As so often, it is instructive to look at the British aircraft industry to note the experience there. Hancock noted that: 'In the… days when aircraft were largely handmade, ease of quantity production could be disregarded. With expansion came also the need for economical design… design calculated to facilitate production by machine tools and jigs, and by a sparing use of 'difficult' components and of skilled labour.'[75] How far this same approach was applied to tank production is difficult to gauge. It is certainly true that design reflected each company's preferences, and this included knowledge of their facilities, processes, real estate, and personnel. So, in that respect it could be argued that 'economical design' was practised. However, where 'economical design' was not practised was in the modernisation of plant, in workspace organisation, and in developing a forward-thinking attitude that would adopt new procedures and where necessary training, and could accept – if not exactly welcome – interruptions to existing production. In other words, 'economical design' where practised only took the short-term view.

Another surprising British design feature was the method employed to produce the technical drawings required for mass production. A wooden mock-up of the proposed vehicle was built to a basic design – often starting out as little more than a sketch or two – under the designer's supervision, which showed the proposed layout. Once approved, one or more mild steel pilots were made by hand based upon the mock-up, and it was only once these pilots had been accepted that detailed technical drawings were produced. This was a case of reverse engineering one's own product. Indeed, the early drawings used to produce the mock-up would be of no use in building the real thing, as so many changes would have to be made.[76]

During the war there were numerous occasions when firms were unable to complete either component manufacture, or even assemble whole tanks, due to the parent company being incapable of supplying the necessary drawings.[77] Skilled draughtsmen were in as short supply as skilled workers, maybe even more so. Hancock wrote that: 'The chief stringency, however, was not in material facilities but in technical personnel. This became more acute as time went on.'[78] Despite all the inexperience of these firms that were brought into tank design from a standing start, there seem to have been few attempts at learning from each other's experiences or helping each other out: 'Little endeavour was made to investigate and mutually to solve common problems of design.'[79] Again, this was probably due to the commercial imperative, although physical separation could also play its part.

Even in a specialist armaments firm like Nuffield Mechanization and Aero – the only other example of course being Vickers – the design department was lacking: the main design capacity for NMA was embedded within its older, sister company, Morris Motors, and even there they had no experience in designing anything larger or more complex than an eight-ton lorry. Part of the reason for this was a pre-war tax arrangement designed to assist the railway companies, which penalised the construction of lorries larger than 2½ tons. This led to light lorries with small engines being favoured in Britain, which was just another unhelpful factor when tank rearmament was required. [80]

Organisation within government

Although a government department existed throughout most of the Second World War called the Department of Tank Design (DTD), its title was somewhat misleading:

> Under the new Director General of Tank and Transport Production, the small Department of Tank Design, recreated in July 1940, was for long restricted merely to modifications in current production.[81]

The responsibility of the department for most of the war was *not* to design tanks – it most definitely did not do what it said on the tin. Rather, it was only there to coordinate the details of each design and to advise companies on production issues. In terms of personnel it was spread far too thin to have much impact. This private-venture approach mirrored the practice adopted by the RAF and which, for the junior service at least, had led to many successes (and also many failures); in large part this was because the companies were experienced aircraft manufacturers already, and only needed a guiding hand. It was not until the A41 Centurion of 1944/45 that

DTD designed its own tank, and this was to become one of the most widely used and battleworthy tanks of all time, and which remains in service (albeit much modified) to this day.[82] It can of course be argued that this success came about because DTD had the opportunity to view all the errors made over the previous years, and was therefore the only organisation capable of seeing the bigger picture.

When in 1936 the post of Director General of Munitions Production was created, many of the functions of the MGO were transferred to that office, including crucially the responsibility for tank production. In 1938 the responsibility for tank design was likewise transferred to DGMP. The Director General was himself moved to within the Ministry of Supply (MoS) in August 1939, taking his responsibilities with him.[83, 84] The DGMP quickly lost responsibility for tanks to a newly created post, the Director General of Tanks and Transport, in October 1939. Most significantly, 'The creation of the post of DGMP was the first of many steps, accelerated after the creation of the Ministry [of Supply] in 1939, to put production in control of development [with] increasing emphasis placed on production as opposed to design.'[85] Tank production was therefore to be in control of design and development, with all the complications that implied; for the first time, quantity was to be rated above quality.

As always with such organisations, the responsibility for a particular specific area implied close liaison, cooperation, and often compromise with other departments; it most certainly did not imply integration at the level that was required for success. From the outset, the need for a close relationship within MoS between the Director of Mechanization and the Directors of Artillery and Machine Tools was clear. As the diagram shows, the fact that the Director of Mechanization was working for a different Director General to the other two cannot have helped the relationship.

The transfer of responsibility for tanks was not to proceed smoothly, and in particular the relationships between design, development, and production which should have been clarified were not:

> with the transfer of both production and development branches to the Ministry of Supply in the autumn of 1939 it was for a time almost obscured. The War Office was deprived at a stroke of all its technical advice and, though it remained the main channel of user requirements and criticism, it could do nothing but pass such quality problems over to the Ministry of Supply for solution...The dislocation was critical in

Ministry of Supply October 1939: the departments with responsibility for tanks

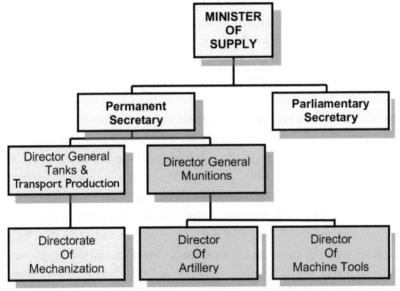

Source: JD Scott & Richard Hughes *The Administration of War Production* (1955) Appendix II.

tank development… to remove the Director of Mechanization into the Ministry of Supply thus cut the last link between the War Office and control of specification policy. There was thereafter a danger – and more than a danger – that the War Office would ask only for what the Ministry of Supply could provide.[86]

The tail was now wagging the dog. The army, in effect the customer for the tanks, had little or no direct control over the products. Once the GS specification had been agreed and issued, it was passed to one of the civilian companies. There was no time even to ask for a number of different companies to submit proposals or to produce outline drawings. This led to 'the abandoning of competitive design, [as] time and facilities did not permit such extravagance.'[87] The company selected was paid to turn the specification into a battleworthy machine, at high rates of production, at minimum effort and with maximum efficiency. Until 1943 most companies failed to deliver any one of these aims, let alone most or all of them. Examples of this will be detailed later. Only once the company had produced its pilot models – or often its first production tanks in those cases where pilots were not made – were the military able to comment on the design: 'Responsibility for the automotive testing of AFV designs rested with the Mechanical Experimental Establishment or MEE at Farnborough, whilst gunnery trials were mostly conducted at the RTC Gunnery School[88] at Lulworth Camp in Dorset'.[89]

Tactical testing of the whole was not conducted, and even these separate trials, conducted by acknowledged and respected experts, were not guaranteed to allow rectification of identified problem areas to take place. For example, the Gunnery School condemned the small machine-gun turret on the Crusader I as totally useless. It was impossible to employ effectively, and was considered to be a waste of time, materials, and stowage space – but hundreds of the tanks were built with them and used in action, whereupon the views of the Gunnery School were endorsed by the crews, who hated the turret. Only after many months was the design modified to remove the item. Because of the way the system was set up, the DTD experts could only offer 'relatively minor help.'[90] And as the troops began to complain bitterly about the quality and reliability of the machines they were receiving, particularly those involved in actual fighting, all the War Office could do was to pass on the complaints to the MoS and ask them for their reaction. The ministry, it must be stated, did little to hasten any improvements or rectifications, as to do so would hinder production and they were under huge pressure to deliver the numbers promised. The personal interest and involvement of the Prime Minister, who almost daily sent scathing memos to the ministry demanding to know why forecasts were not being met, may have helped in terms of quantity but it seems to have been a positive disadvantage in the search for quality. To the MoS, quantity was all. Quality was nowhere to be seen, and this would remain the case for the first four years of the war.

Contracts

By early 1938 orders for complete tanks and tracked carriers had begun to increase, although of course while orders could be placed easily, completed tanks and other AFVs took time. By March of that year nine other firms in addition to Vickers were involved in building AFVs, with the annual value of these orders amounting to around £5.5 million pounds. Compare this to the sum allocated for the same purpose in 1936: £0. The government was trying to create a massive tank and AFV building industry virtually from scratch. One specific problem that emerged out of the hurried nature of such arrangements was that from 1937 contracts were frequently placed without either an agreed target price or a maximum price per unit. This led to manufacturers being able to pass on many additional costs to the Treasury, which would not have happened if a maximum price had been agreed beforehand.[91] Later, around mid-war, the maximum price contract became the usual method, although occasionally fixed-price contracts were issued, using the 'at cost price' plus an agreed margin of profit.

The Contracts Directorates within the Ministry of Supply were responsible for 'securing supplies on the most favourable terms.'[92] Tank contracts were difficult to get right from both parties' perspective, due to the frequent changes in design requirements leading to modifications mid-run, and to the impossibility of placing long production runs over long periods, which clearly would have been the most efficient method, but which would have precluded changes and improvements. However, during the course of the war costs did fall, partly because experience was gained by the firms themselves, partly because of the increased turnover in what remained a capitalist for-profit market, and partly because the MoS, once experience was gained, was able to keep a better eye on costs and see through the companies' arguments.[93] The following table gives an indication of how much the different types might cost:

Basic cost price of tanks

Type	Weight	Contract price (£)	Cost per ton (£)
Infantry Mk I Matilda	11	6000	545
Infantry Mk II Matilda II	25.8	18000	700
Infantry Mk III Valentine	15.6	14900	955
Infantry Mk IV Churchill	38.5	11150	289
Cruiser Mk I A9	13	12710[94]	978
Cruiser Mk II A10	14	12950	925
Cruiser Mk III A13	14.3	12000	842
Cruiser Mk IV A13 MkII	14.8	13800	936
Cruiser Mk V Covenanter	15.9	12000	757
Cruiser Mk VI Crusader	17.6	13700	782
Cruiser Mk VIIIM Cromwell	28	10000	357
Average all Infantry Tanks			550
Average all Cruiser Tanks			743
Average all types			647

Source: Hancock, *Design*. p60.

It can be seen that the average cost per ton gradually fell as the war went on, because experience was greater, design, plant and facilities were improved, manpower was more skilled, and production runs were larger allowing economies of scale. Cruiser tanks were overall more costly than infantry tanks, despite the latter always carrying much more armour. This was probably because of the increased costs associated with the cruiser's engines, transmission and suspension, as they were required to move much faster and therefore required more power and a more complicated running gear. Many of the ancillary components – sights and periscopes, radios, weapons – were the same in both types.

The way that each of the tank-building firms operated was slightly different, not only because of the firms themselves, but also because of the terms of the individual contracts. Much of the necessary ancillary equipment was manufactured under MoS arrangements and issued to the firms under the title 'free issues'. This included such items as weapons, radios, and instruments. Contractual arrangements varied widely, as each type of tank was different in design and manufacture, and prices could not be easily standardised.[95] It is worthwhile examining a few examples of how business was done: [96]

Vickers-Armstrongs, the parent form for the Valentine tank, accepted very little 'free issue' material, but arranged supplies of bullet-proof plate, tracks and turrets either by sub-contract or by making them itself. (This is hardly surprising. Vickers were the major arms firm in the country with massive resources in many fields, so they were able to retain control of as many components as it could either make itself or sub-contract out, in order to maximize profits.)

Components for the Churchill tank were obtained by contracts placed by the MoS itself and were issued free to the members of the group making this tank. Vauxhall Motors [the parent for Churchill] provided the engines [and] sought and obtained capacity for the manufacture of components and the erection of greater numbers of tanks that it could erect itself. (Vauxhall entered the arena of tank building – notice the use of the term 'erection' implying the putting together of components rather than designing and manufacturing components – later than many other firms but were successful in establishing a large group of sub-manufacturers. As the MoS was functioning by this time (during the tank crisis of mid-1940), it was logical for the Ministry to take direct control of contracting for components, even large items such as hulls and turrets, allowing the firms to concentrate on putting them together.)

For the group producing the Crusader, Cavalier and similar types of tank, under the direction of Nuffield Mechanization and Aero Ltd, raw materials and common components were purchased through a central organisation, attached for accounting purposes to [the parent company] Morris Motors Ltd. [Morris then] issued raw materials on repayment and components free to all group members. Its expenses were borne by the MoS, and Morris Motors agreed to forego all profit on its repayment transactions with group members. Contracts [awarded to] individual members of this group were all at maximum prices, but agreed settlements were made within the maximum prices twice a year, each settlement covering production in the previous six months.

Nuffield was always something of a 'funny', in large part because of the intransigent nature of Lord Nuffield. He persistently refused to build other firm's designs, preferring to retain control within his organisation. The foregoing of profit by NMA was not an act of selflessness; it simply allowed it to make its profit not from its sub-contractors, but directly from its contracts with the government.

None of this should be taken as necessarily implying profiteering, although companies of course negotiated with the MoS to obtain the best prices they could. Strict controls were in place to prevent profiteering, and accusations of the practice, so common during the First World War, were a hugely sensitive issue. However, what must be reiterated once again is that all these firms remained commercial organisations, and even in wartime they needed to make a reasonable profit. The definition of 'reasonable', however, was not straightforward but is outside the scope of this work to examine. How did such contracts work in reality? Two examples show that contract forecasts and actual delivery were two very different beasts.

The inexperienced shipbuilding company of Harland & Wolff in Belfast were let Contract T.5325 on 5 December 1938 to build seventy-five A9 Cruiser Tanks. The contract specified that deliveries were to commence on 31 January 1939, and they were to be delivered at the rate of one tank per week. This was not in any way demanding and all seventy-five should have been in the hands of the Army by 3 July 1940. As it was, the first one was not ready until 29 August 1939, some seven months late. (It cannot be argued that there was an unfairly short time between contract let and first delivery, as the contract would have to be agreed by the company.) However, the final one was delivered on 22 June 1940 (the day of the French surrender), thus the contract was actually completed very slightly ahead of schedule and the company might have congratulated itself on a job well done. The army would not have seen this as a reason for celebration, as the delay in the commencement of delivery left the army lacking thirty cruisers that could have equipped two complete squadrons and allowed them to train on the new tanks.[97]

Contract T.4571 for fifty A9 Cruisers from Vickers required that deliveries should begin in January 1939 at the rate of four completed tanks per month for the first three months, and eight per month thereafter. For this the company would be paid £11,280 per tank. Despite the company being the only experienced tank designer and manufacturer in Britain, this was not achieved, and the graph shown compares the contract with the reality:

A9 contract T.4571 deliveries

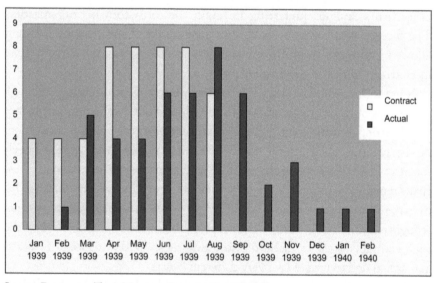

Source: Bovington Tank Museum Contract Card T.4571.

Thus, a contract which was due to be completed by mid-August 1939 was not finished until some six months later. A careful examination of the card also shows that only forty-eight tanks are recorded as being completed; it is not clear if the final two tanks were ever made or not. Also noteworthy is the tailing-off of production to a single unit per month for the final three months.

One of the lost opportunities in the pre-war period was the failure to realise that Canada had the potential to play a huge role as an armaments producer, provided there was substantial investment allied to a forward-thinking policy. Although the Liberal government of that country was opposed to direct involvement in someone else's war, it was clear that public opinion would swing firmly behind Britain when war actually came. The army could have employed the allocations that it was unable to spend within the UK to create a modern industrial base in Canada, stimulating the Canadian economy at no cost to the Canadian government. Despite its anti-involvement stance, it was an offer that it would have found difficult to refuse, if only on purely economic grounds. This base, safe from interference from the Luftwaffe, power shortages and blackout regulations, and with easy access to raw materials and manpower, could have adopted the best production practices to maximise output.[98] It is true that there was little existing surplus plant in Canada, but there was large unemployment and thus great potential from a skilled workforce, the opposite of the position in Britain. The Americans expected such a move; it never happened. Prior to the outbreak of war, the sole AFV production contract placed in Canada was an order for 100 carriers, mainly taken because Canada wished to buy twenty-five for its own use.[99] The first order for 300 Valentine tanks, which had been under discussion since the outbreak of war, was delayed until mid-1940.[100] By the war's end Canada had produced only 5,613 tanks and tank chassis, including 1,420 Valentine tanks, the vast majority of which went to the USSR. Much more could have been made of this potential – and much earlier.[101]

The size of contracts varied greatly, increasing as the war progressed. In the late 1930s the standard contract was for less than 100 vehicles, with fifty or seventy-five typical numbers; this was still enormous compared to the frequently single-figure contracts of a decade previously. By the middle of the war contracts were generally let in three figures, and the largest identified single contract for tanks was for 3,000, to NMA for the production of Centaur, although it is unlikely that this was completed.

Tank design during the rearmament period

In October 1936 the War Office, showing somewhat rare initiative, had looked in detail at the types of tanks that might be required, and the three categories of Light, Infantry and Cruiser were confirmed as policy; until that stage they had been classed by weight – Light, Medium and Heavy.

A lack of direction (and indeed any real possibility that government policy might change) meant that this piece of forward-thinking was not further developed, but neither was it questioned. In January 1939 the Director General of Munitions Production was able to summarise the position:

> The difficulty about the tank has been… to make up our minds exactly what we want… the type of tank you want depends very largely on the theatre of war in which it is expected to be used… Directly you begin to consider a war on a Western basis your tanks become a different business altogether from a war in Egypt.[102]

He was not quite right: the basic design of the tank could actually be the same, but the ability to operate in Egypt would require that the tank was designed *ab initio* with that in mind, so that it could be modified easily in order to suit the conditions. Neither happened. The biggest problem was in terms of the continued muddled thinking that demanded two main types of tanks, cruiser and infantry, with different primary characteristics. Most disturbing of all was that in neither type was 'gun-power considered a primary requirement'.[103]

Armour protection

It became obvious during the late 1930s that the standard protection of around 14mm was too thin to offer sufficient protection from the new anti-tank guns that were starting to appear, and that the new tanks required would have to carry more armour if they wanted to survive. A suggestion was made in February 1937 that it might be possible to extend the life of the ageing Medium II fleet by replacing the existing armour with thicker plates,[104] and to improve the engine and transmission; this was fortunately not taken up but it did at least show that some people were alert to the changed conditions.[105] Where fitting thicker armour did have an immediate impact was in the development of the new series of cruiser tanks. These, it will be recalled, were meant to be reasonably armoured, but their most important characteristic was speed, to allow them to seize fleeting opportunities and unbalance the enemy. The first model of a purpose-built cruiser tank was the A9, designed by Carden to carry only a maximum of 14mm of armour; any more weight would have seriously handicapped its performance, as it only had a power to weight ratio of 12.5bhp per ton when at its lightest.

The A9 was developed into the A10, which with 30mm was still too lightly armoured to be used as an Infantry tank as originally intended, causing it to be reclassified as a heavy cruiser. However, it used the same 150bhp engine as the A9 and struggled to reach a power to weight ratio of 10bhp per ton. The third type of early Cruiser, the A13, had to be quickly up-armoured from the original 14mm to the new standard of 30mm, adding nearly a ton of extra weight, slowing it down and putting more strain on the suspension and tracks.

As we have seen, almost all of the British companies building tanks during the Second World War were simply heavy engineering concerns, not specialist armament firms, and therefore their designs were intended to be simple to build, and flat plates helped to achieve this. Almost all of their designers rejected the use of cast armour, widely used in French tanks, because it possessed certain characteristics that made it difficult to manufacture. A big handicap was that the size of castings was limited in the early war years, but once a casting mould was made, efficient – meaning speedy – production could be achieved.[106] The biggest drawbacks of cast armour were that thicker armour was required to give the same protection than flat plate, and thus weight would increase, as would the demand on raw materials. It was also harder to maintain consistency of quality than plate, and for these reasons cast armour was not much in favour at the start of the war, with the notable exceptions of the one man A11 turret, and the A12 Matilda II turret and nose. The turret on the latter was kept as small as possible to simplify production, with the result that it was terribly cramped and therefore inefficient for the three men who inhabited it. The only way the nose piece could be cast was to make it slightly larger than required, and then manually grind away the excess material – this was a major reason for the slow production of the Matilda II.[107] Operational priorities finally over-rode this objection, and a number of large cast pieces came into use towards the end of the war, including gun mantlets and complete turrets and which often incorporated shapes which added to ballistic protection.

When the first tanks were hurriedly designed and built during the First World War, they were constructed by building a box frame of angled steel, to which armour plates were bolted or riveted on the outside, and which then formed compartments in which the crew, engine and weapons could be installed. This was a simple process as riveting was a semi-skilled operation and widely used in British industry, but it was not entirely suited to the demands of mass production nor indeed of efficient design. Firstly, the frame and rivets added weight, whereas using the armour itself as the frame and chassis was a much more efficient solution. In a typical tank the frame alone could weigh as much as 4 tons and the rivets another 200lb. It restricted the design to simple box shapes and was difficult to make waterproof. Every join between plates was a weak point, and it made the machine inherently more dangerous, as rivets could be struck by hostile fire and turned into projectiles in their own right, flying around the inside of the tank, damaging equipment and causing casualties.

Until just prior to the outbreak of war Britain was still obtaining quantities of 14mm armour plate for cruiser production from Böhler in Austria,[108] and early attempts to obtain replacement plate from the USA were hampered by squabbles over minor differences in specification. However, in general terms the armour quality was never in question; the introduction of nickel-chromium-molybdenum in the 1930s had enabled British armour to perform pound for pound at least as well as any in the world,[109] but how much of it to use and where, and how to impart mobility to it once fitted, certainly were:

> The quality of Allied armour plate was nearly always high. Quantity production and selection of the right sort was more often the problem... the British tended more to the use of jointed, homogenous plate because their industry was already oriented that way and there was no time for vast capital plant reorganization. For this reason largely, they only turned over slowly from riveting and bolting joints to welding them.[110]

We shall return to the issue of welding presently.

Mobility – engines

A select few understood that the weights of tanks were likely to increase during development and on operations, and therefore suitable engines with a lot of surplus power needed to be designed or otherwise procured. This was not easy, as in 'peacetime British motor engineers produced only one or two engines of more than 100 horse-power'.[111] One possible way of overcoming the problem was by obtaining more powerful engines from the aircraft rather than the motor industry, and modifying them for use in tanks. In October 1936 Giffard Martel, the Assistant Director of Mechanization, discovered that the RAF had stocks of 600 surplus Napier Lion XIA engines, each of which developed 465hp. General Elles, the MGO and therefore his boss, refused to provide the limited funds necessary – a mere £500 – to buy an example engine from the RAF, despite the obvious advantages of experimenting in the use of the more powerful engine for the new cruisers. Hugh Elles, if he wanted tanks at all in 1936, wanted only infantry tanks, as he thought that the new cruisers would be too vulnerable to anti-tank fire due to their light armour.[112] This failure of foresight could have paid huge dividends if the Lions could have been developed into efficient tank engines; the potential was certainly there as they were compact in size and they possessed enough raw power to theoretically propel tanks of over 30 tons. A 15-ton A13 powered by a Lion would have a power to weight ratio of 33:1, and even if the engine had to be de-rated to prevent excessive strain on other components, achieving 20:1 would have made the tank incredibly fast. We shall never know, but one cannot help but compare this situation to the later adaptation of the Rolls-Royce Merlin into the Meteor tank engine, a massive success story.[113]

Another problem that bedevilled many British tanks of all types in the early years was poor cooling. Many aircraft engines were air-cooled, as the flow of air over the block in a fast-moving aircraft was sufficient. When this was attempted in the enclosed space of a tank hull, the results were catastrophic, with overheating – even on a chilly Salisbury Plain – a major cause of breakdowns. Put the same tank, without modification, into the North African desert, and the results can be imagined.[114] The answer was clearly to use water-cooled systems, which added weight and volume, and led to some awful design decisions being made. The most prominent of these was the sad tale of the Covenanter. Built by LMSR and using a derivative of the novel Christie suspension, the Covenanter did actually employ a purpose-built engine, a rarity at the time... and since. This was a Meadows 300bhp, which was built specifically for the tank as a very low-profile unit was needed to fit inside the space available. Unfortunately, the resulting powerplant was low but wide, and this left no space inside the hull for the cooling system, meaning that the radiators had to be placed outside the main armour envelope, on the hull front next to the driver where they would be extremely vulnerable to damage, and also massively complicating the 'plumbing'. Fortunately, it was never to see active service, being reserved for armoured formations in the UK, although nearly 1,800 were built. The best that can be said about it was that its terrible reliability forced inexperienced fitters and crew members to increase their mechanical proficiency, which would pay dividends later.[115]

Force development and organisation

The tactics of trench warfare on the 1914–18 model still dominated high places, and the relevance of this seemed at the time to be proved by the impregnable concrete fortification of the Maginot and Siegfried Lines… A more advanced design and development policy during the years 1936–40 might well have been disastrous in the ensuing period: as far as quality factors in many military equipments (sic) was perhaps not really made until after 1940, but at least a false start was avoided.[116]

Professor Hay, the author of this statement, makes an important point. It may well be that it was fortunate that the army did not get new models of tanks earlier than it did, as it may have been saddled with heavy models, designed by the veterans of the First World War, and intended solely for breaching such defensive positions. With production lines turning out tanks designed in the mid-1930s, for the sake of argument the A7E3 design, it would have been very difficult to switch to better designs in the immediate aftermath of Dunkirk. Worries over too-rapid rearmament leading to large fleets of already-outdated aircraft had certainly occurred to the RAF:

The RAF were certainly concerned in the same period [early 1930s] that a too-rapid expansion might take them in an unwelcome direction: What the Air Staff were afraid of was that if pressed to hard the Government might embark on a premature expansion which would saddle the Air Force for many years to come with obsolete or obsolescent aircraft. It is therefore no wonder that political pressure for immediate expansion was resisted by the Air Staff… chiefly for fear of cluttering up the air force establishments with low quality aircraft… The full scale rearmament was successfully delayed for nearly two years.[117]

Once production of unsuitable types was under way, it would have been almost impossible to stop, as later events were to prove. As it was, a trench warfare mentality saddled the army with a preponderance of the less useful infantry tanks for the first half of the war. With such problems of design and production, it is no wonder that the task of equipping Britain's new armoured forces was so slow. The following table shows the build-up once war had begun:

UK tank state 1939

Date	Light Mk VI	Infantry	Cruiser	Total
3 September 1939	834	86	77	997
31 October 1939	1068	90	117	1275

Source: Tank Board Notes and CAB 21/1161

It can be seen that, not surprisingly, building the smaller, lighter but much less capable light tanks was much faster than the more complicated and newer infantry and cruiser designs. Problems with infantry tank production – mainly of the A11 model – can be seen in the table; although the policy at the time was to build two infantry tanks for every one cruiser, only four infantry tanks were produced in the first two months of hostilities, against forty cruisers. We have already looked at the missed opportunity of employing Canadian production, but as well as this and the home market, there were some attempts in the period to investigate other options, and which looked at buying off-the-shelf from the increasing number of tank-producing countries. Among these were France and Czechoslovakia. MEE tested the latter's Praga TNH/P in early 1939, but it was rejected due to its inability to fire on the move. Of course, even if it had been approved, the annexation of that country on 16 March effectively prevented any further development. The Germans were not as fussy, as their doctrine did not require tanks to shoot on the move and adopted large numbers of the TNH/P as the Panzer 38(t). The French had also begun to rearm, and their Hotchkiss H39 was also examined; once again, it was not selected and once again, the surrender of France in June 1940 negated any further exploration of potential from that country. Britain was standing alone.[118]

The other side of the hill – Germany

By contrast to the muddled British thinking and the partition of tanks into three distinct classes that were incapable of performing each other's roles, in 1934 the Germans had decided to build tanks 'versatile enough to be successful in all tactical roles... [their] armour was only thick enough to protect them from armour-piercing bullets'. In fact, the German policy before the war was that each type of tank had to carry only enough frontal armour to make it resistant to its own gun. Their early attempts at tanks, the Panzers I and II, were the equivalents of the British light tanks, with one crucial distinction: they were recognised from the outset to have only limited combat power. Importantly, they served as the basis for starting a tank industry from scratch, for learning design and production lessons, and to develop improved manufacturing techniques. They saw quite a lot of action until 1942 but were thereafter largely withdrawn or used as the basis for specialised AFVs, including as self-propelled anti-tank guns. Larger tanks were required, with better armament and armour protection. Even before the Polish campaign of 1939 the decision had been taken to up-armour the medium tanks to a minimum 30mm, and after the experience of that campaign a further increase, to 50mm, was demanded. This was then increased once more to 80mm in 1942. This enabled the Afrika Korps tanks to resist the two-pounder except at very short ranges, whereas the same weapon had been extremely effective against their medium tanks in 1940.[119] Looking at the continuous development of the two major German medium tanks available at the start of the war, the Panzer III and IV, is informative.

Development started in late 1934 for a fully tracked medium tank to be the medium battle tank in the new Panzer formations. This was to become the PzKpw III,[120] which started life as a 15-ton tank with a 37mm anti-tank gun specifically for killing enemy tanks. Initially it was intended to mount a maximum of only 15mm of armour, with a V12 Maybach engine developing 265bhp; power to weight was therefore a respectable 17bhp per ton. In its final version, the Ausfuhrung (Mark) N, it had increased in weight by nearly 50 percent, mounted a short 75mm gun, had a maximum of 57mm of turret frontal armour, and was powered by a 320bhp engine, still giving it around 12.4bhp per ton.

Its running mate, the PzKpw IV, was developed to an even greater degree. First seen in 1936, this was a 20-ton infantry support tank mounting a short 75mm gun to take on enemy anti-tank weapons, with 15mm of armour, and a 247bhp engine (thus 12bhp per ton). From around 1932 (and *before* Hitler came to power), the Germans had wanted to mount a 75mm gun on their medium tanks.[121] The tank changed role around 1941 to become in effect the medium battle tank for the German army, when the Panzer III and IV swapped roles. By now it mounted a long 75mm dual-purpose gun, carried up to 80mm of armour plus spaced armour shields on hull and turret, and was driven by an improved 296bhp engine. This was the tank that most Allied tank crewmen fought against, and which was often but erroneously reported as being a Tiger. Analyses of German tank engagements in Normandy were to indicate that around 80 percent of German engagements and penetrations were from the 75mm, only 20 percent coming from the 'eighty-eight'.[122]

The Mk IV was reliable and low, but its biggest virtue was the ability to be modified and updated to give better firepower, mobility *and* protection. In particular, it was built with a 64in diameter turret ring, which was critical when more powerful guns needed to be mounted. Although it was never the best tank in the field after 1942, it was available in large numbers and remained in production, only really starting to become obsolete in 1945.[123]

Hitler's support for the new armoured arm was critical. Famously and possibly apocryphally, when he saw a panzer demonstration in January 1934 he exclaimed 'That's what I need! That's what I want to have!'[124] A great advantage lay in this early commitment to armoured forces, giving them a level of priority unheard of in Britain. The Germans were also capable of errors of judgment though: in 1933 Guderian identified the need for German tanks to mount a 50mm gun, but to simplify production and to ensure ammunition standardisation this was not achieved until 1941.[125] Kenneth Macksey thought that:

> The fundamental German superiority in tank design lay in basic design. They paid fastidious (and time-consuming) attention to detailed research on power plants, transmissions, suspensions and tracks, and they finally produced machines which were more reliable than those of their opponents and which, above all, were capable of incorporating... guns of larger calibre.[126]

Macksey was surely correct, but despite many such advantages, David Fletcher noted that in 1940:

> It would be wrong to pretend that German tanks were that much better [than British types]. The two smallest models, Panzers I and II, were as poorly armed and armoured as similar British machines. The Panzer III was undergunned [and under armoured] when compared to Matilda II... and it suffered from recurrent failures of the torsion bar suspension... The two impressed Czechoslovakian models, the 35(t) and 38(t), were tough on their crews, being cramped and very harsh on the suspension.[127]

At the start of the Second World War, the Germans certainly enjoyed a numerical superiority over Britain, possessing 211 PzKpw IV, ninety-eight PzKpw III, and nearly 3,000 other tanks.[128] When the British tank fleet was added to the French, however, the Germans never possessed numerical superiority, and in many ways neither did they possess the technical advantages that they were to enjoy over the next two or three years. But they did use their tanks better tactically and operationally, and that made the difference. And crucially, the results of the victory in 1940 then brought them an unforeseen advantage, one which would enable them to dominate British tanks technically for at least the next two years. When the Germans overran France and the Low Countries in May and June 1940, they were able to destroy or capture almost every single British tank on the continent, and it is probable that many more were captured more or less intact than were destroyed. This allowed them ample time to evaluate the strengths of these types, and to arrange countermeasures. This included the immediate adoption of the 50mm anti-tank gun to counter the Matilda II armour, and up-armouring the two medium tanks to resist the two-pounder. The effects of this were to be felt from early 1941 when the two armies next clashed, in North Africa. We will look at the merits of the subsequent German tanks later, including the two most famous models, the Tiger and Panther.

The other side of the hill – the Royal Air Force

Throughout the war it was the primary object of the supply branches of the Air Ministry and of the Ministry of Aircraft Production to maintain the quality of aircraft at the highest possible pitch even though this was bound to reduce the output.[129]

This approach was the exact opposite of the 'quantity before quality' attitude so prevalent in tank production circles from the late 1930s until at least 1942. The differences are both understandable and explainable. Firstly, the safe performance of each aircraft – its 'airworthiness' – was never sacrificed for ease of production. This was due to an attitude so deeply ingrained in everyone involved in aircraft production that it was probably never suggested at any stage that corners involving reliability – synonymous with safety – should be cut. It is one thing for an engine to misbehave or fail in a tank, quite another in a single-engined aeroplane at 20,000ft. Secondly, the RAF was able to benefit from the head start it had achieved at the commencement of rearmament. Of course, during the Battle of Britain in particular, moments of crisis occurred when it looked as if losses would exceed supply, but this never resulted in safety being compromised. There was an understanding that every component part in an aircraft needed to behave at an optimum level of performance, and this seems to have impacted on the attitude of workers as well as the very rigorous systems of quality control employed by aircraft manufacturers. The same could not be said of the tank producers, as we shall see. And the aircraft industry possessed significant advantages in terms of design:

> In peacetime, before the expansion of 1935 and 1936 raised for the industry the problems of quantity production, most of the aircraft factories were little more than experimental aircraft shops built around their design establishments... the firm as a whole was a mere extension of the design organisation.[130]

Indeed, there were no fewer than sixteen established aircraft-producing companies in Britain, including such well-known names as de Havilland, Hawker and Avro. Additionally, there were four companies who specialised solely in designing and building aircraft engines, with the big two being Rolls-Royce and Bristol. This was hugely different to the tank situation, where not only was there only one firm with experience in designing AFVs – Vickers – but there were no specialist tank engine designers at all. Possibly more critically, many of the companies brought into the tank production sphere were also expected to design, from scratch, their own products. It was a recipe for disaster. In terms of research and development, once again the RAF reaped significant benefits:

> The bulk of the advanced research in aeronautical and more importantly aerodynamic problems was largely done for the industry by other bodies and, to some extent, by other industries. Some of it was conducted in the universities and especially in the aeronautical department at Cambridge... A certain amount was done in the National Physical Laboratory and more important still was the work of the Royal Aircraft Establishment... The RAE largely devoted itself to theoretical problems allied to production, and, in addition, performed experiments, tests and calculations of problems passed to it for solution by the firms... The theoretical frontiers of new design between 1934 and 1943 were set by people outside the British aircraft firms. Within these frontiers the work of the designer was, and could afford to be, very practical.[131]

It should be noted that the RAE did, in some instances, assist with specific problems related to tank design and in particular engines, but because of its chain of command and focus on supporting the RAF, this was rare and cannot have had much influence.[132] This is yet another example of the types of problems caused by the separation of army supply from those of the other two services. In some ways, though, the aircraft industry suffered (at least during the early days of rearmament) with similar problems to the tank companies, in that:

> In a number of (aircraft) firms the legacy of the days when they were little more than design establishments still lingered on, and production continued to suffer from handwork methods... the firms, having been selected on the basis of their achievement in design, proved incapable of handling the purely industrial problems of aircraft production on a large scale.[133]

Production realities could also lead to unfortunate decisions:

> It was an accepted doctrine in the Air Ministry and the MAP that industrial organisations, and above all the labour force, stood in danger of being dissipated every time a factory was forced to reduce its operations. Stop-gap orders were thought necessary in order to prevent the firms from losing their labour, and especially their skilled labour...[134]

This use of stop-gap orders led to undesirable side-effects, such as the continuing in production of the outclassed Fairey Battle light bomber, which was a deathtrap when used against the Germans in 1940.[135] However, it is in the nature of air forces that types no longer suitable for front-line service can often be found useful in other roles. So it was that the Battle continued to be used well beyond its original function as a bomber, both as a trainer and as a target-tug. However, the fact that over 3,100 Battles, a type obsolete even before the start of the war, were made (with production finally ending as late as December 1940) might be considered a greater waste of resources than the 1,771 useless Covenanter tanks. But let us not forget that despite being obsolete as a fighting machine, the Battle remained fundamentally safe and airworthy – in army terms, it was reliable.

Chapter 4

British Tanks Between the Wars

Service medium tanks

At the armistice in November 1918, the army found itself with many hundreds of tanks deployed in France, many more on order, and had eighteen battalions in France to man those vehicles plus seven in the process of formation around Bovington; the Tank Corps, only formed as a unit in 1917, was on the rise. But the cessation of hostilities brought an immediate reduction in both the number of units and the personnel. By the early 1920s the Tank Corps found itself with only four tank battalions, all in the UK, manning the remnants of the the First World War tank fleet, the majority having been broken up for scrap.[1] A small battalion helped to provide muscle to the British Army of the Occupation of the Rhine (BAOR), a few detachments were sent to Russia, and in time twelve armoured car companies were formed to operate in Egypt and India, but the future of the corps remained in doubt. The new – and expensive – designs that had been under development for use in 1919 and beyond were likewise scrapped or scaled back, with the large contracts being cancelled.[2] The Tank Corps needed a new tank, however, and despite the fiscal stringency of the early 1920s, managed to get one; Winston Churchill, the Minister of War, announced during the debate on the Army Estimates in 1920 that the army would be equipped with a new, 20mph high-speed tank. Despite the Ten-Year Rule, the army had somehow managed to obtain £220,000 for forty-two new tanks, and it needed to be spent quickly, or it would be lost.

The company that was to lead the world in tank development over the next decade, Vickers-Armstrongs, had not been involved in the tank story during the conflict, but in 1923 produced its own design, known as the Vickers Light Tank Mk I, given the GS project title of A2E1, the E1 denoting it as the first experimental model of that type. Because of its weight the army classified it as a medium tank, having somewhat arbitrarily decided to classify tanks as light if they were under ten tons, heavy if over twenty, and medium if somewhere in between. The tank therefore came into service in March 1923 as a medium tank, officially the 'Tank Medium Mark I' (Mk I) but known to all as the Vickers Medium. This design, updated over the following years, would be Britain's main tank for the next two decades, with just over 200 being built in Mark I and II varieties. For good or ill, much of what happened in tank design over the next twenty years can be related to the experience gained in operating the Mediums. In terms of production, the Royal Ordnance Factory at Woolwich hand-built the first batch of the tanks,[3] with V-A constructing most of the remainder, as follows:

Vickers Medium tanks

Type and mark (build standard)	Registrations	Qty	Remarks
Medium Mk I	T1–14	14	T1 Mild steel. Made by ROF Woolwich.
Medium Mk I	T15–30	16	T15 Mild steel. Made by V-A.
Medium Mk IA	T31–41	11	Made by V-A.
Medium Mk IA	T42–58	17	Made by V-A.
Medium MK I/II Hybrid	T59–60	2	AKA Indian pattern. Used in trials in India from January 1925.
Medium Mk II	T61–115	55	Made by V-A, although ROF may have built around twenty-one of them.
Medium Mk II	T116–156	41	Made by V-A.
Medium Mk II	T169	1	Made by V-A for Australia.
Medium Mk II	T192–205	14	Made by V-A.
Medium Mk II	T206–220	15	Made by V-A.
Medium II Special	T221–224	4	Made by V-A for Australia.
Medium II Command	T236	1	AKA Medium II Special, known as Boxcar.
Medium II Command	T349–352	4	Probably not built.
Medium Mk II**	T363–365	3	
Medium IIA	T418–427	10	Made by V-A, although ROF may have built six of them. Built specifically for use in Egypt.

Although in many ways the Vickers Medium was an extraordinarily simple, almost childlike, design – a box for a hull with tracks and a turret – it was in fact extremely modern in a number of ways, bearing in mind not only the available technologies and financial limitations, but also the fact that it was designed in haste, and it incorporated a number of features that would become standard in tank design. The hull was a simple box, constructed of a steel frame with a maximum of only 6mm (later 8mm) armour plates bolted to it, less than the First World War Mk V tank. The engine, a readily available commercial Armstrong-Siddeley V8 developing 90bhp was, unusually, air-cooled and gave the 11-ton tank a power-to-weight ratio of around 8bhp per ton: hardly amazing but certainly enough to move it at about 20mph on a good surface, and a bit more if the crew knew how to tweak the engine. The driver sat to the right of the engine, at the front of the hull and in his own compartment, with a bulkhead keeping the worst of the engine heat from him. Early designs of driver's hatch proved to be dangerous, and many an unwary driver was badly injured when his hatch crashed down on him, but this was resolved with a simple redesign.

There was also a genuine suspension – the First World War tanks all lacked this feature – so the crew could start to enjoy if not comfort then at least a slightly less bone-jarring ride, which also allowed them to be able to shoot on the move. In fact, this ability to fire on the move can be viewed as something of a hindrance to subsequent tank development, as the RTC (it was entitled Royal in 1923) adopted the capability with great enthusiasm, and spent a lot of their time training gunners to be able to do this. Unfortunately, there were problems. Firstly, the gunnery practices were mostly conducted over the sides of the tank, driving along at a reasonably sedate pace on a fairly smooth track and shooting at large targets at quite close range – typically about 500 yards. Even under these artificial conditions a lot of training time and ammunition expenditure was required, neither of which could be guaranteed under wartime conditions. Secondly, and as importantly, to aim the gun in elevation the gunner used a shoulder-piece attached to the gun mounting, allowing him to 'ride' with the movement of the tank and anticipate exactly when to fire – he was in a knees-bent standing position, and did not have a seat. The apparent success of this arrangement – the RTC boasted of their abilities in this respect, and no self-respecting demonstration was complete without a line of Mediums hitting target after target on the move – led to many of the early Second World War tank designs incorporating the free-elevation arrangement, rather than using a more complicated but easier to use (and more consistent) elevation gearing system, controlled by a hand wheel. This led to the fire applied from the tanks being less accurate than it might have been, as only pre-war trained RTC gunners could get the best out of the system.

The main gun was a 47mm three-pounder mounted in a fully-rotating turret: such turrets had appeared on British armoured cars and on French Model 1917 light tanks during the war, but this a first for a British service tank, and represented a major advance. In theory the three-pounder was a dual-purpose weapon, capable of firing both AP and HE, but in practice only solid-shot was issued, which was capable of penetrating about one inch of armour at 1,000 yards; for the early 1920s, this was more than sufficient. The killing and suppression of infantry was left to the many machine-guns mounted around the hull, as well as one mounted in the turret coaxially alongside the main gun, another innovation that would be adopted as standard throughout the world. However, the British doctrine, in which machine-guns were viewed as the weapon of choice for engaging infantry and other 'soft' targets, was flawed. Anti-tank guns, when they were developed, were invariably provided with bullet-proof armoured shields which were effective at stopping standard ball ammunition, and in any case the range of the MGs was much less than that of the main gun. The lack of an HE shell for British tanks was not to be even partly solved until the introduction of the six-pounder gun in late 1942 and led to the deaths of many crews fighting in the desert campaigns.

Some of the tanks were classified as close support or CS tanks; instead of the three-pounder, these were provided with a 3.7in breech-loading howitzer, confusingly and inaccurately referred to as a mortar. This weapon was mainly used to fire a 15lb smoke shell intended to provide rapid local smokescreens that the assaulting infantry could use to close onto an enemy position. Although an HE shell was developed, it was rarely used, and again British policy took a wrong turn at this point. Instead of giving the CS tanks an HE capability in order to use them to provide rapid HE fire to support attacks, most shells carried were smoke,[4] and this applied equally to other CS tanks built later – the A9, A10, Churchill and Matilda II, for example. Again, a problem with a root cause located in the 1920s was not solved until a new 95mm weapon with an extremely effective HE shell was introduced in the second half of 1943.

The tank commander was located in the turret, which was better for overall control but caused difficulties with communication to the rest of his crew, particularly the driver; this forced the development of inter-communication (IC) systems, starting with simple speaking tubes in 1927, but eventually leading to efficient radio harness systems with each crewman being able to talk to the others. In order to assist the commander, his position was at the top of the turret, and he was provided with the so-called 'Bishop's Mitre' cupola, another innovation which would lead to the development of a really efficient and world-leading all-round vision cupola – but not until about 1944.

As experience was gained, more tanks were built and these incorporated improvements, with the earlier tanks often being brought up to the latest standard with a workshop programme of modifications; the tanks were thus redesigned incrementally. In many ways the most crucial modification was the introduction of radio transmitters and receivers; this began in about 1931, when the Mk II** models began to be fitted with bulky radio sets. In many circles it was widely believed that it was technically impossible to receive or transmit from a moving vehicle, and although the ranges were short and voice quality often frustratingly poor, the journey had begun, and in the Second World War British radio communication procedures and technology were both at a very high standard. The doctrinal insistence that the radio set must be mounted in the rear of the turret led to issues with finding the space, as well as technical problems in linking the hull and the turret, but this is a doctrine followed to this day and which has been proved to be correct. Another innovation based on the gun tank was the design and production of a special command tank for the Brigade Commander, the world's first Armoured Command Vehicle.

Experimental Medium tanks

Towards the end of the 1920s a limited amount of money was made available to experiment with more modern medium tanks, with the designs intended to produce a tank that could – again, if money was made available – replace the Medium I and II models in service. What happened next was heavily influenced by the development of the only experimental Heavy tank built in Britain between the wars, the A1E1 Independent. Specified in 1922 and ordered from Vickers four years later, the 33-ton tank carried a maximum of 28mm of armour, extraordinary for the time, but the salient feature was the way in which its machine-guns were mounted. Unlike the Medium I/II which had its hull MGs in ball-mounts protruding from the sides and rear of the box, the Independent featured no fewer than four Vickers .303in sub-turrets mounted around the main three-pounder turret, with one either side of the driver at the front, and two more, one each side, at the rear. The need for these small, cramped and inefficient turrets became something of a standing requirement in the tanks to come, and affected not only the design of the experimental Mediums, but also tanks that fought in the Second World War – the A9 and Crusader I cruisers being prime examples – where they were worse than useless, taking up space with a system that poisoned its gunner with toxic gases as soon as firing started. It is a mystery why such a flawed concept was persevered with, but it was, until finally discredited as late as 1942.

Back to the experimental Mediums. The first design was known as the A6E1 but was commonly referred to as the Sixteen-Tonner as this was the top weight that would allow them to use the then in-service military bridges. The first two of three prototypes were built by V-A and delivered in 1928, with different transmission arrangements; another followed just over a year later. Vickers had obviously been affected by the MG turret bug as they wanted to mount no fewer than three sub-turrets, but weight requirements precluded this and they had to settle for two, one either side of the driver – if this wasn't bad enough for the poor gunner, each mounted two Vickers MGs. However, the placement of the turrets meant that the only place left for the driver was at the front, and although his side vision was severely restricted by the two turrets, placing the driver in the centre makes his job easier where width judgement is required, such as crossing a bridge or driving onto a railway flat. But this was a spin-off, not a conscious decision, and it never became policy until adopted for the Chieftain design in the 1950s.

The A6 was capable in many areas; its 180bhp engine could achieve a top speed of 30mph and almost 20mph across country. It was thought of as a good platform for shooting on the move, which remained an important criterion to achieve. But they were expensive, reckoned to cost around £16,000 each, a prohibitive amount if the entire Medium I/II fleet was to be replaced, so none were ordered into service. Thoughts turned to trying to build a tank with similar capabilities, but significantly cheaper. Fitting the bill was the Medium III, which appeared in 1933.

It appears that the Medium III series was not initially developed just in order to be cheaper than the A6, as both types were in fact developed more or less concurrently. The fact that they were called Mediums from the start rather than being given a GS 'A' development number indicates that they may have been procured with the intention of being the first of a line of new service tanks to replace the Medium IIs in service, but as it turned out, once again only three were made.[5] The basic layout was similar to the A6, with a central driver flanked by two MG sub-turrets. But the turret was very new, with curved vertical plates forming the front of the turret, which extended to the rear with what became known as the bustle, designed specifically –

another innovation – to house the radio set. In order to reduce weight new armour, developed by the English Steel Corporation and known as CTA, for cemented tank armour, was used; this was a form of face-hardened armour. CTA was adjudged to be particularly good at resisting small arms rounds, and furthermore it was assessed that 10mm of CTA was the same as 14mm of ordinary plate, making for a significant weight saving so that it could come in at around the same weight as the Sixteen-Tonners. Unfortunately, it was difficult to work with, expensive to produce, and made welding much harder, so the British experiments with CTA on Light Tanks ended before the war, as we shall see. All three crew members in the turret now had seats which were attached to the turret so that they rotated with it, another innovation destined to become standard. For their time, both the A6 and the Medium III were pioneering, innovative machines with many redeeming features; indeed, it is fair to say that when they were produced, Britain still led the world in tank design, and this was to continue with the next – and final – experimental medium tank, the A7.

The A7 was specified in 1928, and initially two models were constructed, both by ROF; the idea was to produce a lightweight medium tank (if that isn't an impossibility!), that was faster and had improved trench-crossing ability compared to the in-service tanks, and was also able to provide a good gun platform – the need to be able to shoot on the move was still being stressed. The tanks were often referred to as the Ten-Tonners, as the intention was for them to come in at 10½ tons, right at the lower end of the medium tank category. Of course, as always happens, the weight of the tank increased during development and eventually they weighed around 14 tons, as they all used the then-standard 14mm plate. Improvements included the introduction of a new, angular turret. The three-man turret featured a commander's cupola and its basic shape was used not only in the contemporaneous light tanks being developed, but was also seen on the early cruisers, starting with the A9. In a break from the design tradition set by the A1, A6 and Medium III tanks, rather than the multiple MG sub-turrets, the hull of the A7 mounted a single Vickers MG in the vertical front plate. Strangely, this was on the right-hand side, as for no reason that has ever been explained the driver was situated off-centre to the left, which must have made road driving in the UK difficult if not perilous. Equally strangely, a driver's escape hatch was positioned in the nose of the hull, immediately under the machine-gun; although the suspension design precluded the positioning of side access hatches, placing one in the front of the tank not only meant that escaping crewmen would be facing the enemy, but also substantially weakened the armour protection in that area. It is probable that the realisation of the problems associated with the design led to the use of under-floor escape hatches in many early war tanks.

In many ways the key use of the A7E1 and E2 models was to trial various types of suspension systems, as both used the same 120bhp engine; this meant that the power to weight ratio was only marginally better than the Medium I of 1923. In choosing the suspension the leading expert in such systems, Sidney Hortsmann, of the Slow Motion Suspension Company in Bath, was consulted. It appears that he suggested trialling a novel idea, the use of torsion bars. When a roadwheel encounters an obstacle, it needs to move up and down, and as many as possible of the forces transmitted to it should be prevented from being transmitted in turn to the hull and the crew. Therefore, the suspension has two requirements: to absorb the shock by some form of spring, and then to damp the oscillations quickly to return the spring to its resting state, otherwise the suspension will cause the vehicle to bounce. A torsion bar does this by using a long bar of treated steel that runs transversely across the bottom of the vehicle hull. It is fixed at the end opposite the wheel it works with. The wheel axle is fitted to the bar, such that when moving up and down the bar itself twists in response to the motion of the wheel. Resistance to this twisting force provides the shock absorption function, and the tendency of the bar to want to return to its resting, untwisted state provides the damping. The system is simple with few external components; but it does take up some of the scarce internal volume at the bottom of the hull and the bars can be time-consuming to change if they break or crack. However, for unknown reasons Hortsmann's idea was rejected; David Fletcher wrote that 'this might well have been one of the most short-sighted decisions on tank design ever made by British tank designers, [it was] used extensively by the Germans throughout the war, and subsequently by the Americans and others with considerable success'. [6] The benefit of hindsight…

The suspension systems adopted all proved troublesome and none were suitable for service tanks, although of course failure brings increased knowledge if nothing else; the final suspension design was adequate at 15mph but could not cope with the 25mph that the tank was capable of. In 1934 work started on the very final inter-war Medium, the A7E3, again produced by the ROF and which was completed in late 1936.[7] Although similar in overall construction to its earlier brethren, the E3 now weighed 18 tons and featured numerous improvements based on the experience gained, including, an extended bustle with provision made for the new No.9 radio set. The A7E3 was required to use a more powerful engine to cope with the increase in weight, and of course, no commercial alternative was readily available. So the decision was made to use a pair of water-cooled AEC bus engines, each of a different design, and linked to the transmission through a complicated gear system. This provided the necessary power output but added to the maintenance load as two engines required servicing, not one; a similar system had been used on the 1918 Whippet fast tank, but the many complaints about the negative aspects of using a linked two-engine system from then had been forgotten only fifteen years later.

To summarise the development of the A6, the Medium III and the A7 tanks: they all contributed to advances in understanding and design, particularly with regard to suspension and turret design. They all reflected the RTC obsession with shooting on the move and were all under-armoured, even if the 14mm or equivalent armour carried was the standard for that time. However, by the mid-thirties the days of the medium were over, as the new categories of cruiser and infantry tanks had now found favour and were to exert their baleful influence on tank design in the period leading up to the next war. And it is interesting to note that while the turret design on the A9 and A10 cruisers can be clearly linked to the A7, it was the Matilda II infantry tank that benefited most from the suspension trials conducted on the medium tanks – and also inherited its problematic twin-engine arrangement because of the apparent success of the experimental layout used on the A7E3.

Experimental Medium tanks

Type	Registrations	Qty	Remarks
A6E1	T404 (ML8698)	1	Mild steel. AKA 16 Tonner. Made by V-A.
A6E2	T405 (ML8699)	1	Mild steel. AKA 16 Tonner. Made by V-A.
A6E3	T732 (MT9637)	1	Mild steel. AKA 16 Tonner. Made by V-A.
Medium Mk III E1	T870 (MT9707)	1	Made by ROF.
Medium Mk III E2	T871 (MT9708)	1	Made by ROF.
Medium MK III E3	T907 (MT9709)	1	Made by V-A.
A7E1	T816 (MT9639)	1	Mild steel. AKA 10 Tonner. Made by ROF.
A7E2	T817 (MT9640)	1	Mild steel. AKA 10 Tonner. Made by ROF.
A7E3	T1340 (BMM117)	1	Mild steel. AKA 10 Tonner. Made by ROF.

Tankettes, light tanks and carriers

Although this family of armoured vehicles does not play a large part in the story, it would be remiss to ignore it completely as it did play a part in the story of design and development. Soon after the First World War, British tanks were divided into three classes according to their weight rather than their capabilities or intended use, and all tanks under 10 tons were classified as light. This did not imply that Britain intended building any tanks in the class, but there was some support for the concept, based on alternative theories of the way that tanks might be used to overcome enemy defences, and, not least, on the French experience. As well as using heavy tanks such as the Schneider and the Saint Chamond, the tank built in the largest quantities by the French was the seven-ton Renault Model 1917, generally referred to by its project code, FT. With a crew of only two men and over 3,000 built before the end of the war, this tank was very different to the heavy tanks used elsewhere: the British Mk IV tank weighed about 30 tons and had a crew of eight. The theory that led to their development was that if an army was able to field hundreds of light, simple and relatively mobile small tanks, then the enemy would not be able to deal with them all and would be swamped by sheer weight of numbers. This led to two British design teams in the 1920s working on vehicles that would allow this, and which would then develop into not only the British light tank models of the 1930s, but also the famous Carrier family of armoured vehicles, including the Bren and Universal models, which were made in the tens of thousands during the Second World War.

One of the first soldiers to become enthused in this mode of warfare was Giffard Martel, a Royal Engineer mentioned elsewhere in this work but who in 1925 was an instructor at the army's staff college at Camberley. Despite this busy job, in his spare time – and using his own money – he set about building a prototype one-man tank, the first in a line of one- and two-man machines that we will refer to here as tankettes, in order to differentiate them from genuine light tanks and the tracked carriers. To some such tankettes were an adjunct to infantry attacks on fortified defences and would be used to bring machine-guns forward under armour (proof against small-arms ammunition only), which would also be able to destroy emplaced enemy machine-guns. In this view they assisted, but did not replace, conventional infantry battalions. Another more extreme view was that whole infantry battalions should be converted so that every attacking soldier was in such a machine. This is not the place to debate these views, and in any case, neither was adopted. What is key is that tankettes allowed much experimentation into simple armoured vehicles and allowed progress to be made at a time of limited funds, particularly in the fields of steering, suspensions, engines, and the like. As Martel was limited in his ability to build prototypes – although he was never limited in his energy, imagination and inventiveness – he formed a partnership with the leading car manufacturer, Morris Motors, who could see commercial possibilities in the venture.

Alongside Morris-Martel, the other significant player was Carden-Loyd Tractors, formed in 1926 by the partnership of John Carden and Vivian Loyd and seemingly inspired by Martel's ideas. Their first demonstration to the War Office was on 8 November of that year, showing their Mk I one-man tankette. Their range of vehicles, basically all experimental types, culminated in the Mk V machine. In total around eighteen of these machines were produced (plus one believed to have been sold to Hungary) before sufficient interest in the firm led to Vickers-Armstrongs purchasing the company in 1928. At that point something resembling production began, and nine Mk Vs were made by Vickers-Carden-Loyd (VCL). It was at the end of 1928 that the significant breakthrough occurred, both in terms of design and production, with the Mk VI. This vehicle became the inspiration for two parallel lines of vehicles, the carrier family and the light tanks. Nearly 400 Mk VIs were produced, mostly at V-A but some by the ROF, with over 100 exported including to Italy and Poland where they became the basis of locally-produced vehicles that saw service in the Second World War. It can be said that by this point, the concept of a one-man vehicle had been discredited and displaced by that of the two-man tankette.

In the mid-1930s a VCL design called the Vickers-Armstrong Dragon 50 (VAD50), developed from the earlier chassis experiments on tankettes, became the basis not only for a new series of Light Dragon tractors designed to tow field artillery guns,[8] but was also developed into an experimental machine-gun carrier to carry a Vickers MMG, which could be dismounted and used in its tripod or fired from within the vehicle. This marked the start of the famous carrier family of vehicles, including the Scout and Cavalry carriers used by the BEF, the replacement of the Vickers MMG with the new LMG to create the Bren Carrier, and then the sensible decision to design a Universal Carrier, which could be adapted without much difficulty into a whole range of roles, including an Observation Post (OP) vehicle, a 3in mortar carrier, a battery starting and charging vehicle and a flamethrower. Sources indicate that the British built around 57,000 carriers of all types, with Ford of Canada building about 29,000 and the US up to 20,000. Australia and New Zealand between them produced another 6,000 or so. There are three points to make here. One is that these 112,000 or so vehicles constitute one of the largest, if not the largest, numbers of tracked vehicles ever built around a particular design family. Secondly, their use imparted mobility to the British and Canadian infantry that was lacking in all other nations in the Second World War and must be considered as a significant success. And thirdly, it is possible that historians and researchers count such tracked vehicles as tanks, and we must therefore be wary of making the same mistake when attempting to work out exactly – or even approximately – how many tanks Britain produced during the Second World War.

Finally, we need to look at the British Light Tank development, as these most definitely were tanks, even though they proved to be extremely vulnerable in terms of protection and lacking sufficient punch in terms of their firepower. It must be stressed that they came about not because Britain saw a role for them (at first), but because they were simple and inexpensive and offered a way of Britain acquiring something resembling a tank force on the cheap. The story really begins with the VCL design called the Carden-Loyd Mk VII: although this was known to have certain weaknesses and defects, it interested the War Office sufficiently for an order to be placed for four modified versions known as Light Tank Mk I in September 1928, these representing the first light tanks to be ordered by the army. Over the next few years the Light Tank evolved through a number of marks, summarised in the table, which demonstrate clearly how improvements were made to tracked vehicles in the days before computers, modelling simulations, and the like; it was done through experimentation and learning from mistakes. In this period Britain had a luxury that was not present during the Second World War: time. It took something like eleven years to develop the light tank from its Mk I form into its definitive Second World War version, the Mk VIB, and even then, despite huge advances being made, the VIB was still not fit for the types of combat it was used in from 1940 onwards.

Overview of British light tank development 1929–1945

Type	Year	Max Armour	Armament	Weight	Mobility	Crew	Remarks
Light tank A4E1	1928	Mild steel	.303in Vickers MMG.	2.5 tons	Meadows EOC 59bhp engine. 35mph.	2	AKA Carden Loyd Mk VII. **One built.** To MWEE 1928.
Mk I	1929	14mm RHA.	.303in Vickers MMG.	3.25 tons	Meadows EOC 59bhp engine. Horstmann suspension. 35mph.	2	**Four built** as A4E2–E5. All four to MWEE for trials Oct 29–Jan 33. No service use. Round turret. A4E2 constructed as an AA tank with twin Vickers .50 HMG.
Mk IA	1930	9mm RHA.	.303in Vickers MMG.	3.25 tons	Various engine, gearbox and suspension systems trialled.	2	**Five built** as A4E6–10. Diesel engine trialled. **Four more built** for trials in India.
Mk II/IIA/IIB	1930	10mm CTA plate.	.303in Vickers MMG.	4.25 tons	Meadows EPC 58bhp engine. Replaced c.1932 by Rolls-Royce 66bhp engine. 30mph.	2	**66 built.** Initial 16 ordered Dec 30: 12 from V-A (V-C-L), four from ROF. New larger rectangular turret. No.1 Wireless set in turret. Subsequent order for 50: 29 x IIA ROF, 21 x IIB V-A. Additionally, **50–59 Mk IIB Indian Pattern built** for RTC Light tank companies.
Mk III	1932	10mm CTA plate.	.303in Vickers MMG. (Some fitted with .50in HMG?)	4.5 tons	Rolls-Royce 66bhp engine. Wilson transmission. Hortsmann suspension.	2	**42 built in 1934:** 25 from ROF, 17 from V-A. 36 served with 6 Bn RTC in Egypt.
Mk IV	1934	11mm CTA plate.	.303in Vickers MMG.	4.3 tons	Meadows ESTE 88bhp. 36mph.	2	**28 built:** 14 by V-A, 14 by ROF. First type to use armour as chassis, rather than using internal frame.
Mk V	1934	11mm CTA plate.	.303in Vickers MMG. and .50in HMG.	4.15 tons	Meadows ESTE/L 88bhp. 32mph.	3	**Two prototypes built** in 1933: L3E1, L3E2. **22 built** by V-A. First 3–man light tank.

Type	Year	Max Armour	Armament	Weight	Mobility	Crew	Remarks
Mk VI	1935	14mm RHA.	.303in Vickers MMG. and .50in HMG.	4.8 tons	Meadows ESTL 88bhp. 32mph.	3	**81 built:** V-A, North British Locomotive, Ruston-Hornsby, Vulcan Foundry, plus 10 not known. No.7 Wireless set in turret.
Mk VIA	1935	14mm RHA.	.303in Vickers MMG. and .50in HMG.	4.8 tons	Meadows ESTB/L 88bhp. 32mph.	3	**115 built:** V-A and ROF. Ten sold to Australia 1937.
Mk VIB	1936	14mm RHA.	.303in Vickers MMG. and .50in HMG.	5.2 tons	Meadows ESTB 88bhp. 35mph.	3	**886 built:** V-A, John Fowler, NBL, RH, Thorneycroft,[9] VF. 60 AA tanks included in the total.
Mk VIB Indian Pattern	1936	14mm RHA.	.303in Vickers MMG. and .50in HMG.	5.2 tons	Meadows ESTB 88bhp. 35mph.	3	**93 built:** V-A.
Mk VIC	1937	14mm RHA.	7.92mm BESA MG & 15mm BESA HMG.	5.2 tons	Meadows ESTB 88bhp. 35mph.	3	**168 built:** V-A, JF, RH, VF.
Mk IIIB Dutchman	1938	NK.	Nil	NK	NK	3	49 built by V-A: residue (majority?) of tanks not supplied to the Netherlands were used by Britain as training vehicles.
Mk VII Tetrarch	1938	16mm RHA.	Two-pounder and 7.92mm BESA MG. Some fitted with 3in CS howitzer.	7.5 tons	Meadows 175bhp.	3	Air-portable light tank, originally a private venture by V-A, known as PR or Purdah. Limited use in Op Ironclad (Madagascar) 1942 and on D-Day. **Two pilots built** (V-A) plus probably **170** service tanks (Metro-Cammell.) Used for first DD trials.
Mk VIII Harry Hopkins	1941	38mm RHA.	Two-pounder and 7.92mm BESA MG.	8.7 tons	Meadows 149bhp. 30mph.	3	**100 built** by M-C. Air-portable light tank designed to replace Tetrarch. No operational use.

Note: production figures are approximate, as the various sources disagree on how production was broken down, particularly from the Mk VI onwards. Figures here are based on the Chilwell census records.

Note: experimental models and one-offs not proceeded with are not shown.

It can be seen that the tanks gradually got heavier, as invariably happens during development, and that the big change came with the introduction of the Mk V, featuring for the first time a two-man turret. It was widely understood by this time that the tank commander could not cope with all the responsibilities forced upon him in a one-man turret – loading and firing the gun(s), dealing with ammunition resupply and stoppages, operating the wireless set, navigating, controlling other vehicles if a section leader, to say nothing of the maintenance burden when out of action. The introduction of the two-man turret handed at least some of these to the gunner who was also the wireless operator, but it would not be until three-man turrets were introduced on larger tanks that the workload was correctly divided. As a result, during the Second World War, a number of infantry and cruiser designs suffered from having a two-man turret, including some marks of the Valentine and the six-pounder armed Crusaders, not to mention the one-man turret on the A11 Matilda.

One experimental design based upon the Mk VI deserves a mention, as it represents a potential missed opportunity. Tank T1667 was fitted with a larger open-topped turret mounting a two-pounder gun, the same weapons carried on cruiser and infantry tanks. The design can be considered as what would later become known as a tank destroyer – lightly armoured and with no overhead protection but carrying considerable firepower for its size. It is not clear why the design was not proceeded with – it may have been something as simple as there not being sufficient guns available to mount on a vehicle for which no official doctrine existed. We can only speculate the effect that such a vehicle would have had, even in small numbers, had it been available to the light tank units in the BEF in 1940, but we can be certain that it could not have made things worse.

It should also be noted how the early light tanks were either built by Vickers-Armstrongs (or one of its subsidiaries), or by the Royal Ordnance Factory, but as war approached, a number of other firms were brought into light tank production using what was known as 'instructional' orders – the nearest that the army ever got to employing a shadow scheme as operated by the MAP. These included Ruston-Hornsby and Vulcan Foundry, both of which went on to produce considerable numbers of larger tanks. The light tank, although not suitable for modern combat, was instrumental in bringing such firms up to speed, and thus contributed indirectly to British efforts to improve tank production. But to conclude, as was noted earlier, light tanks and carriers are not really a big part of this story, and we should now return to the mainstream, by looking at the first two infantry tanks made by Britain in the years immediately before the war.

A11 Matilda infantry tank

The design and development of Britain's first-ever purpose-designed infantry tank, brought into service to support the new doctrine, is in many ways an object lesson in how not to go about designing a tank; the only reason that the tank was authorised for production was because it was built down to an acceptable price. Sir John Carden, the designer, was very conscious of how difficult it was for the army to obtain the funds to develop tanks in anything like the quality and quantity needed, and as a result proposed to the army in October 1935 that he could design a purpose-built infantry tank for under £15,000 in development costs, and then produce service tanks for only about £5,000 each, a budget intended to make the army interested at a time when a 20-ton tank would be expected to cost around £20,000. In the mid-1930s British infantry tank proponents fell into two schools: those who envisaged a large, powerfully armoured tank carrying a gun plus machine-guns, as opposed to others who saw the need for a well-armoured but small and therefore inconspicuous machine armed only with a machine-gun. Because of the limitations caused by working to a tight budget, Carden's design fell into the latter category and so the army got an infantry tank that forced their hand – at least initially.

Famously, Carden sketched out what such a tank might look like: it would be a two-man affair – with all the problems known to exist from such a design – and suggested that it would be capable of a top speed of only 5–8mph; no more would be needed for a tank designed to accompany the infantryman on foot. By using existing components from other vehicles, plus a cheap, readily available Ford engine and gearbox, the A11, as it became known, would fulfil the role without any frills; despite British doctrine, he intended to save money by not including a wireless set, although service tanks did end up with them fitted. Where the A11 was impressive was in the armour it carried, an exceptionally thick (for the time) 60mm frontally, twice as much as German medium tanks. With simplicity came a degree of reliability, although the .50in version of the Vickers MG that some of the tanks mounted was notoriously bad for having stoppages. One user thought that it was one of the tasks of the driver to try to rectify problems by repairing one of the two feed blocks for the gun, even while the commander/

gunner/loader wrestled with the second spare block fitted to the weapon. The inadequacies of the design were not lost on thinking soldiers. Writing in 1945, Brigadier Custance of 8th Armoured Brigade considered that 'this sort of tank, and indeed the idea of an AFV without a gun, was severely criticised by many thinking tank officers at the time... it doesn't pay in the long run [just] to save a few thousand pounds.'

A single prototype, A11E1, was made in mild steel and, with a few modifications to the design of the cast turret and to the suspension, was brought into service as the A11, attracting the nickname Matilda.[10] It was tested at MEE starting in September 1936, and the specification for the production version was issued in April 1937. For unknown reasons, there was then a year's delay, and the first contract, for sixty (enough for one regiment plus a few spares) was not placed until the end of April 1938, with another order for a second batch placed a month later in May, and a final batch of nineteen ordered in January 1939. Despite the worsening

A11 Matilda production

Type	Military Registrations	Civil Registrations	Quantity	Remarks
A11E1 Prototype	T1724	CMM880	1	MEE trials commenced in Sep 1936. Mild steel.
A11 Initial Model	T3433-3492	HMH788-847	60	Morris type radiator used. Simple driver's vision slit. Contract T4319 29 Apr 38. Built between Aug 38 and Apr 39. Majority lost in France 1940.
A11 Second Model	T5551-5610	RMY905-964	60	Ford type radiator used. Flap-type driver's vision device. Contract T5429 May 38. Majority lost in France 1940.
A11 Second Model	T8101-8119	PMX458-476	19	Ford type radiator used. Flap-type driver's vision device. Contract T6458 Jan 39. Contract completed 2 Aug 40. Majority remained in UK.

situation in Europe, production at Vickers-Armstrongs was not rapid, and by 1 February 1939 only thirty-seven tanks had been delivered; by the end of October, with the war nearly two months old, the total had increased to eighty-four, still not enough for two full battalions. In total only 139 service A11s were built, plus the single prototype; nearly 100 of them were to be lost in France in 1940, and the remainder were then used for training before being scrapped. The key attribute of the A11 turned out not to be its cheapness, although of course that was what made the tank attractive in the period before army rearmament started in earnest, but its simplicity was allied to its thick armour. Not many crews were able to say the same about the tanks with which they were to be equipped for the next few years.

A12 Matilda II infantry tank

It is incontestable that the A12 or Matilda II was Britain's best tank in the early war period, due to a combination of its excellent – at the time – two-pounder gun, thick armour, small target profile and three-man turret. It gave the Germans a great surprise in France in 1940 when nothing short of an 88mm anti-aircraft gun could penetrate it frontally, and the Italians had nothing to match it in North Africa. It was also slow and difficult to manufacture, technically complicated, difficult to maintain in the field, and almost impossible to upgrade to any significant degree.

In October 1936, only one month after the A11 pilot started its trials, the MGO, Hugh Elles of First World War Tank Corps fame, ordered that the development of a larger version of the A11 should be investigated, identified as General Staff project A12. This would use a similar pointed nose to the A11 but even more frontal armour, and must be capable of mounting a gun as well as an MG in a frontal sub-turret, plus it had to use a diesel engine and be capable of 15mph. It also needed to be able to cross an 8ft-wide trench, something the smaller A11 was clearly incapable of. Equally clearly, his mind was influenced by his experiences of trench warfare and his fear that the new anti-tank guns being introduced could mean the end of the tank unless armour was improved – it was for this reason that Elles had no faith in the concept of cruiser tank warfare.

By this stage Vickers-Armstrongs was at full capacity and unable to take on the new design or manufacture; the era of 'leave it to Vickers' was over. The War Office looked around for a company that could be given the task of design parent and manufacture, and their eyes fell upon Vulcan Foundry

(VF), a near-failing enterprise based in Newton-le-Willows, Lancashire. As the MAP had snapped up most of the truly excellent engineering companies, the WO had to take what was left. Vulcan had recently been given a number of small 'educational' orders to learn how to produce light tanks, but these were to someone else's design and the firm had no experience of tank design from scratch. In November 1936 they were contracted to design and build the new infantry tank, the A12. It was to prove to be a steep learning curve for the company, and something of a miracle that the tank produced was as good as it was.

Assisted wherever possible by members of the Mechanization Board, who gave a great deal of help with the hull layout, Vulcan was still required to take the lead in the production of general assembly drawings and the creation of a wooden mock-up, prior to the creation of one or more pilot models made from mild steel. They were provided with the drawings of the experimental medium tanks, including the A7E3, plus a complete Medium tank fitted with the so-called Japanese suspension, as well as a number of other components including final drives and track examples taken from the Medium III. It was with a modified version of this suspension and a hull which replicated some features of the A7E3 that the Matilda was designed. Design work started on 21 December 1936, although initially the company was only able to employ two draughtsmen on the project, which greatly slowed this stage of development. This is a good example of how the lack of skilled labour could handicap tank design and production: it took nearly nine months for the team to be increased to eight, which speeded things up greatly.

On 16 April 1937 the early work was approved, and on 25 May authority was given for Vulcan to build two pilots, A12E1 and E2. Fortunately, it was also confirmed that there was no requirement to mount an MG sub-turret, which with the design of the front of the hull would have been a near-impossibility anyway. Vulcan did well to produce a workmanlike design within the constraints they were working to, but the whole project was not in any way straightforward. For example, the company found it increasingly difficult to get sub-contractors to deliver the additional specialist parts needed for the tank. Vulcan lacked the ability of larger companies to persuade or coerce small companies to give them priority or even to meet their contractual obligations, but eventually the Director General of Munitions Production got involved and this appears to have solved the problem to a large degree.

Because Vulcan lacked tank experience, the assistance given by the various official bodies meant that Matilda took on a form that was influenced by the latest work that had been done on experimental mediums, meaning the A7E3. The distinctive mud-chutes were insisted on by the War Office and followed their use on the earlier tanks; although these and the 1in-thick side armour added weight, they did provide some measure of extra protection, particularly in 1940 and until the Germans adopted the 50mm anti-tank gun. Not having to mount a hull machine-gun ran contrary to the doctrine of the time, but there was simply no room to fit one on the quite small hull front, and therefore the driver was placed into a central position, with the advantages that this conferred. The front of the hull was designed as a one-piece nose casting, similar to the earlier (but in many ways contemporaneous) A11, as it was pointed, although the addition of cast tool lockers either side somewhat disguised this by changing the appearance of the front of the hull. The use of cast armour was driven by the specification of exceptionally thick armour on the front of the tank, which prevented the use of attaching armour plates to the internal frame, the standard construction method. The Mk IV Light Tank had demonstrated that by using thicker armour plates the internal frame could be largely dispensed with, but the technology of the day was not able to replicate this on a much-larger infantry tank. After seeking advice from the heavy armour experts in the admiralty, the Mechanization Board contracted Hadfields Ltd of Sheffield to supply much of the plate and cast armour used on Matildas. It is probable that the all of the cast armour components for Matildas, including the turret shells and hull noses, were made in Sheffield and transported to the six firms who were eventually to assemble the tanks, which of course slowed down and complicated production.

A three-man cast turret was designed (by the Superintendent of Tank Design), and although this added efficiency by taking a lot of the burden off the commander who was also provided with a vision cupola, it was again kept as small as possible to save weight and the whole affair was very cramped for the crew. Although not fully realised at the time, the use of cast armour also caused production difficulties; the castings had to be made over-size and required all the excess material to be laboriously ground away by hand, a time-consuming process known as cheese-paring.

The biggest problem with the Matilda II, as it came to be called, was in finding a suitable engine to power what would clearly be a heavy tank. Ignoring the old First World War tanks, and the A1E1 Independent, which weighed around 28 and 33 tons respectively, most of the inter-war work had been conducted on light tanks, with the Sixteen Tonners a notable exception. The new cruisers being built around the same time were being kept as light as possible so the engines chosen for them would not be suitable, and the introduction of the A12 meant that an engine had to be found for a tank weighing over 20 tons. Around 200bhp was required, and in the end it was decided to adopt a method that had been trialled on the A7E3, pairing two engines together and combining their output to give the required horsepower. The engines chosen were described as a 'new type' of AEC 6.7-litre diesel, with two of them coupled via a complicated component called the crossdrive, which delivered the combined output to the gearbox. Matilda was the first British service tank to use a diesel engine, neither common nor popular at the time. There were many experts who immediately recognised the problems that this solution conferred: two engines to be serviced, more spare parts required, and additional weight and complexity added by the crossdrive. The 'plumbing' in the hull – the myriad pipes, cables and controls that were needed – made the layout of the engine compartment a driver's and fitter's nightmare, with many components and sub-systems completely inaccessible. Sprocket rings could not be removed and changed without removing the side armour plates; to solve this, soldiers in regiments would cut them in half, allowing each half to be changed separately without having to remove the armour and all that entailed.

In early August 1938 the A12E1 was sent for gunnery trials at Lulworth. As usual the tank was tested to see how good it was at providing a stable platform for shooting on the move. Not surprisingly for a heavy tank moving at slow speed, it was assessed to be good in this area when shooting over the side, although not when shooting at targets head-on, the most likely and preferred option; the suspension pitched up and down. But other problems were also recognised. The small size of the turret and fighting compartment was noted as impairing crew functioning, and the original design for the turret crew positions was thought to be dangerous, with nothing to prevent them being hit by the recoil of the two-pounder, or indeed to prevent the driver being struck by the power-traverse of the turret. But these problems could be overcome. More difficult to solve was that the fan systems required for engine cooling dragged a lot of grime inside the tank, and within ten minutes the crew and internal components were all coated in dust. It was stated that in Europe this would be a nuisance, whereas 'in Egypt this will be unbearable'.

But such problems were either not recognised at the time or were thought to be unimportant: war was very much more likely in June 1938 than it had been when Elles first proposed the tank twenty months earlier. The first two contracts for nearly 200 tanks were placed with Vulcan on 11 June 1938, but building the tanks was very slow, with the first production tank not available for testing at Farnborough until two weeks after war had been declared. Although by 11 July 1939 contracts had been placed for nearly 700 A12s, by 31 October 1939 only six service tanks existed. This was because in addition to being a technically complex tank, it had also proved to be a complicated tank to build. It had been designed by Vulcan using its own facilities, practices and preferences, and this not only made life difficult for the soldiers operating them, it also applied to the other firms building the tanks to Vulcan's design. As it was apparent very early in the development phase that Vulcan would not be able to singlehandedly produce sufficient numbers of the tank quickly enough, five other companies were brought in to build the tank. These were Ruston & Hornsby (RH); the London Midland & Scottish Railway (LMSR); John Fowler's (JF); North British Locomotives (NBL); and Harland & Wolff (H&W). In total, these firms built Matildas as follows:

Vulcan	610 (plus ten mild steel instructional tanks)
NBL	619
Fowlers	580
LMSR	426
Ruston & Hornsby	395 (plus five mild steel instructional tanks)
H&W	275
Total	2,905 (plus fifteen mild steel instructional tanks – 2,920)

Although the tank was improved while in service, with new engines fitted and other enhancements including attempts at rationalizing the plumbing and changing the locations of difficult-to-access components, the tank was unable to mount the six-pounder gun when it started to become available in 1941, and that doomed it to obsolescence. In any case, better tanks were by then becoming available. But stopping production was almost as difficult as starting it, and the final tanks were not built until mid-1943, at least a year after they were no longer a viable proposition on the battlefield, despite their thick armour and small size. The remaining tanks were used as training machines until they were no longer required, and then broken up for scrap.

Matilda marks – overview

Mark	Engine	Coax MG	Remarks
A12 Infantry Tank Mk II (Matilda II Mk I)	AEC 183/184 (87bhp each)	Vickers .303in	Original service tank with Vickers MG
A12 Infantry Tank Mk IIA (Matilda II Mk II)		Besa 7.92mm	Change in MG to BESA
A12 Infantry Tank Mk IIA* (Matilda II Mk III)	Leyland E148/ E149 or Leyland E164/ E165 (95bhp each)		No change in designation regardless of which pair of engines fitted. E148/149 used aluminium crankcases; E164/165 used cast iron.
A12 Infantry Tank Mk IIA** (Matilda II Mk IV)	Leyland E170/ E171 (95bhp each)		Rigid engine mounting. Increased fuel capacity.
A12 Infantry Tank Mk II (Matilda II Mk V)			As Mk IV but with Westinghouse air servo for gearbox.

The early Cruisers

Three other tanks complete the inventory of those designed before the Second World War and which saw service during the first two years of the conflict. These were the Cruiser Tanks Mk I, II and III, otherwise known as the A9, A10, and A13. The lines of development of the first two were interconnected, but the A13 was a separate beast and very important, as it was from that tank, and particularly its suspension design, that subsequent British cruisers were to be developed, up to and including the Comet.

The A9 was originally conceived of as a new medium tank design, changing its name to cruiser when the designations were amended to reflect the new doctrine in 1936, when it became the Cruiser Mk I. The idea was to develop a new medium tank that was an improvement on the existing and experimental mediums, but much lighter and at less cost, the two things being virtually synonymous at that time – take a ton off the tank, save £1,000. The intention was to bring it in at 7 tons (which of course would have classified it as a light tank!) but inevitably the weight rose and when fully equipped was closer to 13 tons. The detailed work was completed by Vickers-Armstrongs, under the direction of Sir John Carden. A brand-new type of suspension, known variously as Slow Motion or the Bright Idea, was developed from the work carried out on the light tanks and used on the tank, with the idea being taken up by Horstmann's specialist company. The suspension consisted of two externally-mounted units, each with three roadwheels; most unusually, the first and last wheels were larger than the middle four.[11] A big advantage of this type of suspension was that it simply bolted on to the lower hull sides: if damaged it could be repaired quickly in the field, unlike suspension systems that had components built into the hull of the tank.

In order to save weight, the lower part of the hull was almost boat-shaped, giving it good ground clearance but not much mine protection, at that stage not identified as the major threat that it would later become. The policy of keeping the tank small meant that it must have been a cramped affair for its six-man crew, more so for the driver flanked by the two hull machine-gunners either side of him – the compulsion to fit MG sub-turrets was still very strong. Ammunition feed also proved to cause problems, with the belts often jamming the traverse to add to the gunner's woes. Another design flaw was discovered only after the tank had been in action: there were a number of shot traps that tended to deflect incoming fire into vulnerable areas; not least of these was caused by the sub-turrets deflecting fire into the lightly-armoured sides of the driver's hood.

The pilot model, A9E1, was contracted for on 15 June 1934 and completed in April 1936. It went to MEE for trials with its original Rolls-Royce Phantom II engine in July 1936, but this was unsuccessful and it was refitted with an AEC A179 petrol engine in April 1937. The top speed proved to be about 25mph on the roads, but the suspension was inadequate for the speed of the tank moving across country, giving the crew a difficult ride. As Colonel Justice Tilly famously summarised: 'It's a dud. Too small for cross-country work, the crew are too cramped to work their weapons or wireless; it bounces like a rubber ball; the tracks come off.' This last point proved to be a major failing, despite it being a mechanically reliable tank – during trials, at least. Photographs of the tank on campaign in France, and later in North Africa and Greece show many examples of tanks immobilised with broken tracks.[12] In large part this was due to the requirement to keep track width narrow in order to meet the overall width requirements imposed by the railway loading gauge. Another effect of using narrow tracks was to increase the ground pressure to greater than it would have been with a wider design. Track design had not been a major problem on the slower mediums, but as speeds increased the need for more work in the area became apparent. Bob Crisp, who earned a rare DSO as a lieutenant with 3RTR in Greece in 1941, knew the tank well. His first encounter with them led him to describe them as 'impressive-looking, near obsolete cruisers', despite them being no more than two years old. During the brief campaign he offered the following insights into the performance of the A9 and A10 tanks that made up the majority of 3RTR's equipment:

> [After their first move] five tanks were left lying out in the vineyards with hopelessly broken tracks... my right-hand tank edged slowly forward [and I heard a voice] in the ear-phones: 'Hullo Cool, Collected[13] calling, I have broken a track'... I told the driver to start up. The starter whirred and stopped. There was no answering roar from the engine. 'We've had it sir, ruddy petrol pump's unserviceable...' we were about to destroy the tank for want of a flipping petrol pump.

The first fifty service tanks were built by V-A and completed between February 1939 and February 1940; at that time Vickers advertised that it was the largest tank order they had received – a damning indictment of Britain's commitment to its armoured force between the wars. Another seventy-five were made by Harland & Wolff in Belfast between August 1939 and June 1940, bringing the total built to a paltry 125. David Fletcher recorded that there was an opinion that the design was too complicated for the majority of inexperienced firms to be able to cope with.[14]

The A9 holds the record for a number of firsts. It was the first British tank to use a (hydraulic) power traverse system for the turret, and the first to use the Vickers tank periscope rather than direct vision glass blocks; both were to become standard features. It was originally designed to mount the old three-pounder gun, but the introduction into service of the new 40mm two-pounder required that weapon to be fitted; in an era of failures, the two-pounder proved to be a very fine anti-tank weapon, probably the best in its class. Despite its inability to fire a high-explosive shell, it remained the best gun in western Europe until surpassed by the German 50mm towards the end of 1940. Some tanks were fitted with a 3.7in close support howitzer, used mainly for firing smoke. Mounted above the gearbox was a small air-cooled auxiliary charging engine, used to power the ventilation fan in the turret and for charging the vehicle batteries. The tank was also notable for its use of sloping plates, which gave the same performance as thicker armour mounted vertically. The turret was a slightly modified and improved version of that first seen on the A7. Nonetheless, with a maximum of only 14mm armour – as ever, a concession to save weight and cost – the protection was to prove woefully inadequate only a few years later.

The A10 or Cruiser Tank Mk II was a direct derivative of the A9, intended to be more heavily armoured in order to become the first infantry tank, and using the same components as the A9 wherever feasible. Had this been possible, developing infantry and cruiser tanks along similar lines could have proved to be an efficient approach to tank production, but the experiment was not successful. In order to turn a cruiser design into an infantry tank in late 1934 the maximum armour protection was increased to one inch (25mm), at the time considered thick enough, but which would soon be overtaken by anti-tank gun development. This required a redesign of the hull, removing the two MG turrets and redesigning the front of the hull. Initially this produced a well-sloped glacis plate, the raised driver's hood being the only inelegant part of the design, but the War Office then insisted on the tank having a hull MG, and so the front end was redesigned for a second time in September 1938 to produce a stepped plate, necessitating moving the driver from the centre to the left and fitting in a hull gunner to his right. Strangely, the hull MG was a 7.92mm BESA but the turret coaxial MG was a .303in Vickers, meaning that two different types of MG ammunition were required. This was subsequently remedied with the Mk IIA on which the Vickers was replaced by a second BESA. In order to carry the additional armour Vickers took an unusual route: the basic hull was built up from thin plate made of malleable steel, to which thicker panels or armour steel were rivetted to create the necessary thickness. This represented the first use of what would come to be called composite armour.

By 1937 the inadequacy of the design was recognised and the development of the A11 and A12 was pursued instead. The A10 was reclassified as a heavy cruiser – a strange amalgam of weight and role, and which had no place in the supposed tactical doctrine of the day. For unclear reasons but probably based on the realisation that the increased armour would make it a (slightly) harder nut to crack than the A9, the tank was ordered into production in 1937, with 170 being built by Vickers; seventy-five by BRCW; the same number by NMA; and ten by RW Crabtree. Thirty of the tanks were built for the CS role with the 3.7in howitzer. As with its older brother the A9, the tank saw service with the BEF in 1940, in North Africa, and Greece in 1941, by which time it was obsolete.

The story of the development of the third cruiser tank, the A13 (Cruiser Mk III) started in 1936. Giffard Martel, he of the light tanks, had become the Assistant Director of Mechanization and almost immediately was sent to Russia to observe the Red Army tank manoeuvres that September. What was most impressive to him was the demonstration of the BT fast tanks moving at speed across country, using a revolutionary new suspension developed (stolen) from an American design. This was the Christie suspension, featuring large roadwheels with long travel and a system of shock absorbers. Martel was determined to introduce such a system into Britain, but there was no chance of dealing with the Soviet Union. The other option was to work directly with the prickly inventor, Walter Christie, who was trying to interest the US Army in his design. It was at this stage that William Morris – Lord Nuffield from 1938 – another difficult character, became involved. He headed the Morris Motors car company and, in order to become involved in tank design, in 1936 had created a new organisation specifically for the task – Nuffield Mechanizations & Aero, or NMA. NMA acquired the patent rights for the Christie system, allowing Britain to develop it legally. In a series of moves worthy of a novel, a prototype of Christie's tank was eventually bought at a cost of nearly £10,500 and exported to Britain. When it finally arrived in late 1936 it consisted of a nine-ton chassis designed to carry only a machine-gun turret, with a turret ring diameter so small that even a light tank turret was too large for it. Clearly a lot of redesign was required to turn the chassis into a medium/cruiser tank, including enlarging it considerably.

Powering the tank was an American Liberty V12 engine, a 1917 design originally intended for aeroplane use. The engine produced around 350bhp, an impressive amount of power and one of the secrets of the tank's speed, although this was not the engine used in the Soviet versions. As we already know, Martel had investigated the purchase of surplus Napier Lion engines – probably specifically for the A13 project – but this was refused on financial grounds, and so by default the Liberty in its N-L form became the preferred option for the new tank, a decision that made some sense at the time but which would cause a great many problems over the next eight years.[15] There was no doubt that the engine could propel the tank at a good speed, with a governed road speed of 30mph being easily achievable, but problems of cooling, air filtration and reliability were to plague it in service. One feature of the original Christie design that was not required was the ability to remove the track and propel the tank by attaching a chain drive to the rear roadwheel; this was fortunate as it was technically complex, of dubious practical value and would have made the British cruisers using the system even more difficult to produce and less reliable.

Two mild steel pilots of the new NMA-designed cruiser were ordered in January 1937 and delivered in late 1937 and early 1938; these were the A13E2 and E3, the E1 designation having been used for the original Christie tank. The intention was to armour the tank to the then-current 14mm standard meaning that the tank was likely to weigh around 14 tons; maximum use was made of aluminium to keep the weight down, including the roadwheels.

Unfortunately, the team tasked with modifying and developing the suspension worked to this weight, rather than building in the capacity to accommodate a heavier tank at a later stage. This was to cause problems later, as the inevitable increases in weight of the A13 and its successors caused a number of suspension problems, particularly involving damage to the front roadwheel mountings and axles. A new three-man turret design, similar to that used on the A9 and A10, came from ROF Woolwich, with two-pounder and Vickers MG specified.

The A13E3 model became the basis for the first contract, and sixty-five Cruiser Mk III were ordered on 22 January 1938 and built by NMA, with the first service tank appearing at the very end of that year. The tank was later modified to increase the armour protection to bring it up to a 30mm standard and replace the Vickers with a BESA, being renamed as Cruiser Mk IV and IVA in the process. This increase in protection was achieved on the turret by attaching additional angled panels to the turret sides, in doing so becoming the first use of spaced armour on a British tank. Another 240 tanks, all Mark IV or IVA, were to be built by NMA and forty by the London Midland and Scottish Railway (LMSR), shortly to have a go itself at tank design with the truly dreadful Covenanter. Thus, a total of 345 A13s were built, production finishing around January 1941. Indications of some of the problems that were to beset this line of Liberty-powered cruisers started to be seen in France in 1940, when 5RTR, operating nearly brand-new tanks, withdrew from contact near St Valery but lost as many tanks to breakdowns as they did to enemy fire. A report after the BEF experience regarded the A13 as a reasonably good tank – which it was, for its day – but that there were problems with the armour, still regarded as insufficient, 40mm being suggested as the absolute minimum in future; the same report commented that German anti-tank guns were very powerful, being capable of penetrating 60mm of armour. This was certainly referring to the use of the 88mm against infantry tanks, but the writing was definitely on the wall – and would be ignored. Other concerns were with the design of the track, which gave poor grip on wet ground, the steering drums which wore very quickly, and the inaccessibility of many parts which caused considerable delay in maintenance and repair. However, we must not lose sight of the fact that the tank was developed from a concept in late 1936 through to production beginning only two years later, producing a tank that had many good features and was, for its day, a half-decent fighting machine. Its positive side led to it being used as the basis for subsequent cruiser tank development, with, initially at least, much less success.

Chapter 5

Fourth Best? The Crisis of the Early War Years

Whatever else you do, strive to give the military the third best. The second best takes too long.

Robert Watson-Watt

It would be murder to send our Field Force overseas to fight against a first-class power.

Lord Gort *17 March 1939*

The Army, at the moment, is in the position of having cavalry mounted on ponies in operation against an enemy with full-sized horses, or a man having to fight a duel with a dagger against an opponent with a full-length sword.

Gen MacReady, ACIGS, September 1941

It has been estimated that losses in France arrested tank development in Britain by two years.

David Fletcher *Cromwell Cruiser Tank*

The collapse of France in the early summer of 1940 heralded a period of military effort which made the activity of the rearmament years and the phase of operations in France during the winter of 1939 and the following spring seem trifling. From this situation arose a call for quantity which could not but affect the quality of the weapons themselves.[1]

The Great Tank Crisis of 1940

In June 1940 the major tank crisis of the war occurred, and it greatly affected what happened subsequently. This has received scant attention mainly due to its various components being treated as separate events, but it was huge and affected everything else that happened until the end of the conflict. It was this crisis more than any other single factor that caused Britain's tank units and crews to be equipped with tanks that were the inferior of those fielded by the Germans.

A number of separate but associated factors conspired to bring about the crisis, and these require explanation. Firstly, as already noted, British tank production was already well behind the existing modest schedule. There had been no clearly identifiable stimulus to tank production from September 1939, despite the declaration of war. The Phoney War that followed brought a false sense of security, and failed to inspire the tank producers to dramatically raise their output, so that the monthly totals increased only slowly, with total production of all types between the start of the war and the end of April 1940, i.e. just before the German invasion, came to only 572, only seventy-two per month on average, hardly breathtaking work:

Tank production September 1939–May 1940

Month	Production all types	Percentage increase (Sept 1939=100)
Sep 1939	54	
Oct 1939	86	159
Nov 1939	79	146
Dec 1939	95	176
Jan 1940	56	103
Feb 1940	65	120
Mar 1940	68	125
Apr 1940	69	127
May 1940	138	255

Source: AVIA 22/469

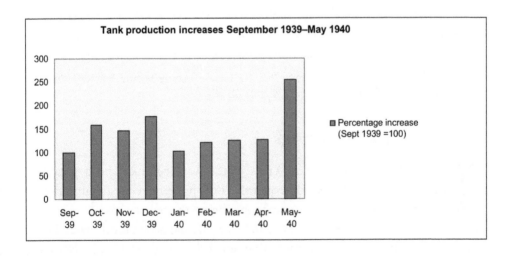

It can be seen from the graph that there was only a very slight increase up to December 1939. Christmas holidays almost certainly account for the subsequent slump (back to the start level) recorded in January 1940, followed by only a very gradual growth for the next three months. The large jump in May 1940 can be attributed to two factors; efficiencies at last starting to take hold, and probably more importantly, the attack on France on 10 May which spurred industry to make a greater effort. The Phoney War was finally over. General Thorne, commanding the Army in Kent, the most likely invasion site, was correct when he observed that 'Germany is organised as a war machine, whereas England has just begun to think about the means of waging a modern war'.[2] As we know, the Germans quickly overran France and the Low Countries. During the period from 10 May until the final day of the Dunkirk evacuation, 4 June, almost all of Britain's stock of modern tanks was lost, as was the last chance of finding external sources of supply within Europe:

[Until June 1940] it was still possible to count on the French Army and French industrial and design resources. The height of the crisis came after Dunkirk, when the country had been denuded of allies, and [the army was] stripped of the meagre harvest of such rearmament as had borne fruit up to that date.[3]

The numbers of tanks that were sent out with the British Expeditionary Force in late 1939 and early 1940 were of necessity pitifully small; the deployment with the BEF over the autumn and winter 1939/40 totalled around 432 tanks, light and infantry, the majority of the latter being the inferior A11 model. The only British armoured division in existence available, the 1st Armoured, was not deployed until 20 May 1940, ten days after the German onslaught, mainly because the production of cruisers with which to equip it was so pitifully slow; it went with around 284 tanks of which only 150 or so were cruisers, the remainder being light tanks used to make up the numbers.[4] The total number of tanks sent to the continent therefore appears to have been about 715 – of these 691 were lost, no more than twenty-four or twenty-five being recovered back to the UK – sources vary.[5] Three light tanks were also lost in the abortive Norway expedition of April, being sunk before they could even be landed.

Tank losses May–June 1940

Type	Lost
Light Mk VIb	345
Light Mk VIc	62
Total Light Tanks	407
A9 Cruiser I	24
A10 Cruiser II	31
A13 Cruiser III	38
A13 Cruiser IV	57
A13 Cruiser IVA	8
Total Cruisers	158
A11 Matilda I	97
A12 Matilda II	29
Total Infantry Tanks	126
Total all types	691

Source: RAC Half Yearly Report No.4 December 1941 Annex M

With the Germans on the Channel coast, invasion was the greatest concern in June 1940 and for the next few months of summer and autumn, before winter weather in the Channel could be relied upon to halt any attempts until early 1941 at the earliest. It is so easy with the benefit of hindsight to disregard the reality of an invasion as negligible, even fanciful. If it seems at this remote point after the event that the threat of invasion was overplayed, it was very real at the time: 'The threats – of invasion, of bombing, of treachery, of chemical and bacterial warfare and of those newer weapons at which Hitler was understood to have hinted – loomed large, terrible and imprecise.'[6]

What effect did this total change in the war situation have on tank production? Figures for production from June 1940 to May 1941 reveal the following:

Tank production June 1940–May 1941

Month	Production all types	Percentage increase (Sept 39 = 100%)
Jun 40	128	237
Jul 40	123	228
Aug 40	148	274
Sep 40	173	320

Month	Production all types	Percentage increase (Sept 39 = 100%)
Oct 40	146	270
Nov 40	150	278
Dec 40	157	290
Jan 41	227	420
Feb 41	205	379
Mar 41	240	444
Apr 41	298	551
May 41	308	570

Sources: AVIA 22/469 and Tank Board notes

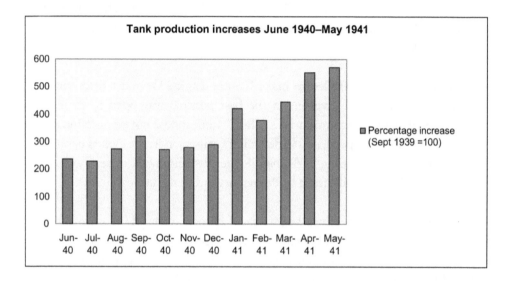

The graph reveals another gradual, although never dramatic, increase. Merely to replace the losses in France (by quantity only) took until the end of October, effectively the equivalent of five months' lost production. The surprising dip after September 1940 is probably explained by human factors. There was, as we have seen, a marked increase in production from May 1940, and this could not be sustained indefinitely using normal working practices. The workers were becoming tired and it became clear that the length of the working week had to be very carefully controlled in order to optimise output. Writing after the event, Churchill said of June 1940 that: 'Men and women toiled at the lathes and machines in the factories till they fell exhausted to the floor and had to be dragged away and ordered home...'[7] Typical Churchillian hyperbole it may be, used to stress the *zeitgeist*, there was nevertheless an element of truth in this. In 1940 industrial workmen generally worked between sixty and ninety hours per week over six days, and this could not be continued indefinitely. In March 1941 the aspiration for each worker to be guaranteed one full day off every seven or eight days was approved, but even then this was not always followed. Later, in September 1943 when the crisis had passed, the 'desirable' limit was set at only fifty-five hours per week, hardly total war.[8] An alternative or additional explanation of the slowdown in the autumn of 1940 may be due to a temporary lack of raw materials or sub-components, a problem that often handicapped production, as well as to the effects of the Blitz in depriving workers of sleep and interrupting shifts, rather than through direct and effective attacks on tank factories. In November 1940 Churchill wrote to his Chief of Staff General Pug Ismay and to the newly-appointed Minister of Supply, Sir Andrew Duncan:

> We have completely failed to make Cruiser Tanks. We must therefore equip our armoured divisions in the best possible way open to us in these melancholy circumstances... The 'I' Tank should not be disdained because of its slow speed, and in default of Cruisers, must be looked upon as our staple for fighting... Meanwhile the production of Cruiser Tanks and of A22 [Churchill] must be driven forward to the utmost limit.[9]

From the design perspective, the lessons of France for the RAC were not at all clear. On 26 May 1940 General Vyvyan Pope (in his capacity as 'Adviser AFV' to the BEF) sent a letter from France to the AFV department in the War Office summarising the technical lessons that he had identified so far. He thought that the light tanks were 'clearly useless'; the two-pounder gun was 'only just good enough'; the armour on all tanks was too thin, needing to be in the region of 40-80mm; the 'I' Tanks were too slow; and the Cruisers were horribly unreliable.[10] The use of typical British understatement could be unhelpful: his comment about the two-pounder may have been interpreted later to support the argument that just good enough was the same as good enough, and may have actually hindered the calls for the introduction of the new six-pounder gun later in 1940. To suggest that Cruisers were unreliable was one thing; to have offered facts and figures and to demand investigation into the reasons would have been more useful in the months to come. But overall, he was absolutely correct and had highlighted the majority of the technical problems that were bedevilling British tanks and would continue to do so for years to come.

Of course, many of the tank commanders and crews directly involved in the actual fighting had been killed or captured and were thus unable to state their opinion, and there was still a great deal of uncertainty at the highest levels as to why things had gone so badly wrong. Was the root of the problem technical, or was it tactical? Was it that the tank force was simply inferior in numbers to the Germans? If the latter, then it would be easy to overlook or disregard any mechanical failings, in the belief that sheer weight of numbers had prevailed. Macksey reported that it: 'would become nearly a year before the 88mm gun became identified as the weapon which could easily overcome even the latest Matilda II, even though it had been employed during the Arras counter-attack.'[11] Indeed, in his letter, Pope had unhelpfully suggested that 'the Boche has succeeded solely because of his mass of tanks... man for man we can beat him any day.'[12] At the time therefore, there was a general feeling that the Germans had simply enjoyed a considerable quantitative advantage, but it is now clear that was not so. The French alone fielded around 4,000 tanks of various sizes and capabilities, while Guderian suggested that a total of around 2,500 German tanks were involved, only 627 of which were the modern Panzer III or IV. Fletcher summed the situation up thus:

> Without a captured German tank of their own to evaluate under controlled conditions, the British could only fall back on rumours, highly coloured opinions, and vivid imagination to explain their defeat. From this early debacle... can be traced the origins of the Panzer myth that soon permeated all allied armies to the end of the war and beyond.'

A formidable legend had been born.[13]

One thing was clear: Britain needed weapons in unprecedented quantities. The losses in France meant that even the regular army had more men than guns, let alone the Territorial Army or the new units being formed. Britain needed tanks to have any hope of resisting invasion, and any kind of tank was better than no tank at all. On 1 June 1940, the total number of AFVs held by units in the UK was recorded as follows:[14]

Infantry Tanks	110
Cruiser Tanks	103
Light Tanks	618
Obsolete Mediums	132
Total	963

Of course, none of these were sent out to the BEF as the Dunkirk evacuation was coming to its end, but of the nearly 1,000 tanks in Britain at this point, only the hundred or so Cruisers plus the approximately sixty Matilda IIs could be counted as modern tanks, fit for battle.

On 10 June 1940 Mussolini declared war on Britain. This immediately turned the Mediterranean and in particular Egypt into a theatre of war. Churchill had always maintained that if Italy did enter the war, Britain must strike hard immediately.[15] Britain had a Mobile Division (soon to be renamed 7th Armoured Division) in Egypt, and early successes were achieved against a numerically superior but often technically inferior Italian army in eastern Libya. However, this increased the requirement for tanks in that theatre, both to replace losses as well as to build on success. Despite the threat of invasion, Churchill knew that some of the precious supply of new tanks coming off the production lines would have to be sent to Egypt and gave the order. On 4 August 1940 therefore, the number of tanks with the forces in the UK was:[16]

Infantry Tanks	189
Cruiser Tanks	173
Light Tanks	336
Total	698

Compared to the figure of 1 June, it can be seen that total figure had dropped by 265 tanks, despite the production of 251 tanks in the same period. This indicates both the importance and the effect of dispatching tanks to Egypt. On 18 June 1940, as the scale of the tank crisis was becoming clear, Churchill told Ismay: 'I gave direction that the 8th RTR should be immediately equipped with infantry and cruiser tanks until they have fifty-two new tanks... What has been done about the output of this month and last month? Make sure it is not languishing in depots...' [17] This can be interpreted as the Prime Minister ensuring that all necessary actions were being taken, or, alternatively, as typical Churchillian meddling. Why did he bother to specify Infantry *and* Cruiser tanks? To mix the types in one unit made no sense, and probably indicates Churchill's imprecise use of terminology, which could (and often did) lead to confusion.

While the only enemy in North Africa remained the Italians British tanks enjoyed a qualitative superiority. One irony was that it was their early success that forced Hitler to deploy a highly mobile and armour-heavy army into North Africa from February 1941, the famous Afrika Korps/Panzer

Armee Afrika, and the resulting battles quickly brought questions of quality sharply into focus. British tanks were not good enough when fighting the Germans, and quantity had nothing to do with it. The only tanks that came out with any credit were the Matilda II (because of its heavy armour) and the Valentine (because of its armour and reliability). The Cruisers were just plain bad – under-gunned, under-armoured, and totally unreliable, particularly when used in the unforgiving desert conditions. This tended to reinforce the old argument favoured by Elles when MGO, and still in vogue with many, that called for many more infantry tanks to be built than cruisers, and which would hinder the equipping of the armoured divisions for at least the next year or so. It also wasted precious time and resources on research and development of super-heavy tanks mounting enormous amounts or armour, including the First World War throwback TOG.[18] The War Office simply knew too little about tanks:

> In its ignorance the War Office was in no position to refute many spurious arguments, for the tank experts in the Ministry of Supply were out of touch with the latest operational requirements and the newly set up Armoured Fighting Vehicle Directorate in the War Office was not strong enough, as yet, to make its influence felt.[19]

In the light of this situation, it was impossible to consider any kind of policy other than to simply maximise production of what was currently available; the next generation of improved tanks would just have to wait. 'The best is the enemy of the good' was a ministerial argument which had brooked no reply as early as April 1939, and in the circumstances of the second half of 1940 held even more weight; the problem was that the good was nowhere near good enough. In June 1940 the Cabinet ruled that 'The immediate task to which more distant requirements must be subordinated was to expedite delivery during the next five months of everything required to make good deficiencies of essential items of equipment.'[20] 'At this stage in tank production', wrote Churchill in November 1940, 'numbers count above everything else. It is better to have any serviceable tank than none at all.'[21] The precise meaning was very clear: 'serviceable' was meant to be used in the wider sense of 'in the hands of the troops', not in the narrower sense of 'battleworthy'. It was to be second-best today, tomorrow and for the foreseeable future, and this decision, as much as any other single factor, was the root cause of the inadequate quality of Britain's tank force.

Quantity before quality

There is a saying that the quantity has a quality all of its own: with regard to British tanks in the Second World War, that is not necessarily so. During April 1940, there was no resistance from either the General Staff or the Ministry of Supply to a key conclusion formed by the War Cabinet committee dealing with the overall coordination of defence:

> The tank programme must not be interfered with either by the incorporation of improvements to the approved types, or by the production of newer models.[22]

This was a critical moment in the story, which came even before the Germans had started to move westwards. Quantity was the policy; quality was nowhere in sight. As the tank crisis unfolded, this position was reinforced and became the *modus operandi*, which suited the companies building the tanks. Thus, many thousands of tanks were built which were known to be obsolete, or under-armoured, or under-gunned, or unreliable, or all four:

> In factories fully employed on well-established types new types could only be produced at the expense of old ones. While new types were coming in, the losses in the old types were for a time bound to be greater that the output of new [types], with the result that total output declined.[23]

Although this statement actually relates to aircraft production, exactly the same situation applied to tank production. It was simply impossible to make a transition to a complete new type (or even major changes resulting in a new mark) without losing many months of output – and potentially therefore some of the workforce who would stand idle while retooling was conducted. The main reason for this was the lack of floor space, which would have allowed tooling-up to be prepared in parallel, ready for the new type, and simply requiring the workforce to switch their tasks onto the new line. This policy led to a number of unfortunate second-order consequences. The most crucial was the reluctance – certainly by industry but also on the part of certain sections of the ministries – to develop and introduce new tanks or even to make major improvements to those already in production. The reason for the unacceptable delay to the introduction of the excellent six-pounder gun was exactly this. The gun had received design approval on

9 September 1940, but the first order was not placed until May 1941, and mass production only commenced in November 1941, fourteen months after it should have been. This was because 'experts' within the Director General of Munitions Production had claimed that the production of the newer gun would result in only one-sixth as many guns being made, compared to if two-pounder production continued unabated. It was subsequently found that the larger gun could be made twice as fast as the two-pounder: 1,293 man-hours against 2,682 for the two-pounder.[24] When this was realised in mid-1941, the cry 'Six pounders at all costs!' could be heard, but the opportunity to out-gun the Germans in 1941 had been lost, along with many lives.

Secondly, that there was bound to be a drop-off in production following any major change was a given: how to reduce the time required to ramp up production back to acceptable levels to the absolute minimum was the real challenge. Therefore, the tank-designing manufacturers were more likely to produce new tank designs that were of an evolutionary nature, and were therefore able to make as much use as possible of existing plant and processes, not to say trained manpower. This evolutionary process could eventually lead to capable tanks being designed, as in the Comet finally emerging from the A13 – Covenanter – Crusader – Cavalier – Centaur – Cromwell lineage, but it took an awfully long time and was not in any case guaranteed.

Thirdly, it tended to perpetuate the 1940 attitude that quantity was always more important than quality, a position which was, as previously noted, unfortunately sometimes reinforced by the Prime Minister's acerbic notes on the subject. It was a mindset that needed changing at all levels.

As well as working out how to introduce improved models without dramatically affecting production, other methods had to be found to increase productivity. One possibility was to involve more firms: those which were not yet involved in tank production but were available to take on the type of work. However, as David Fletcher noted: 'If there were any such firms in June 1940 then the chances were that there was probably something seriously wrong with them.'[25] There were indeed a few such firms, and there were usually very serious reasons why they should not have been allowed to build tanks, let alone design them. But needs must when the devil drives, and such companies were thus brought into the programme, not only as assemblers but more often as suppliers of sub-components. On the face of it the design parents should have supervised the output of these firms, but as skilled manpower was lacking quality control often went by the board, which was to impact seriously on the reliability of these machines in the years to come.

Even worse than this, one of the most damaging results of the tank crisis was the placing of the so-called 'drawing board order'. Rather than build pilot models which would be tested by people who knew about tanks, and thus could be refined before mass production commenced, firms would be asked to design a tank to a GS specification, and as a result of their drawings alone, a contract would be placed for large numbers of tanks. Even the finest tank designs would suffer from teething problems, and the designs that were affected by this system were not of that ilk. Hancock noted:

> The 'Drawing Board' order... in its essence this consisted of approving an equipment for production before it was fully designed, let alone tested, so that the manufacturer would tool-up with the certainty that production would start. The 'drawing-board' order was *only* applied extensively to AFVs.[26]

A new series of tanks to be called Heavy Cruisers were considered necessary in late 1940.[27] These had much better frontal armour than previous specifications, the 75mm of frontal armour all but matching that of Matilda II. However, the tired old Liberty was the chosen engine, as the Tank Board stated on 17 January 1941 that it required the new tank to be in production by spring 1942. This was an impossibly tight schedule for a completely new design, so the design had to be based on old models already in production, however flawed they might be. As Kenneth Macksey summed it up:

> Controlled by the Prime Minister's policy that every resource must be concentrated on production, to the exclusion of research and development, the British went on churning out a mass of obsolescent weapons while cutting back on development of the next generation. In 1940 parity in numbers and quality could have extended into a lead but for the incontrovertible need to replace the losses of Dunkirk regardless of quality. But once that lead in quality had been surrendered, the chances of regaining it got more remote with every day that passed.[28]

The policy of ordering off the drawing board was most noticeable when applied to the Churchill infantry tank. It was ordered in 1940, and the Prime Minister himself gave orders that its introduction was not to interfere with the production of other types then being built. This was an impossibly tall order and as a result the early marks were plagued by unreliability. The tank came very close to being cancelled after 3,500 were produced, but a vast and complicated rework programme (which absorbed huge resources) eventually turned it into a successful tank. The phrase 'more haste less speed' comes to mind. In the dark days of 1940 taking such a risk was understandable, but it seems incredible that the lessons of ordering off the drawing board were not sinking in a year later. At exactly the same time that the MoS had to report that two companies who were meant to be producing new Churchills were fully employed in reworking hundreds of the faulty early marks, other parts of the same ministry were arguing that the policy that had caused the situation was still correct.[29]

The effect of the Great Tank Crisis on design and production

Equipping the Army…could only be done by resolutely foregoing the luxury of placing quality above quantity.[30]

On 9 August 1940, as the Battle of Britain was being fought over England, Churchill told Beaverbrook: 'If it came to a choice between hampering aircraft production or tank production I would sacrifice the tank.'[31] In the context of the time this was absolutely the correct decision; one does not gamble on the outcome of the immediate battle in favour of a future battle that may not even be fought. What is not clear is how much impact this statement had upon tank production, but it certainly did not help. Quite the opposite: any additional delays, however small, that were caused would have the then-invisible effect of postponing the day when a battleworthy tank would become available.

The location of many of the companies selected to produce tanks laid them open to attack from the air. Many of them had already attracted the attention of the Luftwaffe in their own right, as builders of locomotives or road transport, or as steel producers; knowing they were now building tanks simply made them more attractive as a target. They also tended to be located in industrial areas that would naturally be attacked anyway: London, Glasgow, Belfast, Birmingham, Sheffield. However, the Blitz was not about precision bombing, and any disruption to production seems to have been caused more by the reactions to an impending air-raid that by any real destruction. In the early stages of the 1940 Blitz, it was commonplace for an entire factory's workforce to decamp to the shelters as soon as any sort of alarm was sounded, leading to the loss of tens of thousands of hours of construction time. This situation improved as experience was gained and later alarms were only sounded when bombers were nearing the locality, but there was always a fine balance to be struck, particularly as the workers themselves were not prepared to take risks with their own lives.

Sometimes though, the Luftwaffe struck lucky and managed to hit a tank builder. On Friday 30 August 1940 the Vauxhall works in Luton were heavily bombed, killing around forty workers, mainly hitting the drawing shops, and stopping production. The extensive bombing of the Metro-Cammell factory in April 1941 caused the abandonment of the remainder of an order, luckily only for the unimportant Tetrarch light tanks.[32] Another side effect came from the deliberate targeting by the Luftwaffe of the means of aircraft production. When this occurred, the MAP had the power to switch production of sub-components to firms engaged on MoS work which was of a lower priority. As this could also include tank components, tank production was adversely but unquantifiably affected by this practice.

A priority system to properly organise all the conflicting requirements between the competing ministries was not in place at the start of the war. It was not until the Production Council was set up on 22 May 1940 that something approaching clear direction was given. This stated that there were only two priority categories: 1A, for aircraft, bombs and small arms ammunition; and 1B, for field guns and ammunition. There was no designated category below this, but in effect it existed for 'other work required by the Armed Forces and which could be completed by 1st September 1940.' This priority system extended to the prioritisation of the labour force, especially relevant for the recruitment of skilled tradesmen.[33] It can be seen that tanks were not even mentioned, and this was to be the case for over a year, furthering hindering efforts to increase production in those companies already building tanks. The MAP were not shy in extending their claim for priority into any area of production, however mundane. For example, the supplies of a paint pigment used to produce green shades known as chromic oxide became scarce during 1940, and so by the end of that year the specification for the painting of military vehicles changed from using matt Khaki Green G3 to a new brown colour called SCC2 Brown; this was to stay in place until 1944 when a new colour similar to the US Olive Drab was adopted. A similar occurrence happened with the aluminium paint used for the inside of tanks: the MAP claimed priority and so the army had to paint the inside of its tanks white instead. The army did not think that brown was a better camouflage colour than green, quite the opposite, nor indeed was it too worried about the switch from silver interiors to white, but the priority system meant that it had no choice.

Medium Tank Mk I. Entering service in 1923 and subsequently developed into the improved Medium II, this type of tank was the mainstay of the RTC until just before the start of the Second World War. It was simple and therefore easy to build by hand and for the first time featured a fully-revolving turret with a co-axial machine gun. It was also the first to be designed to carry wireless.

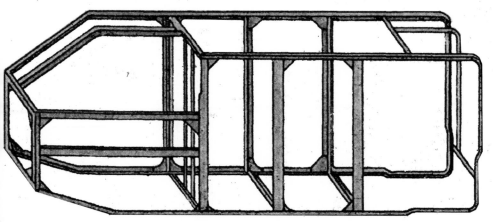

The framework used to make up a Medium II tank. Flat armour sheets would be bolted or rivetted to the framework, which added weight, and the rivets themselves could become sub-projectiles if hit by enemy fire. Despite the advantages of welding, this type of construction remained common in Britain, only partly because of a lack of skilled welders in the workforce.

The A1E1 Independent. Although intended as a heavy tank, many aspects of the design influenced subsequent medium and cruiser tanks, including the insistence on including one or more machine-gun turrets; the Independent had four.

An early Morris-Martel two-man tankette. Although valueless as military vehicles, the experimentation with such designs led to the development of light tanks and the carrier range of tracked vehicles.

The first cruiser tank, the six-man A9. Designed as a medium, it was too lightly armoured, and the suspension was not suitable for its role. It was the first tank to carry the excellent two-pounder gun but was encumbered with two MG sub-turrets on the front of the hull.

An A10 of 3RTR abandoned in Greece in 1941, probably not through enemy action but because the track broke, as so often happened. Intended to be the first infantry tank and based on the A9, it fell between two stools and quickly passed into oblivion.

The first cruiser to use the new Christie suspension was the A13. A great improvement over its predecessors, it was nevertheless still too lightly protected, even when modified to take extra armour. It led to the development of the useless Covenanter and also the Crusader, later to the Cavalier/Centaur/ Cromwell tanks, and eventually to the Comet.

The A13 Mk III or Covenanter was the supreme example of wasted effort in British tank production. 1,771 were built of which not one saw action. Its dreadful unreliability relegated it to training roles only, and from 1943 onwards the entire fleet was scrapped.

The rear engine decks of the Covenanter were clearly a mess, and anyone who saw such an appalling design arrangement on the outside of the tank could probably guess how the tank would perform.

A brand-new Crusader II. This was a Wolseley-built tank, and this is probably outside the large Ward End Works. Lord Nuffield purchased the company in 1927 and it built tanks for the NMA group. This example is still fitted with the horrendous MG turret which was hated by the crews and often removed in the field.

An A15 Crusader on exercise in the UK, *c*.1942. All too typically, this one is being recovered due to a breakdown. Inconvenient in training, frequent breakdowns led to a loss of combat power in action, not to mention the death or capture of many crewmen.

A Crusader being repaired in North Africa, almost certainly due to a broken water pump. Such trivial items kept many tanks out of action, and a lack of spare parts made the fitters' job much harder than it should have been. Despite complaints, a reliable water pump was never satisfactorily designed for the Crusader.

The Nuffield Liberty engine was the preferred tank engine in the NMA group. It was designed as an aircraft engine in 1917 but despite a nominal horsepower of 340, it never performed well. The bolts for each individual cylinder can be seen at the base of each, which tended to come apart when used cross-country. The exposed valves can also be seen. Despite its known failings, the Nuffield group continued to recommend its use, even when the Meteor was developed.

A new Churchill hull being transported. A great failing of the British system was that not all tank builders were also manufacturers, and therefore many components, large and small, needed to be transported around the country to where they could be assembled.

A 75mm-armed Churchill. Despite its archaic appearance and notoriously bad initial reliability, the A22 tank was developed into a reliable and well-armoured vehicle that remained in service until the end of the war and beyond. Statistically, Churchill crewmen suffered fewer casualties than in any other tank type and as a result the tank became a popular vehicle.

The Valentine was a private-venture tank that was only grudgingly accepted into service by the army. Despite this, it was well-liked by its crews for its small size, thick armour, and above all, reliability. Most Valentines used diesel engines, a rarity for the time. The suspension, very similar to that used on the A9 cruiser, was much better suited to a slower and heavier infantry tank.

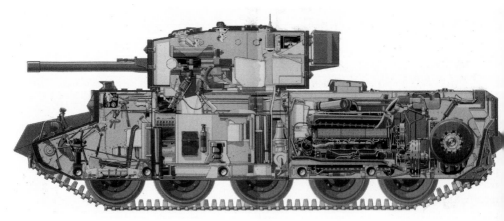

A six-pounder armed Cromwell, with its outstanding Meteor in the rear. For the first time the Cromwell gave British tank crews a fast and reliable cruiser, even if its armour was not particularly thick. Early Cromwells still used the shoulder-controlled free elevation system for the gun, although this was later changed to a modern geared version.

A welded Cromwell: many of the type were still built using the old-fashioned and flawed rivet and bolt technique. Although a technique for the welding of armour had been developed in Britain by 1934, the resistance of many of the tank-building firms meant that it did not come into widespread use until 1944.

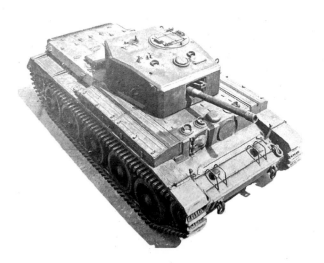

The A30 Challenger was an attempt to mount the excellent seventeen-pounder gun onto a Cromwell chassis. Although the tank looks too high and somewhat ungainly, it was in fact no taller than the US Sherman. Only 200 were built.

A hero of the war: the Meteor petrol engine was developed from the famous Merlin, suitably modified for use in tanks. The persistence and ingenuity of W.A. Robotham and his team of engineers at Rolls-Royce was one of the few high points of tank design during the war.

An A34 Comet in service in early 1945. The Comet was a perfected Cromwell and mounted an outstandingly accurate and consistent 77mm gun developed for the tank. Although it was to be surpassed by the Centurion, the Comet was undoubtedly the finest tank that Britain fielded during the Second World War.

The main drawing board office at English Electric, Stafford. By no means were all of the companies involved in building tanks so well equipped, and the lack of skilled draughtsmen slowed down the design of some tank types.

Component manufacture: Valentine suspension units being made in a small workshop. Many of the firms involved in building tanks were reliant on receiving a steady flow of sub-components from a myriad of such companies. A lack of quality control in some plants led to infuriating problems for troops using the tanks.

A lathe operator at work. The supply of machine tools was an essential component of production, as was the training required to bring new employees into the workforce and turn them into at least semi-skilled workers.

Grinding. One of the downsides of using cast armour components was that the pieces had to be cast over-size, and then laboriously ground down to the correct size and shape, a process known as cheese-paring.

A Valentine being tested post-production. Although all the factories claimed that rigorous testing was part of their quality-control procedures, in fact many tanks arrived at units with a myriad of different faults.

A Valentine production facility. Nearly twenty hulls are in various stages of manufacture, and the typical engineers' workbenches alongside the line can be clearly seen. One tank has just had a turret shell placed on it.

Filling a Valentine with oil. The oil drum has been moved to the tank, and a hand-pump is being turned; this is clearly not a modern production line operation. Instances were recorded of tanks leaving factories without any oil or coolant.

Matildas being assembled at an unidentified factory. Here the hulls are at least being moved along on rails, although the construction sequence still appears somewhat random.

A completed Matilda II, without armament, outside a factory; many of the nearly 3,000 Matildas built were sent as aid shipments to the USSR and others served with the Australians. The small rectangle on the top of the nose is the brass manufacturer's plate, used to identify the individual vehicle.

A Covenanter being shown off at the EE testing ground on Cannock Chase. The two-pounder is not fitted, as it was common practice not to fit some of the so-called 'free issue' items such as guns and wireless until the tanks arrived at an ordnance depot prior to issue.

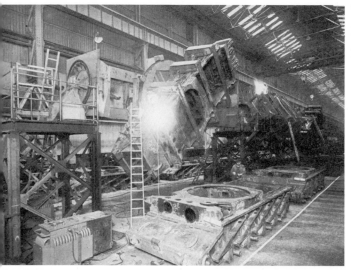

Three manipulators in action at EE Stafford, being used to weld Comet hulls.

Comets nearing completion at Stafford. The large rings are the ball-bearing races that support the turret on the hull. Very careful machining was necessary to ensure that these items were placed horizontally onto the hulls.

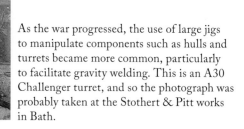

As the war progressed, the use of large jigs to manipulate components such as hulls and turrets became more common, particularly to facilitate gravity welding. This is an A30 Challenger turret, and so the photograph was probably taken at the Stothert & Pitt works in Bath.

Still at Stafford, the track is being joined to the suspension of a Comet which appears to be nearly complete. It is muscle power rather than machinery that is completing this job. The idler appears to be of the early rubber-tyred version, which was found to be faulty in use and brought the whole fleet to a standstill in early 1945; it was quickly replaced by a cast version.

Captured German tanks – here a Panther – were subjected where possible to trials to investigate their capabilities. Note the armour thicknesses marked on the side. Despite their thick frontal armour, German tanks were much more vulnerable to attack from the flanks.

English Electric employees leak testing the hull to ensure that it was waterproof; this was only employed once welded hulls were developed. All welded seams were coated internally with a sealant compound to assist in this, as all tanks after mid-war were required to be able to wade in six feet of water (with 18in waves) for six minutes, enough time to wade ashore from a tank landing ship or similar.

The War Office and the MoS continued to fight their corner with the MAP but with little or no success before the middle of the next year, 1941. On 9 July the newly-appointed MoS (and former MAP) Lord Beaverbrook wrote:

> Tanks and tank spares, and 2 Pdr and 6 Pdr guns and AP ammunition (but NOT armoured cars), have been given Priority 1A[34]... I have given a pledge to [the MAP] that nothing will interfere with the production of bombers and fighters... whereverso there is any conflict, you will give way at once in favour of fighters and bombers... nothing in this priority will interfere with: torpedoes, Oerlikon guns, [and] any other item of 1A Priority now held by the Admiralty.[35]

This was agreed by the Production Executive the following day; the decision was noted as being influenced largely by considerations of providing a 'psychological impetus to tank production' – implying that a physical impetus could not be expected, which, considering the tone, was unsurprising.[36] However, a report of mid-1941 contradicted this assertion:

> 297 infantry and cruiser tanks have been produced in May [1941], and it is hoped to obtain between 275 and 300 in June... difficulties due to the lack of priority for work on tanks were now largely overcome, though the mentality created by the old priority system still made itself felt throughout the industry.[37]

The critical point about this decision was that the RAF and Admiralty still retained the right to trump the MoS whenever it suited them to do so; in effect their Priority 1A was more important than the Army's 1A. They both continued to play their cards strongly, the MAP in particular, and there was never a serious attempt to change the balance of power. This would have required Churchill's agreement, and that was never likely – the concerns regarding RAF production during the Battle of Britain had given way to concerns over the Royal Navy and the Battle of the Atlantic. As in so many ways, the MAP were simply doing business so much smarter than the MoS:

> It cannot be repeated too often that the progress of British aircraft was the work of both the industry and the Government... none of the new entrants (the non-established firms who were now producing aircraft under the 'shadow' scheme) however undertook the work of design and development.[38]

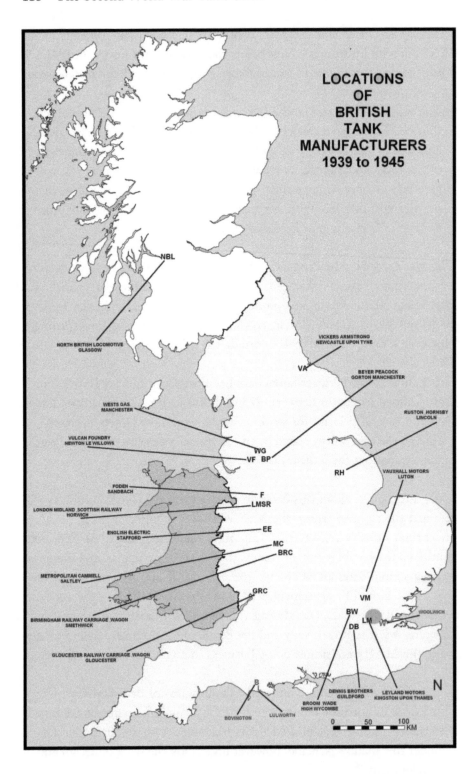

LOCATIONS
OF
BRITISH
TANK
MANUFACTURERS
1939 to 1945

NBL

NORTH BRITISH LOCOMOTIVE
GLASGOW

VICKERS ARMSTRONG
NEWCASTLE UPON TYNE

VA

BEYER PEACOCK
GORTON MANCHESTER

WESTS GAS
MANCHESTER

RUSTON HORNSBY
LINCOLN

VULCAN FOUNDRY
NEWTON LE WILLOWS

WG
VF BP

FODEN
SANDBACH

RH

VAUXHALL MOTORS
LUTON

F

LONDON MIDLAND SCOTTISH RAILWAY
HORWICH

LMSR

ENGLISH ELECTRIC
STAFFORD

EE

MC
BRC

METROPOLITAN CAMMELL
SALTLEY

GRC

VM

BIRMINGHAM RAILWAY CARRIAGE WAGON
SMETHWICK

BW   LM

WOOLWICH

DB

GLOUCESTER RAILWAY CARRIAGE WAGON
GLOUCESTER

B

N

DENNIS BROTHERS
GUILDFORD

LEYLAND MOTORS
KINGSTON UPON THAMES

BROOM WADE
HIGH WYCOMBE

BOVINGTON   LULWORTH

0   50   100
                  KM

Lies, damn lies, and production forecasts

[As production forecasts were constantly not met there was a] general scepticism as to the value of such lengthy short-cuts. If quality and mechanical efficiency were [more] important rather than mere output, it was hardly economical to avoid trials... As a critic [in the House of Commons] put it, we were not avoiding the manufacture of prototypes, we were manufacturing nothing else.[39]

There were two main types of tank production forecast used within official circles. One of these was the Target Figure, the other and lower figure was known as the Reasonable Anticipation programme, which was meant to better reflect the realities of the situation – the former generally reflected an optimistic view that would have surprised even Mr Micawber, the latter that of a realist, if not quite a pessimist. Between August 1940 and June 1941, the target was for 1,478 'I' tanks and 520 cruisers to be produced.[40] In the same period, the Reasonable Anticipation figures were 1,048 and 425 respectively, representing around 74 percent of the higher figure. A comparison between these figures and actual production achieved gives a reliable indicator of how badly the tank production scheme was doing in terms of sheer quantity, and how both figures could be wide of the mark:

MoS production forecast August 1940 to October 1940

	Target (Set 16 Jun 40)	Reasonable anticipation (Set 5 Aug 40)	Actual production
August 1940[41]	167	157	143
September 1940	194	135	116
October 1940	222	160	127
Total	583	452	386

Source: PREM 3/426/8

It can be seen from this snapshot that in the first months of the tank crisis, actual production was lagging behind even the Reasonable Anticipation Programme by 15 percent and the Target Figure by 34 percent. A comment under these figures noted that output would have to increase massively just to attain the Reasonable Anticipation figure by 1 April 1941. One of the reasons for the over-optimistic figures was stated as an assumption that tank production would be given 1A priority status, which as we have seen did not come into effect until 9 July 1941 and then only with caveats.[42]

Production in August 1940 was described by the PM as 'lamentably small'. On 2 September 1940 he was moved to 'enquire the reason for this shocking failure in output'; the answer given was that the weekly output figures did not reflect true production over a long enough period; they only showed issues to troops, and did not show those tanks sent to the ordnance depots, in transit, and so on. The optimistic theory was also raised that one week's poor figures were likely to be immediately followed by a much better week; the numbers gave the lie to this. In fact, no real answers were given. The question that should have been asked was very simple: what needs to be done to maximise tank production? Juggling the way that the figures were displayed was not the answer.[43] The same situation persisted into the new year:

MoS production forecast January to March 1941

	Target (Set 17 Sep 40)			Reasonable anticipation (Set 17 Sep 40)		
Type	January	February	March	January	February	March
Covenanter	62	76	78	41	41	48
Crusader	14	25	38	14	20	22
Matilda II	105	115	120	66	66	95
Valentine	130	130	130	80	80	80
Churchill	106	152	227	70	100	180
Totals	417	498	593	271	307	425

Source: PREM 3/426/8

Again, unreasonable optimism clouds the table – production of the brand-new Churchill did not actually begin until June 1941, with the first 350 units expected to be produced under the Reasonable Anticipation programme not being completed until mid-October 1941, six months late. The Target Figure was not actually met until the end of the year – nine months late.

As the war went on the methods used to collate and display the figures frequently changed, which is never the easiest thing for the historian to contend with and make sense of. In some cases, it was displayed by broad classification (Cruiser, Infantry etc), while in others it was done by name. Until mid-war the figures were generally monthly, thereafter weekly.[44] Some figures are missing from the files, hence the gaps in the tables below. In mid-1941 the two types of forecast were replaced by one, presumably because the use of the Target Figure was making everyone concerned with tank production look bad, and presumably therefore the Reasonable Anticipation figure was used.

MoS production forecast from April to July 1941

	Apr	May	Jun	Jul	Total
Light Tanks	15	15	13	13	56
Cruisers	91	103	134	134	462
Infantry Tanks	200	170	200	200	770
A22 Churchill	8	54	88	130	280
Totals	314	342	435	477	1568

Source: PREM 3/426/2

MoS production forecast from November 1941 to March 1942

	Nov	Dec	Jan	Feb	Mar	Total
Matilda	120	120	120	120	120	600
Valentine[45]	172	172	172	172	172	860
Churchill	155	155	155	155	155	775
Covenanter	65	65	70	70	75	345
Crusader	73	75	80	85	90	403

Source: PREM 3/426/2

The next factor that added great stress to the production situation of mid-1940 was that it had been realised that the size of the Royal Armoured Corps (RAC) was much too small, and that a massive expansion would be needed. At the outbreak of war, there were eight battalions of the Royal Tank Regiment, plus most of the regular cavalry had been or were in the final process of being mechanised – eighteen regiments. (Three regiments remained mounted until as late as 1941.) Six regiments of 'war-raised cavalry' were all formed as armoured units *ab initio* in late 1940 and early 1941, and there were initially eight (later increased to nearly twenty) Yeomanry (territorial cavalry) regiments which were converted from horse to tanks and AFVs, the decision to do so being made in spring 1939.[46] Another sixteen battalions of the RTR were raised from scratch or by converting territorial infantry units. In total then, around seventy battalion-sized units were (theoretically) operating AFVs by early 1941, and each required around sixty tanks or armoured cars to bring it up to strength.

Thus, the most basic mathematics indicated the immediate need for about 4,200 tanks and armoured cars of all types, ignoring training pools, reserves, loss replacements and the like. The average production in early 1941 was only around 200 tanks per month; with around 2,000 already 'on the books' at that rate it would take until early 1942 before all these units had received the tanks they so desperately needed to start to train with. From November 1941 another thirty-three infantry and seven Foot Guards battalions were converted, adding another 2,400 AFVs, mainly tanks, to the army's requirement. Finally, following the entry of the USSR into the war in July 1941, Churchill promised Stalin that from October 1941 250 tanks per month were to be supplied to Russia, another 3,000 per year.

Another problem was also beginning to surface, which would have grave implications for tank production. Between August 1940 and February 1941, 3.25 'I' tanks were being built for every cruiser.[47] This was because until late 1940, if not a little later, the received wisdom was that many more infantry tanks than cruisers would be required by the army. However, as a result of the German use of armour in 1940 and the much more mobile warfare in North Africa, the demand for cruisers suddenly rose, with many fewer infantry tanks being required. Until February 1941 the army was intending to raise ten Armoured Brigades (operating cruisers) and ten Army Tank Brigades (with infantry tanks). In that month the requirement was suddenly changed, to twenty and eight respectively. This change of priority came at the same time that production was getting into something approaching full swing, and the MoS therefore strongly resisted the requests of the user, in order to prevent interruptions and delays in overall production. What everyone had missed was the opportunity to design and build a dual-purpose tank, which was well armoured but also mobile and with good firepower, not to mention reliable: the Germans had managed just that with their improved PzKpw IV. It was not until much later, when General Montgomery put his weight behind the call for such a 'Universal' or 'Capital' tank, that anything was done, although production did start to favour cruiser output from around 1942, a year after the priorities had been turned on their head. At one point, in mid-1942, it appeared that a ready-made answer was to be found from the USA, in the shape of the new Sherman medium tank.

It had become obvious to many by early to mid-1941 that British production alone would not be sufficient to meet the Army's need in quantitative terms, let alone qualitative. Churchill therefore personally arranged the supply of US tanks under the Lend-Lease programme, which began in March 1941. At first sight the new US tanks appeared to be the answer: 'By the end of 1941, it had become clear that for many months, if not years, to come, the

British Army would have to depend upon American Medium tanks...to meet its cruiser demands.[48] From late 1941 the British army, initially in North Africa but later everywhere, began to receive large numbers of US tanks: Grants, Lees, Stuarts, and especially Shermans. These gave the soldiers much needed reliability and firepower, but over-dependence on them caused problems only three years later, and nearly led to another Great Tank Crisis in 1944. At the start of the Second Battle of El Alamein in October 1942, the Eighth Army recorded that it had 1,351 tanks. Of these, 48 percent were of British manufacture, mainly Valentines and Crusaders, whereas more than half were US Shermans, Grants and Stuarts. It is probably fortunate for the outcome of the battle that this was so.

The reasons for delays

One question that must be asked is why the production forecasts were so wrong. One simplistic answer, which nevertheless contains a large amount of truth, is that the manufacturers and the MoS were simply too optimistic and failed to factor in the possible delays to production. The tank industry was not working in isolation though; it was competing for resources, especially skilled manpower, with all the other industries in the country, and as we have seen, with the higher priorities successfully claimed by the MAP. However, some specific causes are identifiable, and this section will provide a flavour, if not the whole picture, of the reasons for delays. The effects of actual bombing, other than those already noted, do not appear to have played a major part, but the loss of productivity caused by the raids (loss of sleep, loss of production time), most certainly was.

Machine tool availability continued to bedevil the producers throughout the war. In some instances, there were sufficient available across the country, but they were not always in the right place. A June 1940 report stated that 'The census of machine tools shows that although there may be shortage of one type in one district, there are no types which are worked to the full in all districts, so that redistribution might ease the problem.'[49] There is no evidence that this was actually done. For one thing, more tank producers were being brought into the programmes, so the problem could only get worse unless additional tools were made. Next, the machines that were not 'worked to the full' would still be in use, even if not at maximum output. Lastly, redistribution might seem attractive on paper, but ignored the real difficulties of moving plant between commercial firms even on a temporary basis – there was no government desire for this sort of compulsion. An October 1940 report was unable to give any more cause for optimism: 'The fulfillment of [the forecasts quoted] is dependent on better supplies of machine tools than we are present obtaining.'[50]

In the autumn of 1940 at the height of the crisis there were a number of problems caused by restrictions in raw material supply, especially particular metals. The overall deficiency in the thick (1in to 4in) armour plate that was forecast for 1941 was 10,417 tons, even assuming that all the plants available would get the raw materials needed and were able to work at maximum output. As the Navy was likely to get all 14,000 tons it had requested, the shortfall would have to be met by the army, which represented 31 percent of the total required not being available.[51] There was a slight surplus of thinner armour plate (less than 1in); whether the knowledge of this deficiency in one area and a surplus in another led to compromises with design and/or construction is unclear, but must remain a possibility, as light tanks could continue to be constructed without being affected by shortages of thicker plate. On 1 December 1941, the Prime Minister noted that 'Armour Plate is [still] the tank bottle-neck. We are short 400 tons per month for production of the Churchill tank'.[52] Presumably he was referring only to the thicker plate.

Another specific bottleneck was caused by problems with the supply of drop forgings in the first two years of the war. This was not only because of competition with other weapons and in particular with the MAP, but also because of the comparatively low wages in that trade, drop forging operators only being required to master a simple technique of using a hammer to shape metal pieces over a die. This led to many workers leaving to take up better paid employment in other trades, which only exacerbated the situation. Eventually, the Minister of Labour had to agree to direct labour, a form of compulsion, to where it was most required.[53]

Clearly, a restriction in the supply of individual specialised components could cause a whole production line to slow or stop. At one point it was reported that: 'the drop in Churchill [production] is due to the production lag caused by late arrival of ball bearings. These are beginning to arrive from America and will be worked into final drives at once.'[54] Similarly, a lack of Rackham clutches and gearboxes caused problems for Matilda II production during August and September 1940.[55]

Later in the war, in November 1942, the following reasons for poor production over the previous year were identified:[56]

- The January forecast for 1942 production was much too optimistic.
- Reworking Churchills caused two of the companies that had been planned to produce tanks to be turned over entirely to repair and reworking.
- With Crusader, as a result of a plethora of complaints regarding faulty workmanship, an increased inspection regime slowed delivery; there had been late deliveries of armour plate; and the production line had been 'robbed' of parts required to be used as spares for the frontline.
- The switching of tank-producing firms to locomotive production had cost 918 tanks per year.

This last point requires some further explanation. We have seen how failing locomotive builders had been identified as having the means to build tanks, and that a number of them were put to that work. By the height of production, in mid-1943, at least twenty-four major companies were or had been involved in tank and large AFV production, with a few others on the periphery and literally dozens of others acting as sub-contractors; of these, ten were locomotive or rolling stock construction firms. However, by late 1942 it had been realised that the destruction being wrought by the RAF on the continental railway network would cause logistic problems when Europe was liberated. Therefore, from that year a number of tank producers were moved back to their original and more familiar task and began building locomotives once more, a policy that was both foresighted and necessary for the overall progress of the war.

In the same month, November 1942, a report by the MoS to the Prime Minister began by stating that the intention of producing 1,000 tanks per month had failed for three main reasons.[57] (In fact 1,000 per month, an arbitrary figure used for impact akin to the 'thousand bomber raids', was never reached: the highest monthly total ever achieved was 919 in May 1943.) The reasons given were:

- The shift to locomotive production in preparation for Operation Bolero, meaning the build-up to and operations after the invasion of Europe.
- The increased production of spares.
- The changeover to Cromwell production.

A different list of poor excuses for poor production was passed to the Prime Minister on exactly the same day, 17 November 1942:[58]

- Production tends to be high towards the end of a month, so deliveries are always low in the first week of each month. (This suggests that a cyclic working practice had evolved, although it is not at all clear whether this was due to raw material delivery, supply of sub-components, labour control, etc).
- A number of defective Valentine assemblies that were only identified during final testing.
- Covenanter and Matilda are getting toward the end of their production runs, naturally they are slowing down.
- Cromwell is not yet in full production.
- Churchills are awaiting delivery of ball bearings from USA.
- Churchill production has been affected by demands for spares.

Industrial action, stoppages, go-slows and strikes were surprisingly frequent during the war years. The 12 December 1942 weekly production report to the Prime Minister commented that Matilda production figures were low due to 'the stoppage at the North British Locomotive Works', but no details were given.[59] In fact Matilda output declined monthly from April 1942 until production finally ceased in the middle of 1943, so it is unlikely that industrial action was the only reason, rather a natural running-down of capacity, although why this could not be explained in the report is not clear. After the Matilda order was completed, NBL made no further tanks, returning to locomotive production, so it could also be that NBL was now focussed on its new task to the detriment of building the final tanks. The same report ensures that the PM understood the MoS position by concluding:

> The achievement therefore of the one thousand tanks per month must depend upon the extent to which production capacity can be kept fully and regularly harnessed on clearly established designs, with the introduction of the minimum of modifications.[60]

This can be taken as yet another appeal by the Ministry to ignore the urgent requests from the troops for better tanks and for modifications to the existing and flawed designs, in order to keep the numbers up. There is little doubt that some personnel in the MoS thought only in terms of figures and were not at all concerned with the fighting qualities of the tanks and the often-fatal effects upon the crews.

The comment about industrial action is one of the few mentioning this type of delay. Although the number of days lost to strikes increased as the war progressed, there is little to suggest that overall this was a major problem for tank production. However, holidays could frequently affect production. In summer 1940 the government remembered – a little late – the lessons from the First World War of potential burnout if workers were not allowed sufficient rest, and tried to restrict the total hours worked by different categories of worker. On the other hand, too many holidays could be as damaging as too few. On being shown the poor weekly production figures in August 1942 and being told that the reason was 'again due to holidays in the factories', Churchill wrote 'Dreadful' as his sole comment, prompting Beaverbrook to ask his assistant to 'please see that this is passed on to those whom it may principally concern.'[61] Similarly, the weekly report issued on 26 December 1942 comments that the figures 'reflect the effect of the Christmas holidays'. In the big scheme of things holidays probably only affected production very slightly, and the morale impact of allowing them was more beneficial in the long term. After all, Britain was not a totalitarian state using slave workers, and reinforcing this distinction was important to the propaganda war.[62] As an example of how holidays did disrupt production, an examination of the production of Churchills by Dennis Brothers in the Christmas period 1 December 1944 to 22 January 1945 needs no further explanation:

1 Dec–22 Dec	14 completed	= 0.63 tanks per day
23 Dec–27 Dec	Nil completed	= 0 tanks per day
28 Dec–31 Dec	2 Completed	= 0.5 tanks per day
1 Jan–22 Jan	12 completed	= 0.54 tanks per day

Shift working was never able to reach a level of output one might expect from a nation seemingly engaged in total war. One of the main reasons for this was simply that there were often not enough skilled or semi-skilled workers to go around for a single shift, so there was not the spare capacity to use up in this way. But failing to introduce genuine round-the-clock shift working was a huge loss of potential – one calculation showed that if a three-shift 24-hour working day was introduced in a plant, not only would output rise, but also half of the jigs and one-third of the tools could be released for use elsewhere.[63] Workers' wages went up quite dramatically during the course of the war, with wages rising from an average of 75s per week in late

1938 to over 140s per week in early 1944, a rise of 88 percent.[64] But despite the rise in wages hours worked remained remarkably static, an average week rising from 47.7 hours in late 1938 to a peak of 52.9 in mid-1943, an increase of a mere 11 percent.[65] And despite what the Prime Minister might have liked to portray, in general privately-owned factories never operated around the clock, and the norm seems to have been one long shift per day, rather than two shorter ones. This differed from the state-owned factories, as the ROFs had introduced round-the-clock working in 1941.[66] Overall, there was a marked reluctance to introduce shift working in the tank industry, despite its apparent attractions for increased productivity, with the unions very vocal on the issue. These objections included:

- A loss of overtime pay by the workforce.
- Women and young men were forbidden by law to work nights; although exemptions to this could be claimed, these were rare.
- Additional strain on the limited managerial, supervisory and maintenance staff.

On those occasions when a second shift was used it tended to be much less effective, as it was often much smaller and therefore less productive than the first or main shift. For tank workers the second shift was assessed to be only 17 percent of the size of the main.[67] So it was more business as usual than total war: 'Even as the Nazi subjugation of Western Europe was making headlines... the machinery of daily life in Britain was ticking steadily away. In the tank factories work continued as usual, albeit on a round-the-clock basis.'[68] In this last statement David Fletcher may for once be wide of the mark. There is scant evidence of any round-the-clock working by the vast majority of firms, in part at least because of the shortages of skilled or semi-skilled workers which could allow this to happen. Additionally, the production of tanks depended in many cases on the flow of sub-components into the factories. It only took one stoppage of a critical component to bring the whole production line to a halt, regardless of the number of shifts.

Chapter 6

The Tanks of the Early War Years

The A13 Covenanter

The next tank to examine was almost certainly the worst tank that Britain produced during the war; nearly 1,800 were built and – luckily for the crews – not one of them was committed to action. This was the A13 Mk III, given the name Covenanter. If ever there was a story of how not to build a British tank, this is it. Even the name given to the project, A13 Mk III, may have played its part in the tale of woe that ensued.

In late 1937 the Mechanization Board began investigating a new heavy cruiser, A16, that would use the new Christie suspension, be powered by Nuffield's Liberty engine, and use some of the best features of the experimental A14 tank then being built by LMSR to a design from DTD. A14 was intended to use a Horstman suspension, but during trials in early 1939 it was assessed as too complicated, too heavy, too noisy and too slow, and was subsequently abandoned. Development of the A16 was likewise stopped, and LMSR was instead instructed to look at how they could improve the existing A13 design that it was building, but which would be both lighter and cheaper. It was for this reason that the Covenanter, as the tank would later be named, was referred to as A13 Mk III rather than given its own A project number.

Up to this point LMSR had only built tanks to other's designs, specifically Nuffield's A13, and, just underway, Vulcan's Matilda II infantry tank. With very limited experience therefore the company was requested to become the parent for a new cruiser tank with a 30mm armour basis, and would thus be responsible for the detailed design of the hull, as well as having responsibility for sub-contracts and the oversight of production by other firms. LMSR, described as a 'large and unwieldy company', had only been formed in the previous decade by the amalgamation of many smaller locomotive companies. The main production factory was in Crewe, with a subsidiary facility in Horwich near Bolton that was used for tank production. LMSR possessed extensive facilities for administration and had already made some preparations for expansion of its tank work by creating a drawing office in the company headquarters in Euston, which might in part explain the decision to award the firm the parentage. This drawing office had been involved in the A14 project, but for some reason it was the Derby office that was instructed to carry out the work on Covenanter.

Having been given the task, LMSR moved quickly. A wooden mock-up (possibly only of the hull) was shown to representatives of the War Office, including the Christie enthusiast Martel, on 13 April 1939, and it must have looked like a fabulous tank to the audience: low, sleek, looking every inch a thoroughbred. Because the tank was thought of as a derivative of the A13 already in production, and was meant to use the 'maximum number of known components', the Director of Mechanization, Major General Davidson, noted that the General Staff (for it was their decision, not his) needed to decide if the tank could be ordered into production without the need for trials of a pilot model. Four days later the GS did approve the first contract to be placed with LMSR for 100 tanks, off the drawing board, and without waiting for the results of trials on the pilot model, one of which was included in the contract.[1] This was the first time that this had been done and was one of the major reasons for the dreadful mess that was to ensue. It was hoped that because the new tank was (or was thought of as) a direct development of the existing A13, risks would be minimal, and any faults found early on, once the pilots were trialled, could be quickly rectified on the production line. In both cases this proved terribly wrong. There was little commonality with the A13, and it could be that something as incongruous as the project title was unhelpful here, giving the staff not familiar with the details a feeling of confidence that the risk was worth taking. Incidentally, during the same meeting, the requirement for a heavier type of cruiser to be developed concurrently was discussed; the A14, A16 and A18 models were formally rejected and this led to the decision to instruct NMA to develop the A15 Crusader, using a common turret design developed by Nuffield for both tanks.

It was also decided that rather than use the Liberty engine of the A13, the Henry Meadows company of Wolverhampton would be tasked to produce a bespoke engine for the new tanks, and while this was accepted by LMSR for the Covenanter, Nuffield refused to do the same for the Crusader. The engine design was very much influenced by the space available for it to fit into: as the tank was meant to be low and narrow, the engine compartment was consequently restricted in size in all three dimensions. For the task, Meadows modified and enlarged their existing engine used in the Vickers

PR (Tetrarch) tank, to produce the DAV flat-12 engine which developed a nominal 300bhp, plenty to move a tank expected to weigh no more than 14 tons. Because of the limited space it was found that there was no room under the armour for the main engine cooling components, and therefore the radiator had to be placed somewhere else, this being in the nose of the tank to the left of the driver's hood, with armoured covers for the air intake mounted above it. It is not clear if the wooden mock-up had included this feature as, it if had been, it seems inconceivable that the experts would have let the arrangement stand.

The War Office had ordered maximum use of welding to save weight as much as to speed up production, but in October 1939 LMSR pushed back against this, citing concerns over the technique as well as the lack of skilled welders. They recommended that the more traditional rivetted construction be used, at a weight penalty of an estimated two hundredweight, and this was accepted – missing the opportunity to experiment with armour welding techniques that would have paid dividends later. However, to be fair the war had just started and although the Great Tank Crisis was still in the future, there was a clear imperative to maximise production of new tanks. Composite armour construction would be used, as on the A10, with thinner inner plates of IT 110 specification carbon manganese steel, with thicker plates of higher quality IT 70 homogenous armour bolted onto them. For some reason, the inner plates were measured in fractions of an inch, whereas the outer plates were in millimetres. The near-vertical front outer plates of the turret and the hull fronts, for example, were ¾in thick, and the outer plates 21mm. (This gave a combined thickness of 40.05mm, the maximum used on the tank).

The first pilot, of welded construction and made by LMSR, was delivered (without the turret, which was not ready) to MEE on 23 May 1940, a fortnight after the German invasion of the Low Countries. The initial trial report came out on 1 August, after the tank had run 700 miles, three-quarters of it across country. The tank had already gained weight, and at an estimated 15 tons 17cwt was now nearly two tons over the weight specified. [2] The narrow track used gave the Covenanter a higher ground pressure than the much heavier A22 Churchill being developed. [3] The report criticised the inaccessibility of components (à la Matilda), the tendency of the petrol tanks to leak (with the tank actually catching fire during one trial), the lack of lagging on the cooling pipes connecting the engine with the radiator and which ran through the crew compartment, a cramped driver's cab and, not least, difficulties in steering which made it very difficult to keep the tank in a straight line. The pneumatic steering was thought to be both complicated and vulnerable to damage, as a failure of the compressor or pipes would make the tank difficult to recover. For some reason the tank featured horizontal steering tilers working around a pivot, rather than the more conventional levers, and, even more bizarrely, had the accelerator pedal in the middle, with the clutch pedal to the left and the foot brake to the right. There was even a problem with the Triplex vision blocks; there were a number used on the tank, but no one had thought that it would be a good idea to standardise the size used. The report went on to identify the problem that would bedevil the Covenanter: engine and transmission cooling. The engine always ran very hot, which brought up the oil and the fuel temperatures.

Trials on the second pilot tank, this time with a turret, started in September 1940 and while some of the more minor problems had been solved or at least improved, there were a lot of problems with difficult gear-changing and the gears jumping out of mesh under load. The engine was found to run even hotter than previously, causing, on one notable occasion, the petrol in one of the tanks to boil. In other ways the tank must have impressed the trials teams. The Leyland pilot tank was found to be capable of nearly 37mph on roads, although with erratic steering characteristics, how confident the crews felt at this speed was not recorded. An end-of-year progress summary made it clear that because of the continuing problems with cooling, the tank was not suitable for use in tropical climates. Moreover, the design was now considered to be at the maximum weight for the suspension, and therefore no more armour could be fitted.[4] The intention to mount a driver's BESA machine-gun within his hood was deleted at this point, fortunately. By the end of March 1941 another report claimed that 'substantial progress has been made'; that might well have been the case, but the tank was still suffering from serious problems and was now in the hands of field units, with eighty-eight having been issued. These units discovered the same problems identified during the trials, but writ large. Even the moderately warm summer temperatures in Britain in 1941 made things worse, and engine fires were frequent, caused by the over-heated petrol, and as an expedient they tried to improve cooling to the engine compartment by wedging the 7mm thick armoured doors open with pieces of wood. The handbrake had no safety device and had an alarming tendency to release itself.

The primary problem remained one of cooling and was not caused solely by the location of the radiators. The engine was, by design, crammed into a tight space, with fuel and tanks and transmission components in close proximity, meaning that over-heating tended to affect all of them. Insufficient air flow was another major issue. To get anywhere near solving the problem, Leyland Motors was employed and instigated a complete redesign of the cooling and ventilation systems, including a radical design for the rear decks. (Fortunately, it was this work that led Leyland to become so disenchanted with British tank design that Rolls-Royce was contacted by them.) Two modification schemes were developed and can be referred to as Interim and Full. The Interim scheme was retrospectively applied to the first batches of Mk I machines made, with the intention of making things better, whereas the Full scheme would be applied to a new-build tank, the Mk III, which would improve cooling to the maximum extent found possible, but at the cost of adding over half a ton to the already overloaded chassis.

By late 1941 it was clear to many that the tank was even more of a dud than Tilly had declared the A9 to be. The increased weight was now causing front axles to bend, as the majority of armour weight was, naturally, on the front of the tank. The tank would eventually be assessed as having a service weight of nearly 18½ tons, 30 percent more than originally intended, despite only carrying a relatively thin maximum 40mm of armour. Nonetheless, a large re-work scheme – taking up valuable productive capacity that should have been used to build new tanks – was implemented in April 1942 to rebuild hundreds of Mk Is. The modifications led to the Covenanter going into four marks. The original Mk I, the production Mk III using the Full modification package and two hybrids. The Mk II designation was used for a reworked Mk I incorporating the Interim modifications, and Mk IV was a new tank built to the Mk II standard but also incorporating some of the improvements on the Mk III, including the clutch modifications. Clear as mud. Each mark had some 3in CS versions built, in addition to the standard two-pounder-armed tanks.

There was some hope that the introduction of the Mk III would make the tank suitable for service in overseas climes, and while this became official around the end of 1941, only five tanks were ever sent overseas, to Egypt for tropical trials. The story of these tanks gives us some indication of other problems that affected British tank performance. When a batch of four (presumably new) Covenanters arrived in Egypt, a solitary Mk I having been sent out towards the end of 1941, the trials could not be started immediately as the batteries were flat and spare parts – of which there were none – were required to repair the tanks. This was unfortunately typical of problems with transportation: brand-new tanks were frequently sent on long sea voyages loaded onto open decks, not sheeted down (good for security as well as protection from the elements), and requiring many man hours of labour before they could be used. This was primarily caused by the lack of supervision of the dockers who loaded the tanks and could very easily have been remedied, but the problem persisted. When the batch of four trials Covenanters arrived at the MEE outpost in Abbassia outside Cairo in summer 1942, the Mk I that was already there should have completed its trial by then but a replacement engine was still required, about six months after it had been requested. The new tanks, three Mk IIIs and a Mk IV, could not be used immediately as there were many faults that had to be rectified first. These can be put down to poor quality control at the UK factories, including sub-contractors. One tank had a water pump leak that was caused by the absence of a critical spring; another water pump lacked a locking device which also caused leaks; a petrol pump was rusty, and two of the tanks had even had their tracks put on back-to-front.

As production came to an end in late 1942 the three companies had, between them, produced 1,771 Covenanters including the three pilots. By this time many of the initial problems had been rectified to a large degree, but by then the tank was under-gunned, under-armoured, and had a woeful reputation for reliability. The suggestion sometimes advanced that this was, in the longer term, beneficial for the crews and fitters because it taught them valuable lessons about maintenance techniques is a spurious one and should be ignored. Tanks are built as weapons of war. Although some Covenanters persisted in training establishments, in 1943 the order went out that tanks no longer required were to be scrapped; it is to be hoped that some of this scrap was recycled into the much improved tanks of 1944 and 1945. The last word on the Covenanter, and the policies of the drawing board order and quantity over quality, is left in the capable hands of David Fletcher:

> The War Office was offered the pathetic explanation 'quality is desirable', but if quality does not get past the drawing office or the test bench, it will neither do us much good nor the Germans much harm. On that basis production of the Covenanter might just as well have gone on until Doomsday.[5]

The A15 Crusader

Despite a persistent myth, the Crusader was a contemporary of, and not a development from, the Covenanter. On 13 April 1939 Nuffield was asked to take the lead on the development of a new heavy cruiser, given the project number A15 and later named the Crusader – an earlier option rejected was to call it the Python. The first contract for one pilot (A15E1) plus 200 tanks was issued on 27 June 1939, nine weeks before the outbreak of war. Despite a desire to use a new Meadows engine common with the LMSR Covenanter, NMA, led by its aggressively focused William Morris, now Lord Nuffield, refused and insisted on using the old, tired Liberty design that the firm possessed the license for. There is no doubting Nuffield's patriotism or his generosity, but he was determined to run his companies according to his own rules, and frequently clashed with the War Office; when confronted by this extraordinary personality, the WO generally backed down and decisions were made that they often came to regret. However, there is some suggestion that the WO originally wanted NMA to build Covenanters, but it refused, leading to the design of the Crusader; if true, then we must applaud Nuffield, as the Crusader gave valuable if flawed operational service.

The A15 was built around the 27-litre Liberty petrol engine, developing a nominal 340bhp. Designed for aircraft, it had been first used as a tank engine in the Mk VIII design of 1918, and of course was already in service in the A13. For some reason, possibly to simplify production when the A13 was replaced by the new tank, Nuffield was completely wedded to the engine, although it was to become regarded as the weakest part of the tank, as we shall see. The Christie suspension was adopted, but with the inclusion of a fifth roadwheel pair which helped to take the weight and reduce ground pressure. The design was marred by the inclusion, once more, of a BESA MG sub-turret on the front of the hull, which came with all of the problems already known to be associated with it. Fortunately, after a short time in action common sense prevailed and the monstrosity was removed from production during the building of the Mk II version, following the practice of crews in the desert who had already taken some of them off. This created more space for ammunition stowage at the loss of some weight and no efficiency. The turret was the three-man two-pounder armed design from NMA, also used with some detail differences on the Covenanter. This featured sloping sides, as that way the armour specification could be met by using thinner plates set at an angle. Unfortunately, this design created shot traps on the underside, leading to enemy fire being deflected into the vulnerable turret ring area. Many British reports from actions in North Africa were later to refer to jammed turrets and guns, or worse, and led to the adoption of a slab-sided turret on the A24/A27 tanks.

The single mild-steel pilot, A15E1, was completed by NMA and arrived at MEE for trials on 9 April 1940, a month before the first turretless Covenanter, despite a later start. The first production contract for 200 Mk I Crusader tanks had already been issued concurrently, another drawing board order. Nevertheless, in some ways the Crusader was a workmanlike design, certainly at the time of its operational debut with 6RTR in June 1941. True, it was under-gunned, as the Germans had started to field the 50mm gun on its Panzer III tanks, and also under-armoured, at a 40mm basis constructed using composite plates as on the Covenanter. But it was fast and agile, with a low silhouette and the advantages that the three-man turret conferred, despite lacking a commander's vision cupola for closed-down use. It was certainly an improvement over the A9, A10 and A13 tanks that armoured regiments had been used to until that point, even though it was nearly 5 tons heavier than the A13 and thus not as fast, with an officially governed top road speed of 27mph.

However, the Liberty engine, insisted on by Nuffield, was to cause endless problems and gave the Crusader a deserved reputation for unreliability. On the face of it the engine was a good choice, with nominal 340bhp on tap for a tank weighing around 20 tons, which should give a power to weight ratio of 17:1, a very reasonable figure. However, what was not widely appreciated at the time was that this figure did not represent the real power available, as a lot of horsepower was actually used up in ancillary operations including cooling the engine. Typically, a Liberty engine needed nearly 18 percent of the nominal power just to cool itself.[6] But the real problem was reliability. The construction of the Liberty was at fault, as each of the twelve cylinders was individually made of cast-iron and then bolted together; when moving at speed over rough terrain the engine would tend to work itself apart, fracturing the oil galleries and causing leaks that invited sand into the engine. Cooling was also inadequate for the desert, as sand was able to get into the system and caused frequent coolant pump failures which immobilised the tank. The exposed engine valves and chain-drive for the cooling fans also wore rapidly due to sand ingress. The air-cleaners for the engine were mounted on the rear trackguards, just the place where the tank, despite its sand shields, would produce the most dust. These had been changed from a concertina filter type to an improved oil-bath design, but they were still positioned badly; each air cleaner could collect as much as eight pounds of dust an hour. It was only as a result of such experience that it became fully apparent that air-cleaners functioned best by being inside the engine compartment, and better still, that drawing air in through the turret acted as a first stage of filtration, prolonging filter and thus engine life.

To make matters worse, on arrival in Egypt the tanks suffered from the same problems as already noted for Covenanter, with inadequate shipping methods and instances of tanks being driven round the docks with no coolant in the system. One shipment of forty-one tanks that arrived in February 1943, many months after the first complaints had been raised, had not a single tank that was fit for use. Thirty of them required up to 300 man-hours of work to put right – providing of course that the spares were available. The other eleven needed between 300 and 500 hours. (Bearing in mind that the official NMA figures for building a new Crusader from scratch in 1943 was 6,050 man-hours, these figures are truly awful.) An undated report, using information extracted from Middle East Liaison Letters and Technical Reports, had this to say:

A most damning report has just gone home on a recent batch of Crusaders. We wish the manufacturers would pay us a visit. The Crusader is wasting precious lives as well as time, energy, manpower, workshop capacity and transport in initial preparation, recovery, and repair... An analysis made by a REME officer of the defects on 350 Crusader tanks which passed through his hands is given below:

- Ignition & carburettors   29%
- Water pump   27%
- Oil galleries   24%
- Gearbox selectors   22%
- Fan   20%
- Power traverse   14.5%
- Compressor   14%

The defects were all of the known and reported varieties... the other important piece of equipment is the Crusader Mk III with the 6-Pdr gun. This, like all previous Crusaders, is marred by the faults which are still uncorrected, i.e., 60 man-hours of work has to be put into every tank on arrival in order to ensure that faults in the original assembly are corrected. A reliable water pump has not yet been achieved, nor are spare pumps, spindles and water seals yet being received in sufficient quantities in spite of frequent demands by cable.

This must have been immensely frustrating for all involved – with the exception of the companies building the tanks back in the UK which were still churning out faulty goods and getting paid nonetheless.

In an attempt to improve the protection on the tank the Crusader Mk II was introduced during 1941 with a modest 6mm increase to the nose and 10mm on the turret front to bring it up to a maximum standard of 50mm; many Mk IIs were also built without the MG turret, although this was not an official part of the upgrade at first. Additional applique armour panels were also produced that field workshops could fit on the glacis of the tank and were mainly used on the later Mk III. The one feature of the Crusader that prolonged its service life for a while was that the turret ring was large enough – just – to allow a 6 Pounder gun to be mounted as the Mk III. The anticipated early appearance of the 6 Pounder-armed A24 Cavalier led to a delay in the decision on up-gunning the Crusader, but when it became clear that the Cavalier was not going to be ready as soon as had been hoped, the Crusader Mk III was produced instead. The development of this started in September 1941, with Nuffield once again rejecting the official scheme offered to them and producing a design of their own, still using 50mm of armour. Although it looked similar to the earlier version, the turret had to be enlarged and despite this, the larger gun and ammunition meant that there was now only room for two men, with all the control problems that brought. In most regiments therefore the troop leader continued to operate from a Mk I or II for reasons of command and had to forego the advantages of a good tank-killing gun.

Production of the Crusader was conducted by NMA as the parent and, in addition, was farmed out by NMA to eight other companies, including two belonging to the wider Morris stable, MG Cars and MIE.[7] Excluding the single A15E1 pilot, it seems that a maximum of 5,699 service tanks were contracted for, although not all of these were completed. In total, 3,618 gun tanks of all three marks were built (although Mk III was in the minority with only just over 1,000 made), as well as 668 OP tanks. At least 685 anti-aircraft tanks in three marks were also built on the production lines. Conversions of the tank, which had been made obsolete as a gun tank by early 1943, saw some additional service as gun tractors or as Armoured Recovery Vehicles (ARV), many of which were still in service in 1944.

The A24 Cavalier

In late 1940 the MoS requested NMA and Vauxhall to offer designs for a new heavy cruiser. This was to feature much heavier armour (75mm on the turret front and 65mm on the hull front), the new six-pounder gun, a more powerful engine to deal with the expected weight of 24 tons, and not least, greatly improved reliability. In January 1941 Vauxhall offered the A23, a scaled-down version of the A22 Churchill infantry tank then under early development, which was rejected, and NMA offered a development of the A15 Crusader, known as the A24. A drawing-board order for 500 vehicles was placed in June 1941 on the understanding that the new tank must be in production by spring 1942. The Director of Tanks and Transport, Geoffrey Burton, tried to disagree with the placing of another drawing board order as he had seen the shambles that had resulted from previous ones, but was overruled.

Confusion still reigns about the name: originally referred to as the Cromwell I, the name was changed to Cavalier in August 1942 when the Cromwell II was renamed to become the Centaur, and the Cromwell III became the Cromwell I... how could that possibly cause problems? (At one point before this there was a suggestion that the A24 might be called the Tiger, but it was pointed out that the Germans had got there first.) A new six-sided composite turret was designed to eliminate the shot trap problem of the Crusader, and this survived to see service on the two A27 models. Although a 410bhp Mk IV version of the Nuffield Liberty engine was developed and the hull front redesigned to give a slightly larger turret ring and better ergonomics for the crew, the much heavier Cavalier at over 26 tons was markedly slower than its predecessor. In any case, by the time it appeared the Liberty had been thoroughly discredited in the minds of the users. Despite the promises of early production its development was so slow that the vastly better Meteor-engined Cromwell was ready for initial trials two months before it. Although documentation is scarce, one source indicates that the heavier A24 was even more prone to breakdown that the Crusader, probably due to the fact that the mechanical components were under much more strain caused by the extra weight. Despite this, Nuffield still tried to intervene on behalf of 'his' tank, listing a number of advantages that he claimed made it superior to the Centaur. The final 340 built were produced as Observation Post (OP) tanks for the Royal Artillery; other than some of these, no Cavaliers saw service. Excluding the three pilots, only 500 examples of the A24 were built by NMA. It was not as bad as the Covenanter, but it still represented a massive waste of time and resources.

The Valentine

The Valentine was not allocated an A project specification number as it began life as a private venture design, which was offered to the British army and which was – initially at least – repeatedly declined. Despite this it went into service and must be considered as one of the more successful British designs operated during the Second World War, with nearly 6,000 gun tanks being built, plus many variants. It was also, uniquely, built in Canada.

Vickers-Armstrongs had, by the late 1930s, not only produced a whole range of light tanks, but had also delivered the A9, A10, and A11 designs to GS specifications, all of which were in service. This experience led the V-A leadership to conclude that it was possible to combine the best features of these tanks into a small, three-man tank that would be a useful addition to their export catalogue. Such a tank would be reliable and compact, but still be able to carry an exceptional amount of armour and a gun. One description of the Valentine tank, as it was to become known, called it 'a shortened, thickened-up version of the A10'.

Under the direction of the V-A chief designer, Leslie Little (who had replaced Carden when he was killed), the Valentine took shape as an infantry tank. The key design principle that was adhered to throughout its life was that it must be kept to within the weight limits that the engine, transmission, and suspension could bear, and that any attempts to overload the tank would be resisted; this was to prove to be inspired, and stopped the tank gaining more and more weight in the way that all of the previous examples we have looked at did. The compromise this necessitated was that the tank was small, both a blessing and a curse – it was small and hard to hit, but very cramped for the crew. The suspension to be used would be very similar to the slow-motion design used on the A9 and A10 cruisers, but the expected lower speed of the new tank meant that this design should provide a much better ride for the crew, and so it proved.

On 10 February 1938 V-A revealed the design to the War Office. At this stage the A11 was a reality but the A12 Matilda, or Infantry Tank Mark II, had yet to make an appearance, although much was expected of it. Vickers announced that the new design would be armoured to a 60mm basis and that it had already loaded a modified A10 hull to the expected weight of 16 tons and run it for 600 miles without major problems. The firm also wanted to arm the tank with a new weapon that it had developed, a 40mm automatic cannon. Vickers had great faith in this, believing it to be better than the service two-pounder, also 40mm, and pointing out that it meant that the loader could be dispensed with. The firm tried to seal the deal with a cost estimate of £10,000 per tank, then considered to be cheap for a 16-ton tank. The WO representatives were not convinced. They (rightly) did not want to introduce a new and untried weapon that would complicate ammunition supply; one of the advantages of the two-pounder was that the basic weapon and its ammunition were common to both tank and wheeled mountings. Furthermore, and a little bizarrely in the light of what was happening elsewhere, they did not like the idea of a two-man turret. Further meetings followed in which the WO tried to increase the amount of armour on the sides of the turret, to add a vision cupola, and to hang armoured side skirts and mud chutes on it, but Little was adamant; the design must not be overloaded. The WO remained sceptical but still ordered a Valentine mock-up which was completed by 24 March 1938. This still featured the 40mm cannon, but the firm did state that it was capable of mounting the two-pounder if required. The WO representatives said that they could not accept into service a tank with no cupola (the A11 had no cupola), insufficient armour (the A9, A10, A13, and all the light tanks had much less), or poor trench-crossing ability (a problem for the A11 and the light tanks).

However, by April 1939 the situation had changed, and the WO suddenly showed interest in the tank, accepting the penalty of a two-man turret with a two-pounder gun if rapid production was assured. V-A thought that it could have eight tanks a month coming off the production line by April 1940, and that clinched it. Further attempts by the WO to meddle with the design and add weight – for example by fitting 3mm side armour that would have added 4cwt – were resisted by Vickers, which knew that rapidity of production was the tank's key attribute, although the maximum armour had been increased slightly to 65mm. The firm even cheekily suggested to the WO that it might prefer to produce the A12 instead of the Valentine, knowing full well that this would cause further delays and that the current estimate was that they could produce two Valentines for every Matilda. The WO settled for the Valentine. The CIGS was told that producing the Valentine not only increased the overall output of infantry tanks (this being the period when many more I-tanks were required than cruisers), but that it gave them a fallback should the A12 be found to have 'grave defects'. The tank was to be known as the Infantry Tank Mk III, and received the name Valentine later at Churchill's insistence, as he – along with many others – was confused by the complicated nomenclature.

As a result of the meeting the first tentative order was placed for 100 tanks in the same month, April 1939, and in order to fulfill the anticipated further orders two more companies were brought into the scheme, Metro-Cammell and BRCW, both of which received their first contracts for 125 tanks each on 29 June 1939. On 29 September 1939, less than a month after the war had started, Canada expressed an interest in producing tanks, again raising the question of why this resource had not been considered before. Eventually 1,420 Valentines were to be built in that country, the majority going to the USSR. The first V-A-built Valentine was delivered to MEE in early May 1940, and the first ten service tanks were produced by the parent during June. Peak production was not to occur until December 1942, by which time the Valentine was obsolete.

The tank was small and cramped, had a two-man turret (initially), and could only reach a maximum speed of 15mph, but it was small, rugged, reliable, and easy to produce. Furthermore, it was able to be incrementally upgraded in both engine and armament throughout its life and eventually rank to eleven marks, mounting a 75mm gun and a good diesel engine. It was also used as the basis for a Duplex Drive swimming tank, two types of self-propelled gun, and a bridge-layer. In total, excluding the Canadian production, 5,248 gun tanks were built by the three companies; just under 4,000 were built with the two-pounder gun, and nearly 1,300 with either the six-pounder or the 75mm. Additionally, excluding prototypes converted from normal tanks, 647 DD tanks were made, all by Metro-Cammell. Therefore, 5,895 Valentine tanks were built in Britain during the war. For all its faults, it was a success. It had the distinction of being the only British tank that existed at the start of the war and which was still in British front-line service at the end, albeit in specialist roles with the Royal Artillery. Above all else and most importantly in the context of this book, it was easy to produce, simple to maintain, and reliable.

The A22 Churchill

The genesis of the A22 was in an earlier tank, the A20. Firmly rooted in the experiences of the First World War, the A20 was sometimes described as a 'shelled area tank', designed to be both large and heavily armoured, and able to cross battlefields where there was so much hostile shell fire as to render other means of movement impossible. The concept was entirely flawed and unsuited for modern warfare, and the A20 project was to be halted after a single prototype hull had been completed by Harland & Wolff. Of interest to subsequent developments is that in order to power the A20 a Meadows Flat-12 design was proposed, in preference to an H&W diesel design. Additionally, Vauxhall motors had been asked in January 1940 to assist Harland & Wolff with the design for the suspension, despite Vauxhall having no experience in the subject, and this probably influenced what was to happen next. The A20 also seems to have been the first tank for which a drawing board order was proposed; it did not come to that, but Brigadier Hollebone, the President of the Mechanization Board, as early as September 1939 had proposed just this – even before Dunkirk. David Fletcher stated that 'the idea of building new tanks for production, straight off the drawing board, seems to be a terrible gamble, and it was one that the British lost every time they played.'[8]

A new infantry tank project, known as A22, was then authorised, with the specification under consideration at the end of June 1940, just as the Great Tank Crisis was unfolding. The tank was clearly going to be much larger than those in service, although not to the extent of the A20 which was about to be sidelined and then cancelled. Despite the immaturity of the A22 project, in early July the Prime Minister demanded that at least 500 of them were to be built by March 1941, a somewhat arbitrary figure, but the date was worrying. How could a new tank be brought into service, with 500 in field force units, in only nine months? Clearly the answer was that it was impossible, but the effect of this pressure was to hurry the A22, soon to be known as the Infantry tank Mk IV and much more famously the Churchill, into production. The initial problems with the tank mainly stemmed from this decision. At some point soon after this, Vauxhall agreed to take on the parentage and thus the detailed design of the A22. At that stage Vauxhall Motors was heavily involved in producing lorries for the British army, clearly a growth industry. With a new factory built at Luton, the Bedford part of the company had been asked by the WO in about May to design a new petrol tank engine capable of not less than 350bhp, possibly intended as a contender for A20. Apart from its suspension advice to H&W, the company had no experience of the task but had seen the A20 design and presumably the pilots under construction; not surprisingly, therefore, the layout of the A22 was heavily influenced by what the firm had just observed and also by the new engine under design.

The wooden mock-up was approved in September and the first pilot hull was partially complete the following month. As the A22 was much larger than any other of the service tanks being built at the time, it was agreed that it could mount both the 3in CS howitzer and a two-pounder, with the former in a hull mounting alongside the driver, and the latter in the turret. This was a terrible idea; as well as the inadvisability of carrying two types of ammunition, the gunner for the 3in not only had to load it, but also aim and fire it, making rapid accurate fire an impossibility. The traverse and elevation/depression were also severely limited, but it was in this form that the Mk I Churchill went into service. (As it happened, there were insufficient 3in guns and some Mk Is were built with a BESA MG instead, which would become the standard layout.)

The first production contracts were issued on 5 October 1940, a very large drawing board order for 500 tanks involving Vauxhall as the parent, but this total was then broken down into batches to be completed by six other companies, only two of which had built tanks previously. Later, in December, three others were brought into the scheme. The first pilot tank was completed in Luton before Christmas, with a second pilot ready in early January 1941. In itself this was a remarkable feat; to design a tank and produce a pilot from scratch in about six months was exceptional, but of course many of the problems of reliability and design stemmed from the fact that the Churchill was a complete rush job. In its early days, the tank was going to be called the Victoria, and some Canadian tank crews who received very early tanks had even started using the name, only to be told of the change. Although Churchill's personal preference was to call it the Cromwell, Beaverbrook fiercely resisted this and so it became the Churchill. The Prime Minister must have been pleased, although he preferred to intimate that the tank was not named after him but his ancestor John Churchill, Duke of Marlborough.

The tank was unique in many ways. Although the basic layout of three men in the turret and two in the hull was conventional, the (initially bolted, later welded[9]) hull had side sponsons either side of the main hull that the suspensions units were fixed to and which the exposed track ran around, giving it an old-fashioned look.[10] This made the tank terribly noisy for the crews, but did allow lots of stowage space inside and two escape hatches were included, one either side and which later saved the lives of many escaping crewmen. The toothed idler wheel was mounted at the very front creating two 'horns' that blocked the driver's vision to the sides and meant that guiding the driver was a major preoccupation of the commander. The driver steered the tank not by a tiller lever either side of his seat, but rather using a tiller bar in front of him that resembled a bicycle handlebar. The Bedford engine was difficult to access with some components buried out of reach, but, like the Matilda, this was remedied on later marks. From the Mk III the six-pounder was fitted, the 95mm CS howitzer was used on some tanks (Mk V and later the Mk VIII), and gun tanks from the Mk VI mounted the British 75mm gun. The cast turret used on the Mk I was the first attempt to build a fully cast turret: the two Matilda tanks both had cast shells but with a flat plate bolted on to form the roof.

Initial problems were manifold. Many bolted components worked themselves loose; failures of suspension springs and the roadwheel bearings were legion; the track links cracked and broke apart; the air inlets which pointed downwards sucked up mud and dust and leaves; the gearbox jumped out of top gear; the fuel pre-vapourised due to the poorly thought-out pump and fuel line locations; pipes corroded creating myriad oil leaks; the air outlets picked up dust from under the tank and blew it under the hull and into the driver's face, blinding him; clutch failures were common – the list went on and on. Maintenance levels were also exceptionally demanding of the crew – each side had twenty-two roadwheels that needed individual greasing, for example – and the tank sometimes 'ran away', a terrifying outcome that occurred when the hydraulics failed with the gearbox in neutral. Even when working as designed, the ride was dreadful; at anything above 8mph it pitched and made firing on the move impossible, and at the top speed of 15mph it jolted the crews furiously.

When the tanks were issued, from around June 1941 on, Vauxhall famously included a lengthy apology in the user handbook, explaining why these faults had happened and assuring the crews that they would all be remedied, which to be fair they were – but this took time and the tank's reputation suffered as a result, and very nearly led it to being cancelled. The apology ended with the words: 'Please do not draw the wrong conclusions from this frank statement of defects... The only abnormal factor is that, having found them, we are not in a position to put them right before production begins... instructions have been received to proceed with the vehicle as it is rather than hold up production'. The apology thus drew attention to the part that the MoS had played, which was fair, if more than a little unusual.

One of the doctrinal problems with infantry tanks stemmed from the original specifications, which stated that top speed was not important, as all the tanks had to do was keep pace with an advancing infantryman in the attack. This ignored two other factors. Firstly, tanks spent most of their time not actually attacking anything but rather just moving from place to place.

A reasonably high speed would reduce the time spent on road moves and make them more flexible. Secondly, the thought that tanks should always be tied to the bootlaces of the infantry they were supporting was fallacious; in order to best support them the tanks needed to manoeuvre into positions of advantage where they could use their weapons to best effect, and that require battlefield agility. The Churchill was not a fast tank, but it possessed elements of agility that belied its size and design and made it a useful battlefield weapon. It was found that it could move over broken ground that would stop most other tanks and – discovered during the Tunisia campaign – its hill-climbing ability became the stuff of legend.

But the problems still needed to be fixed, and of course the Ministry of Supply was, initially at least, insistent that production output must not be affected by modifications. A huge rework programme was ordered in November 1941 to correct the many faults on the early tanks and bring them, where possible, up to a more modern specification, often involving up-gunning with a new turret and armament. Conducted by Vauxhalls and Broom & Wade, officially the scheme intended to introduce only three modifications: fitting mudguards over the tracks; changing the design of the air inlets; and amending the design of the air outlet. Eventually, however, over seventy items were included. It was agreed that the first 300 or so tanks were beyond redemption and should not be reworked. Without going into the full details, the scheme was successful in remedying many of the faults, but of course this came at the expense of production, which must have made introducing the scheme a difficult decision for the MoS. By the end of November 1942 over 1,200 Churchills had passed through the scheme, gaining an R suffix to their registration numbers and, hopefully, a lot more reliability.

Despite the known problems, the tanks continued to come off the lines in huge numbers despite many officers doing what they could to scrap the design. On 9 December 1941, at a meeting of the Tank Board, the specification for a new infantry tank was on the agenda, and it was stated that 'it was not intended to develop the [Churchill]', although it was accepted that the A22 could still be useful, if armed with the six-pounder and made reliable.[11] At the point when no fewer than 3,500 tanks were on order, in May 1942, the policy was that production was to stop when that number was scheduled to be complete, in March 1943. In October 1942 the Tank Board once again stated that the A22 was obsolete and would go out of production. However, on 20 January 1943 another 500 were ordered, and they would not be the last. In April it was recommended that another 1,000 should be ordered, on the basis that the tank had now been greatly improved and had been demonstrated as effective in combat. This brought the total up to 5,000, and in time would exceed that – although by exactly how many is not known. Recent research gives an overall figure of 5,589 gun tanks, which excludes the five pilots and the forty-nine or fifty gun carrier tanks, which were not tanks at all! Churchill remains the most difficult tank to quantify, for three main reasons: Vauxhall's use of sub-contractors and their conflicting records; frequent alterations and cancellation of contracts; and the effects of the great rework scheme and the conversion of many gun tanks to other roles. In short, the records are a mess, and it is unlikely that it will ever be possible to state a definitive figure with confidence.

Famously, many of the gun tanks built were later converted into specialist roles for use with the 'Funnies', the 79th Armoured Division, including Crocodile flamethrowers, ARVs, AVREs, bridge-layers[12] and the like. The definitive mark of the Churchill as a gun tank was the Mk VII or A22F, essentially an all-welded, perfected Churchill that came into service in 1944, and weighed 40 tons. By now the Churchill had become popular. 9RTR were able to report after action in Europe that 'the Churchill stands up well to anti-tank fire. If set on fire it burns slowly and the crews have a good chance to bail out.' It was even intended to build a scaled-up Churchill, the A43 Black Prince, just to mount the seventeen-pounder gun, but this was thankfully scrapped post-war.[13]

The following description of how one manufacturer, in this case the A22 Churchill design parent Vauxhall Motors of Luton, went about the process of building tanks, was presented as a lecture to the Institute of Engineers in London on 14 December 1945. The transcript of the talk offers a fascinating insight into how some of the problems were tackled, although the use of a brand-new tank to tow literally hundreds of tons of other partially-completed Churchills behind it cannot have done them much good! It is also probable that the description applies to the process once it had time to settle down and mature, rather than at the start when issues of poor quality control were rife.

Tank assembly in the Luton works was purely an assembly operation, because there were no facilities for carrying out the heavy engineering work involved in making the hull and similar parts. Nevertheless, as this works was the Parent concern, it was responsible for the production of this vehicle by all other assemblers and sub-contractors, and it was essential to create an organisation to control the ordering, scheduling, and distribution of all materials and sub-assemblies throughout the group. In order to keep a strict control on the quality of all materials and sub-assemblies, everything, with the exception of the hull, was delivered to a central depot housed in the Luton works, where it was inspected and checked against purchase orders. A large fleet of lorries was necessary to take the precise number of inspected parts to the various assembly plants. This procedure involved a lot of double-handling.

To coordinate the activities of the main vehicle assemblers, three senior executives were appointed liaison engineers. These men kept the assemblers informed of all technical developments in design and production methods, and also advised component manufacturers of troubles which occurred with their products. Similar liaison engineers were working with the various Army units using these vehicles, with the dual object of instructing the troops in the use and maintenance of the vehicles and at the same time providing much useful information regarding the behaviour of the vehicle in service.

The actual method of assembling the vehicle differed to some extent in each plant owing to the different facilities available, but in the main all manufacturers followed the general principles developed at Luton. The hulls were delivered by road or rail straight into the building at the commencement of the assembly line, the first operation being that of sealing all the joints below a certain line with a waterproofing compound. After this operation the hull was lowered into a tank of water to test the waterproofing. Next the bogie wheel assemblies were fitted to the hull and the vehicle was lifted by crane onto rails running the full length of the building. It was then connected to the tank in front by chains. There were vehicles in progressive stages of assembly on this track and as work was completed at each station the whole line was towed forward one station. The toeing was accomplished by the completed vehicle at the end of the line, which was driven off under its own power and pulled all the vehicles behind it, leaving space at the far end for a new hull assembly. At the various stations along the line the different components, such as engine, gearbox, final drive assemblies, radiators, and petrol tanks were fitted, and also the turret seating ring.

The fitting of the turret seating ring gave a considerable amount of trouble in the early days because it was essential for the smooth and easy operation of the turret through a full circle that this seating ring should be absolutely true. Owing to joints in the armour plate the hull was far from flat and level, so some means had to be devised to machine it. First of all, a master ring was bedded onto the hull with blue marking, and the high spots removed with a portable grinder. This was a tedious operation, taking anything up to 102 hours, but by designing and making a special machine which was fixed onto the hull a true face was machined with a single-point tool. By the use of this piece of equipment the time for this operation was reduced to forty-six hours. The final operations on the assembly line were the fitting of the track and the turret... The turret was built as a complete sub-assembly with its rotating mechanism and gun deflection stops and tested on an electrically-operated test stand. The complete time for the tank assembly was 500 hours.

The vehicle was taken out for its first test, which consisted of fifty miles over roads and rough ground. It was then returned to the works and, after being washed, was driven down a ramp into a concrete tank full of water in order to give the hull a second test for leaks. It was then taken to the rectification bay where any defects were rectified, guns fitted by the RAOC, and then finally painted. The finished vehicles were finally dispatched by the Army either on railway flats or by road on the now well-known tank transporters.

Chapter 7

Playing Catch-up 1942–1943

No tank existed after four years of war that was fit to go into a tank battle.
A.J. Smithers, *Rude Mechanicals*

The pooled production resources of the United Nations are now becoming sufficient to permit the emphasis to be put on quality rather than quantity.
RAC Half-Yearly Report, June 1942

In 1943, we are unlikely to produce a single tank fit to go into battle in the hands of the troops overseas.
Winston Churchill, September 1943

By 1942 the British Army was equipped, worldwide, with up to sixteen different models of tank... with but one exception, the Sherman, all suffered to some degree from poor design, outdated construction, or chronic unreliability...
David Fletcher, *The Universal Tank*

The customer complains: the Great Reliability Crisis[1]

By late 1941 the overall war situation had changed; Britain was not going to be invaded that year or indeed at all. Russia had survived the initial German onslaught and was using the winter weather to its advantage. The USA had just joined the war. Increasingly large numbers of US medium tanks were being supplied to the British armoured forces in North Africa and others would soon start to arrive in the UK as part of the invasion build-up. But as the war in Britain began its twenty-ninth month in January 1942, the damaging effects of the pre-war lack of investment in tanks and of the Great Tank Crisis of 1940 were still being felt. British production was growing only very slowly and would not reach its peak for another seventeen months. And while some of the demands for quantity were now starting to be satisfied, another word was starting to be heard again and again: reliability. Quality had been deliberately sacrificed in favour of producing sheer numbers. The Tank Board minutes recorded that:

> Every tank produced was taken off the assembly line to give to field units awaiting equipment. No interference with production, in order to introduce major modifications or new designs, could be accepted. Nor was there time to carry out the engineering tests required to establish the reliability of the main mechanical components or any new designs put into production.[2]

It was no surprise that ordering designs off the drawing board; avoiding the construction of prototypes and pilot models; restricting the user's ability to test the early production models; and then ignoring the subsequent proposals for modifications as they would interfere with production would lead to this near-disastrous situation. The early marks of Churchill were chronically unreliable, with the builders Vauxhall having to insert what amounted to an apology into the user handbook. Covenanter was a mechanical nightmare, so completely un-battleworthy as to be permitted no part in the desperate fighting in North Africa, despite the frequent calls for more cruisers from that theatre. Crusader was slightly better, but suffered badly from appalling reliability, and extremely poor quality control: 'Crusader in particular was repeatedly criticised for its faulty assembly.'[3] The other tanks in volume production, Matilda II and Valentine, were either obsolete or about to become so. No British tank carried a gun larger than the two-pounder until 1942 other then the smoke-firing close support weapons.

The comments about Crusader are worthy of expansion, as many of them derive directly from a lack of quality control and testing by the parent, in this case Nuffield Mechanization & Aero. On 7 February 1942, the Commander in Chief Middle East (CinC ME) complained about poor Crusader reliability and its inaccessible engine, even suggesting that the slower but more reliable – and better armoured – Valentine infantry tanks should be considered to replace Crusaders in future shipments, Valentine having by now acquired a good reputation for reliability. When this proposal was discussed by the Tank Board four days later, the opinion was that reports from the theatre were 'apt to be contradictory', and no action was taken. The damning of Crusader reliability by the troops finally led in May 1942 to the Baird Report, the authors of which visited the Middle East in order to see things at first hand and gather evidence. NMA claimed in the report that the main problems with Crusader were a lack of maintenance by crews, misguided instruction on the vehicle, and a shortage of spares. It even went so far as to suggest that a system of ground crews similar to the RAF be adopted. In the first paragraph of this top secret document the author made the unwise claim that Crusader was considered 'by all to be a very fine fighting machine'; but written by an unknown hand in red pencil next to this was the comment 'A patent lie!'.[4]

Although NMA's wild claims reflected Lord Nuffield's strident approach and refusal to admit any liability or responsibility, the rebuttal did contain one grain of truth. One of the maintenance issues outside the direct control of industry was the falling standard of technical training of the crews. Pre-war, the RTC had built up an enviable reputation for producing technically adept crewmen who knew their machines inside out. The requirement for preventative maintenance was inculcated into them, and this to a large extent explained the lack of complaints about poor reliability in the first year of the war, as the soldiers, both tank crews and the maintenance fitters, were expert at keeping the tanks going. This was because of the amount of time and effort put into the basic training of these soldiers, as well as the unflinchingly high standards demanded by the professional officers of the RTC. However, when the RAC expanded massively and the trainee was now a conscript with less time to be trained in the necessary skills, the design shortfalls of the tanks became glaringly apparent. Hancock commented that:

As the war went on the mechanical aptitude and experience of tank crews tended to decline; the drivers and other members of tank crews trained before 1940 were far more expert in getting the best out of their vehicles; this undoubtedly accounts in part for the high reputation acquired by Matilda.[5]

David Fletcher echoed the sentiment:

Crews with more experience of their charges soon got used to their more wayward traits and learned to detect and remedy them at an early stage... in the Western Desert [they] often traveled hundreds of miles on their tracks without any trouble at all... it had a lot more to do with a higher standard of maintenance and crew care [than with the design of the vehicle].[6]

Once the trainees gained experience though, the overall reliability of the tank fleets increased due to better maintenance on their part as well as better designed tanks. In part this came about as industry was able to find sufficient spare capacity to be able to deliver training for military drivers and mechanics on each particular type, often at their factories. However, it was only in the last twelve months of the war that British tanks shed their reputation for poor reliability and enjoyed high availability, starting with the introduction of the Cromwell and then followed by the Comet.

But it was not all about the crews, despite what Nuffield might wish to imply: quality control in factories was, in many cases, atrocious to the point of being non-existent. Another cable from the CinC ME arrived on 16 June 1942, complaining of faults found on brand-new tanks on arrival, some having been wrecked as they had been driven in the UK without any coolant in the radiators. More complaints on 30 June noted frequent cases of 'careless assembly and poor workmanship'. Crusaders arriving in mid-1942 were taking an average of 200 man-hours each in workshops to render them fit for issue. Faulty workmanship issues that could not be readily detected by visual inspection then frequently manifested themselves within the first 100 or so miles of use, requiring yet more rectification and repair. The CinC finished the telegram with the desperate plea: 'Can you insist on rigid inspections and tests on assembly lines at makers' works?'

The question of inspection of workmanship (quality control) was raised again in July 1942, with the wishy-washy request to 'consider and discuss with the War Office.' On 4 August it was reported that 'internal inspection arrangements of firms were being tightened up.' Whatever that meant, it would be many months before the troops noticed it. On 25 August 1942, out of the approximately 2,500 tanks in the Middle East, around 1,100 (44 percent) were in workshops being repaired.[7] Some of these repairs were doubtless due to enemy action, but a significant number and probably a majority were due to poor workmanship in the British production facilities, although inadequate methods of shipping and storage were also to play a part. On 28 November 1942, the CinC ME finally reported in exasperation that his: 'troops have no use for Crusader 2-pounder owing [to its] unreliability and inferior armament and armour'.[8]

The companies involved were often the cause of ill-will following such complaints, as they, seemingly as a matter of policy, refused to accept any liability: replies to such official correspondence are littered with evasions of responsibility and blame-shifting. On 17 August 1942 Mr Thomas of the

Nuffield Group building Crusader wrote to Lt Gen Weeks, the DCIGS, to enquire if the General Staff at the War Office were prepared to 'sacrifice ten gallons of petrol capacity to allow for the installation of a much-improved air filter' – an extraordinary misuse of the chain of command. Not surprisingly, the tentative answer was yes, but Weeks went on to say that this was only his personal opinion and that the matter should be referred through the correct channels; he then took the opportunity to tell Nuffield that he had received 'the most appalling indictment of Crusaders'. Mr Thomas then replied to what he called this 'broadside' (it was no such thing, it was polite almost to the point of being ineffectual), claiming that the tanks being discussed had been built 'before they started their intensive campaign against oil-leaks etc.' He was correct; they had been built earlier – by his organisation! A Tank Board meeting over three months later, on 8 December 1942, recorded that the new air cleaner was still nowhere in sight, even though the Crusader gun tank would go out of front-line service within four months; because of problems elsewhere, in May 1943, the Tank Board had to reluctantly endorse continued production of Crusaders into 1944.

Why was it that so many complaints could be raised by the crews, but hardly anything was done about them, and even when things were done, the time taken was unbelievably long? Hancock, referring specifically again to Crusader, asserted that:

> What was never satisfactorily resolved was the gap between the bulk issue of a vehicle and the arrival of dependable user comment on it, which [only] came when production was well in hand and when modifications were most resented by the manufacturer. To equip a [single] division …340 tanks were needed: by August 1941, when this number of Crusaders had been delivered, production was at a monthly rate of 65 machines. By February 1942, when user reports were arriving thick and fast, production was running at 130 machines a month and by March, when field criticism was [finally] being translated into modifications, production was ranging between 170 and 200.[9]

Once again both the MoS and the manufacturers raised objections to modifications, citing reduced production as the reason for failing to make improvements, either in design or in quality control. And even at this middle stage of the war, when the immediate tank crisis had passed, the same tired old excuses continued to be heard. As late as October 1942, referring to the new A24/A27 series tanks (Cavalier, Centaur, and Cromwell), the MoS could still unblushingly state that:

> It will be seen from the above that these three new types of machine were put into production before Acceptance Tests were completed. Under wartime conditions it is right and necessary to take this risk in view of the delay that would occur in producing new types if we were to await completion of Acceptance Tests before planning production.[10]

But by this stage the General Staff should have refused to accept these arguments and insisted that the time had come to reintroduce quality as the most important virtue. Some tentative steps had been taken; as early as August 1941:

> reliability was stated by the War Office to be 'the most important requirement in the new Churchill tank. By January 1942 the General Staff applied the new criterion to *all* AFVs. 'In view of Middle East reports', General Weeks informed the Tank Board that 'reliability must be considered more important than numbers.'[11]

Having returned from commanding Eighth Army, at a Tank Board Meeting on 4 August 1942 General Neil Ritchie stated that 'the German tanks appeared to have greater reliability than ours... mechanical reliability was *the* outstanding requirement'.[12] Hancock, in his study of weapon procurement and production, noted that: 'No-one [in Britain] ever specified that an artillery weapon, an aeroplane, or a battleship should be mechanically 'reliable', as it was so self-evident that such a statement was not thought to be necessary.'[13] But in the case of the tank, seemingly uniquely, that was exactly what was needed, in order to spell it out to the manufacturers and designers. In the past this had not happened: neither the specifications for the A24 Cruiser nor the new heavy infantry tank in June 1941 mentioned the word 'reliability'. This would have to change, and quickly: quality was by now becoming synonymous with reliability, and rightly so: high quality in terms of design and production would almost guarantee high reliability, and therefore availability for battle. The army required tanks which would not break down.[14]

For the want of a nail… the spare part saga

On 15 July 1941 there were eighty-three badly needed tanks in the UK that had been in workshops for over fourteen days simply for the want of a spare part.[15] Common sense would have suggested that putting a spare part into these tanks would represent a more efficient use of resources than putting it into a partially-built tank that would not be in the hands of troops for weeks or even months. No one seems to have suggested this, certainly neither the manufacturers nor the Ministry of Supply, as they would not support anything that would affect their already hopelessly optimistic delivery forecasts. The lack of spare parts for tanks remained a constant criticism, at least until late in 1942. The army was seeing the worst of both worlds: it was being given tanks that were mechanically unreliable, but the tank producers were under great pressure to finish completed vehicles rather than to supply a proportion of spare parts to allow repairs to be made in the future. This was because of the system being operated: provision of spare parts was chaotic because in those tanks ordered 'off the drawing board' the requirements for spares had only been calculated by analogy with other vehicles and not from the results of trials, and then probably using the most optimistic figures – what these days would be referred to as 'spin'.[16]

Churchill was clear that because of the pressures for new tanks the army could not have it both ways and he preferred the situation whereby the army had maximum numbers, meaning that provisions for the supply of spare parts had to be sacrificed. Despite this, a number of documents refer to having to slow production in order to furnish spares, particularly for the Middle East, and there were heated arguments between government departments as to the truth of the situation, with the MoS quoting policy and targets, and the military responding with examples of reality, as typically one-quarter of tanks in the hands of troops were unusable.[17] CinC Home Forces, General Martel, told the Prime Minister in February 1941 that 'there was a serious deficiency of spare parts for the tanks in the hands of the troops'. The Prime Minister tasked General Ismay to take up the matter with the MoS, and he was able to report back a week later that 'entirely satisfactory arrangements have now been made for the supply of spare parts.'[18] Unfortunately it was easier to promise it than to do it, and the situation continued to dismay the troops. The army was adamant: they still needed more spares, not only to effect repairs, but also in order to carry out preventative maintenance designed to stop tanks breaking down once committed to battle. The CIGS General Sir Alan Brooke put the situation forcefully in mid-1941:

We were at present living in a fool's paradise in that our formations had a considerable number of tanks without any reserve on which to come and go, and without any stocks of spare parts immediately available to replace breakdowns. Our goods were entirely in the shop window.[19]

The army in North Africa had reorganized itself by this time, to adopt a policy called 'Assembly Exchange' in the field, in order to effect swift repair of those tanks that could be salvaged quickly and then put back into the line.[20] This relied on the simple concept of swapping one complete damaged part for a new one, rather than wasting time trying to find or repair a fault in situ. This relied entirely upon a sufficient supply of spare parts, without which a policy of cannibalisation had to be implemented, leading to the complete stripping out of components from many tanks that should have been repairable, but which ended up as useless hulks.

In August 1941 David Margesson, the Secretary of State for War, wrote to Churchill saying that: 'no armoured formation can be considered as having 100% fighting capacity until it has behind it a 25% maintenance reserve of tanks, *and* [my emphasis] the necessary cushion of spare parts in the echelon.'[21] This was a sad indictment not only of the inherent unreliability of the tanks themselves, but also of the inability of the system to supply spares. The intention was to stock (for the total tanks held) 25 percent spare engines, 15 percent other major assemblies, and 'an agreed scale of parts for a year's maintenance. As you are aware, the MoS have so far been unable to meet this demand...'.[22]

Beaverbrook, now the Minister of War Production, stated in the House of Lords on 12 February 1942 that 'practically all spares asked for by the army in Egypt had been supplied'. This was a barefaced lie, and caused an incensed Margesson to write a very strongly worded letter to the Prime Minister, copying the letter to Beaverbrook and to the Defence Committee (Supply):

On the contrary, essential tank spares are in such short supply that it is difficult, particularly at home, to keep the tanks on the road. The true position has been consistently reported to the Ministry of Supply... last October I acquainted Lord Beaverbrook with the actual position... he promised to produce an immediate acceleration in the production of spares... since this date the weight of spares has increased but corresponding vehicle production has [also] increased, with the result that the net position is substantially unchanged... At the present moment there are demands outstanding for Middle East to the extent of approximately one hundred tons... the [Churchill gearbox] position has deteriorated for months and is now so bad that the manufacturers are so choked with gearboxes awaiting repairs that they have not even sufficient storage capacity to hold them.[23]

However, the lessons of spares production were sinking in, albeit very slowly. An MoS document discussing forthcoming production of the Cromwell series from late 1942 confirmed – possibly for the first time – that: 'provision will be made for adequate spares to be produced concurrently with the tanks.'[24] The RAC Half-Yearly Report No.6 agreed that: 'There has been a general improvement in the spares situation, though a shortage of some items still exists.' The big challenge remained how to translate the desire to maintain quantity of tank production as well as improving quality. An early attempt by the Tank Board to record the history of British tanks during the war opined that: 'There came a time, roughly coinciding with Russia's entry into the war, at which some selectivity became possible.'[25] In fact, there is scant evidence that *any* selectivity took place as early as summer 1941; quality considerations only began to be implemented from 1943.

Tank design and production: mid-war

The brief campaign in France in the spring and summer of 1940 had done little to instruct opinion in the equipment lessons of the new warfare... It was from North Africa that user experience was transmitted in increasing volume during 1941... Though at first experts hesitated to make general inferences concerning weapon policy from the somewhat odd conditions of desert warfare, it was evident that many of the assumptions which had guided development during the rearmament period were outmoded.[26]

Of such [unbattleworthy equipment] AFVs were the most important; it was [now] possible to end that series of interim models which had dominated the rearmament period. It was not so easy to decide on a method of ending it.[27]

It is time to look at the major developments that occurred in the mid-war years, which finally led to the end of the tank and reliability crises, and which eventually bore fruit by producing something approaching battleworthy tanks once again. Despite all the problems outlined above, tank production figures showed a general upwards trend into 1942, with the table showing how the production of tanks, in percentage terms, was climbing gradually. By mid-1942 the monthly cost of the tank production programme was nearing £20 million.

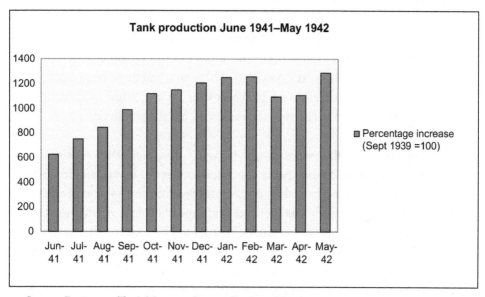

Source: Bovington Tank Museum Census Cards and Registers

However, by 1942, it had become clear that quantity was not everything. The Tank Board review of the tank situation on 26 October 1942, after more than three years of war, was able to summarise this disastrous situation with regard to the main British-produced tanks:[28]

COVENANTER	Obsolete
CRUSADER	Unreliable & unbattleworthy
CAVALIER	Not yet passed acceptance tests or in production
CENTAUR	Not yet passed acceptance tests or in production
CROMWELL	Not yet passed acceptance tests or in production
VALENTINE	To be superseded
MATILDA	Obsolete
CHURCHILL	Obsolescent[29]

The Select Committee on National Expenditure, in its first investigation into British tanks, recorded that: 'Apart from the Valentine used in Russia and the Churchill in Tunisia, no British tanks during 1943 have been considered worthy of a place in the main battles.'[30] It should be noted that both types mentioned were infantry tanks, which were in less demand than cruisers; in addition, Valentine had started life as a private venture by Vickers rejected by the army and the Churchill had come within a whisker of being cancelled the previous year.[31] The introduction to the RAC Half-Yearly report No.6 dated 31 December 1942 noted that:

> The demand for increased reliability, simplicity of operation and maintenance, heavier armament and ammunition, coupled with the maximum armour protection possible, will persist and those responsible for tank design must always have their eyes on the future and work persistently to develop the types of tank selected for production.

This appeal, carefully worded as it was, disguises the continuing dissatisfaction with the tanks being produced in Britain. It was not aimed at the manufacturers directly; rather, it was intended for the higher echelons of official circles, particularly the General Staff and the MoS. At the heart of this was the dawning realisation among many, but by no means all, that what was really needed was a single tank, fast enough for cruiser work, armoured sufficiently to allow it to be used for the close support of infantry, with a good dual-purpose gun, adaptable to be used in other specialised roles – and reliable.

> As early as June 1940 [it had been] stated that the General Staff had agreed 'that future design of tanks need no longer be hampered by attempts to get a big trench-crossing performance.' The results of this were not merely to change Army demands from a majority of infantry tanks to a majority of cruisers, but also to lead to the comparatively fast speed of the new infantry tank [Churchill] and the heavy armour of the new Cruiser [Cromwell].[32]

So even in 1940 there were indications that the pre-war dichotomy of two main types of tank was flawed, but unfortunately the logic was not taken to its ultimate conclusion – a single universal type capable of both roles – for another three or four years. Other hurdles had to be overcome:

When the War Office in January 1941 drew up a list of 'some factors for consideration in future tank design', armour came first, then armament, and then 'simplicity of operation'. In May 1941 the Tank Parliament was informed that insistence on speed and the addition of thicker armour were the two most troublesome prerequisites in tank design.[33]

That may have been so, but the solution to both problems – at least in part – was to provide an efficient and powerful tank engine, specially designed for the job. Until the Rolls-Royce Merlin was adapted into the Meteor, this was not to happen. And the adoption of the Merlin into a very fine tank engine was a story in itself; it was first proposed in 1940 but was not to enter service until 1943, as we shall see. Hancock reiterated the point that by 1942 the: 'North African experience had demonstrated the absolutely vital need for mechanical efficiency in AFVs.'[34] However, the introduction of the Churchill into service had been so dogged with reliability problems, some so serious that a complete rework programme had to be initiated and which diverted firms from production, that the tank was very nearly cancelled. A letter from Deputy Prime Minister Clement Atlee to Churchill in August 1942 informed him that the decision had been taken to cease Churchill production in June 1943, once the existing order for 3,500 tanks was complete, in order to concentrate on Cromwell and despite it not being a like-for-like replacement and causing an overall loss of 400 tanks from the 1943 programme.

In early August 1942 the Tank Board were informed that the 'qualities of a tank' should be put in the following order:[35]

- Reliability
- Armament
- Speed
- Radius of action
- Armour

This is not to say that armour was unimportant: the crews certainly did not see it that way. But at last the way was open to design a better 'balanced' tank, one capable of destroying enemy armour and supporting the infantry. This suggested order was then amended and developed slightly to become the 'General Staff order of priority of requirements in design' dated 10 August 1942, as follows:

- Absolute reliability. The standard required MUST be given in the specification.
- A first-class anti-tank gun, also able to be as efficient as possible against personnel and lorries (e.g. it must have a High Explosive capability).
- Equality (with the Germans) in speed.
- Useful radius of action.
- Armour – the best possible once the previous requirements had been satisfied, with a laid-down minimum.
- A good fighting compartment.

Hancock also took time to comment on the poor state of relationships between the private manufacturers and the official bodies, after over three years of allegedly cooperating:

> More ambiguous than the relations of maker to designer, necessarily tense at the best of times, was the relationship of the parent firms to the MoS and the Tank Board. Not unnaturally they resented being absent from policy making meetings at which their design work was considered, and where their future programme of development might be upset. In September 1942 a group of heads of firms connected with tank design approached the MoS with the suggestion that industrial representatives should attend Tank Board meetings. The MoS naturally had to turn this suggestion down...[36]

Which of the firms got together to make the suggestion is not recorded, but it does show that the tank-producing firms were in communication with each other, sufficient to establish that they had certain common grievances. How far this communication extended in helping each other to produce tanks more efficiently is unclear; it can be assumed that where such cooperation did not affect their commercial interests, then it could be forthcoming. And why was it 'natural' for the MoS to turn the suggestion down? It appears that the Ministry wished to keep the manufacturers compartmentalised, with liaison activities conducted through the DTD. This was short-sighted; to officially prevent a potentially productive method of cooperation – on what was proving to be the single most difficult weapon of war to get right – was bureaucracy at its worst, particularly as the Ministry must have known that such communication was going on unofficially anyway. Despite this, progress was being made, and in:

October 1942 it was laid down [by the MoS] that at least six pilot models of new designs were essential… such pilots were to take precedence over production and were to be subjected to a 2,000-mile test at FVPE.[37] Moreover, a prototype having passed its acceptance test, the DTD must ensure that a small percentage of production vehicles is subject to a protracted endurance test.[38]

At last a sensible system of pre-approval and rigorous testing was once more to be used, the first since the start of the war; the 'drawing board order' was finally dead. And 'there was much closer integration from 1943 until the end of the war between Ministry of Supply and War Office on weapon development policy.'[39] But 1942 still had some bad news up its sleeve, as production figures reveal:

Tank production 1942 as at 9 November 1942

	Forecast for 1942	Total Produced 1942[40]	Difference
Matilda	1340	1366	+26
Valentine[41]	2235	2185	-50
Churchill	2058	1739	-319
Total Infantry Tanks	5633	5290	-343
Covenanter	990	1014	+24
Crusader	2465	2343	-122
Cromwell	348	35	-313
Total Cruiser Tanks	3803	3392	-411
Total	9436	8682	-754

Source: PREM 3/426/15

Two types of tanks were now being built faster than the forecast; the trouble was they were the obsolete Matilda and the useless Covenanter. This yearly production trend showing the deplorable state at the end of 1942 is largely substantiated by a table from the RAC Half-Yearly Report No.6, covering 1 July–31 December 1942:

Tank production second half 1942

	Forecast	Total Produced	Difference
Cruiser Tanks	1948	1608	-340
Infantry Tanks	2436	2395	-41
Total	4384	4003	-381

Source: RAC Half-Yearly Report No.6

On the face of it, tank production in 1942 missed its goal by around 8 percent. However, even this poor result is not the whole story. For one thing, production was being compared only to the Forecast, *not* the Target. As the Forecast reflected the previous Reasonable Anticipation (what might be built) method rather than the Target (what is actually needed) of 10,964,[42] the figure was more like 20 percent below the desired end state. Secondly, the one tank with really poor figures was the one that was most sorely needed, the new Meteor-powered Cromwell cruiser. In fact, of all the tanks apparently made during 1942, only the Crusader III can, by any stretch of the imagination, be considered battleworthy; the Matilda and Valentine infantry tanks were virtually obsolete, the Churchill was still suffering from its too-hurried introduction into service, and the Covenanter was only fit for training. Production of the latter was not to be completed until 30 January 1943.[43] There was also some degree of spin applied to the figures; that given for Churchill production in the file is 2,128; a footnote admits to this including 389 reworked tanks, so the true production figure was actually 1,739, and the Valentine figures may even include those from Canadian production.

In early 1943, the US suggested that Britain should halt production of its own failed types, switching to Sherman manufacture instead. There was a body of opinion within the UK, reinforced by Montgomery's views from the Mediterranean, that the Sherman could be the answer to the need for a universal tank. The GS Policy Committee on Tanks, on 22 February 1943:

> recommended considering manufacturing Shermans in UK, [but] Director AFV preferred Cromwell and got his way... Valentine capacity should be converted as soon as possible to Cromwell. The GS policy is now to produce only one type of Cruiser tank.[44]

The US request was therefore 'politely refused', the government firmly of the belief that Britain must continue to be able to make her own tanks.[45] As the Sherman grew relatively less and less effective as the war continued, this was one of the few policy decisions that in hindsight can be adjudged to have been totally correct. Had Britain adopted the US suggestion – even assuming that British production methods were capable of making Shermans – the army would not have received the Cromwell, and the much better Comet and particularly the Centurion would never have come about. In autumn 1943 'essential parts of the tank programme were finally given equal first priority'.[46] As we have seen, on paper this equality had existed from July 1941, but at last, and too late, the MoS could finally battle the MAP on something approaching equal terms.

Welding – protection and production

Although attempts had been made to weld armour plate during the inter-war period, including by the research department at Woolwich from 1927–1930,[47] it had proved to be difficult to achieve. It tended to either weaken the armour around the weld or to cause the armour to crack, or both. After more work the problem was finally solved at Woolwich by 1934. The weld had to be the same depth as the plate, which for increasingly thick armour plates meant that welding had to be done from above, using gravity to assist in 'filling' the gap. Until large jigs (manipulators) were designed which enabled the largest components, the hull and turret, to be manipulated into position at will, the majority of British manufacturers continued to prefer to build riveted tanks with internal frames, despite the known disadvantages, and no one in the War Office or MoS seemed inclined to force the issue. Indeed, throughout the war there was recognition that many of the tank builders were incapable of improving their manufacturing techniques to employ such new methods, and there does not appear to have been any suggestion that the government might assist them with either capital or plant to rectify this. One of the reasons suggested for Britain not adopting welding was that 'existing surplus capacity for riveting was a powerful argument against the adoption of welding.' This is a striking example of industrial logic hindering development. As noted in 'The Design & Development of Weapons': 'The widespread use of welding was only accomplished with the reduction in the tank programme in and after 1943.'[48] In other words, it came too late to have any effect on the speed of production, although it did confer protection and waterproofing advantages that the crews came to appreciate.

The lack of MoS insistence on introducing welding techniques earlier was another mistake. Welded tanks were lighter, had better protection and were naturally watertight. Crucially, production time was significantly decreased; it is possible that the MoS simply failed to appreciate this as they lacked experts in the field. Adopting welded construction for the Churchill had been discussed during the design stage, but in 1940 the technique was deemed to be too risky, despite early firing trials in July 1940 being 'highly satisfactory'. The story continues:

It was about this time that the decision was made to arm the Churchill with a 6-pdr. gun and as this required a larger turret than the cast one then in use, it was decided that this change provided a suitable opportunity for introducing welded construction in production. Accordingly, in May 1941, Babcock & Wilcox Ltd [a pioneer in developing welded steam boilers and the use of x-rays to examine welds] were asked to construct a welded turret for a firing trial... The results were so favourable that a production order for 100 turrets was placed with Babcock & Wilcox Ltd. forthwith (August 1941)[49]

At the same period, a parallel investigation was in progress on the experimental hulls... In the meantime, a comparison between riveted and welded construction had been made from the production angle. An analysis was made by the Department of Tank Design, in collaboration with the contractors concerned between the current production data on riveted Mark IV hulls, built by The Whessoe Foundry & Engineering Co Ltd, Darlington, and Metropolitan-Cammell Carriage and Wagon Co Ltd, Old Park Works, Wednesbury; and the welded prototypes built by Babcock & Wilcox Ltd... In a report prepared by the Welding and Gas Cutting Branch in March 1942, it was concluded that welding would save 20 per cent. in man-hours and 4 percent in weight, as compared with riveting but required 50 percent more floor space in the fabricator's works. This additional floor space would be largely counterbalanced by a reduction in space required at the plate maker's works, due to the greatly reduced amount of drilling required. The additional floor space was, therefore, not regarded as a serious drawback in the circumstances but the savings in labour and material were vital considerations. Subsequent experience showed that [an even] greater saving in welding man-hours was effected than had been estimated, and the allowance for floor space had been over-generous.[50]

Welding techniques also allowed the reasonably simple addition of appliqué armour, the technique of attaching additional plates to the outside of existing vehicles in order to increase thickness post-production. Later marks of the Cromwell were of welded construction, and by the end of the war welding was firmly established as the only technique to be used, with riveting only used in certain limited circumstances. Only the Comet and Centurion were of all-welded construction.

The tank engine revolution

Until 1943, one of the main elements that had handicapped British tank design was the failure to supply a reliable engine of sufficient horsepower to move the vehicle around the battlefield. In many cases industry was told, via the GS specification, exactly which engine they were to use. Using what was handy was the way things were done, wasn't it? The unwillingness of many to look beyond using commercially available engines, incapable of producing more than 280bhp and notoriously unreliable to boot, did much damage. The solution had been staring everyone in the face – modify an aeroplane engine. These tended to require high horsepower and to be compact, both critical requirements.

The solution was to – eventually – adopt and adapt the famous Rolls-Royce Merlin engine (of Spitfire fame) into the Meteor tank engine, pushing out at least 500bhp (even on the low octane pool petrol used by the army) and thus able to deliver the required 20bhp per ton in tanks weighing around 28 tons. This solution had been initially proposed in October 1940, but had been turned down on the (then very reasonable) grounds that aircraft production came first; one cannot help but remember the request by Martel in 1936 to purchase the surplus Napier Lion engines, which had been turned down on cost grounds by Elles, and wonder what would have happened had the moderate funding requested been made available.

It was not until 1941 that the first Merlin engines became available for conversion into what would become the Meteor. This involved the removal of the supercharger and substituting many of the aluminium components with cast-iron versions. The crankshaft direction also had to be reversed. Many of the first Meteors were made from Merlin parts that had failed the strict quality-control and tolerance tests used by Rolls-Royce. Early trials in a Crusader showed a frightening turn of speed, with one driver being booked for speeding at 57mph. Eventually quite excellent reliability was achieved after a few teething problems were quickly overcome, but the development and production of the Meteor was hampered by the Air Ministry's insistence that Rolls-Royce gave them priority at all times. In other words, only spare capacity could be used to make Meteors. At an MoS meeting held in April 1942, the record showed that twenty-five Meteors had been completed, with another 500 expected by the end of the year, and fifty per week to be produced thereafter. Eventually, the Meteor was to power the reasonably successful Cromwell and also the last of the true cruisers and the best British tank of the war, the Comet, as well as the first universal tank, the Centurion.[51]

Of course, by adding more weight to a design, particularly when adding extra armour but also by fitting larger guns, the strain on the automotive components increased beyond the original design parameters. This applied not only to the engine and transmission, but also to the suspension. Many people realised that there was enormous potential for future trouble in this approach, and when the Cromwell series of cruisers was being designed, a suggestion was put forward by the military (probably DTD) that the chassis should be always ballasted overweight to investigate the effects upon the suspension, but this was rejected by the MoS, which 'assured them that everything would be alright'.[52] In the light of previous experience, this was an incredible decision, and once again, one soon proved wrong as Cromwell – like almost every tank before and since – gained more and more weight. The new Meteor engine had power to spare, but the suspension was still the Christie type with vulnerable torsion bars and spring units. All that could be done was to suggest fitting slightly wider tracks in order to reduce ground pressure.

The other side of the hill – Germany

Despite the well-known advantages that the German panzers enjoyed, particularly in terms of firepower, there were some notable similarities to the British experience of tank production, particularly regarding reliability and the insistence on hand-building of tanks. For example, the much-vaunted Panther had been rushed through design and the earliest models were sent into action without the benefits of testing or rectification of known faults:

> The first batch was sent into battle before development work was complete. All 325 had to be returned to Berlin for modifications... the level of technical quality of the new tanks was such that they were difficult to produce and maintain... like the other German vehicles [tanks] were difficult to repair. The Tiger tank required a small army of mechanics to keep it in the field, while the ratio of spares produced was derisory. For every ten Tiger tanks [built], only one spare engine and one transmission was produced.[53]

Reliability for the Germans worsened as the war progressed, partly because the apparently successful designs of the Tiger and the Panther were technically complex. After the war, estimates by German generals of typical German tank losses due to breakdown and mechanical failures were: Heinz Guderian 60–70 percent and Sepp Dietrich 30 percent, whereas Paul Hausser reckoned that 20–30 percent broke down during route marches, and 15 percent of the remainder during action. The official German reports described these mechanical casualties as 'miscellaneous, non-enemy action'. An average figure therefore would give around 50 percent of German tanks breaking down before or during battle. Jarymowycz constructed a table assessing the causes of German tank losses in a more scientific manner, indicating a similar 43 percent rate for mechanical failure. These figures led to Jarymowycz describing German engineering as 'the most accomplished slayer of German tanks'.[54] He went on to add that 'German engineering proved so precise that it was a disadvantage. The engineering simplicity of the Soviet T34 may have placed it behind the Panther in overall performance, but it proved the more reliable machine and capable of being maintained by any kulak'.[55]

There are also indications that the German insistence on the highest possible build standards added many hours to a tank's assembly, even as late as 1944 and 1945. This was the opposite of the British method, where quality control and thorough testing of the finished tank was only really a feature from 1943 on. The German manufacturers also suffered to some degree from too much hand-finishing, to the extent that the same component from one tank could not be easily swapped with those from another. However, despite the strategic bombing campaign conducted by the RAF, 'effectively there were no labour or machine tool shortages, at any rate before the closing months of the war, and German equipment scarcely at all reflects any concessions to "ease of manufacture": to the end much of it was highly elaborate and difficult to produce.'[56]

Industrial action and strikes of course did not affect German tank production as they did in Britain, but manpower shortages certainly did, particularly as skilled labourers were not as protected from military service as those in the UK, and were frequently – increasingly as the war progressed and casualties mounted – called up, to the horror of the industrial bosses, who found themselves losing the argument with the Wehrmacht. The use of forced and slave labour compensated for this to some degree, but poorly fed and brutally treated workmen could not be expected to produce the high-quality build standards required. The German policy was not to use women in industrial factories, so another source of labour was denied to them. And of course the Allied air raids, increasingly round the clock from 1943, were much more effective than the Blitz had ever been, with a much greater tonnage of bombs and consequent destruction, coupled with more effective targeting of key industries and better bomb-aiming; all these had a large and increasing impact on output.[57] And of course, there are the effects on sleep, ration supply, absenteeism, safety, and morale: these are hard to quantify, but nevertheless had negative effects on both quality and quantity.

The Germans preferred to use face-hardened (FH) armour plates on their tanks, and from June 1940 (at the end of the France campaign) the Weapons Office mandated the use of FH plate; until that point manufacturers had the option of using homogenous armour steel. This was because experience led the Germans to believe that face-hardened plate was able to break up incoming projectiles on impact, which was, at that point in the war, quite true. However, when the British introduced the six-pounder gun, particularly with the APCBC[58] ammunition introduced in 1943, FH armour was adjudged by British experts to offer only 'poor' defence. Increasingly it was the thickness rather than the inherent quality of German armour that was needed to resist the improving Allied guns and ammunition. Face-hardened armour also took more time during production, as the flame-hardening process might require three weeks to finish a single plate. British tanks always used the easier to produce homogenous plate, which maintained a constant quality throughout the thickness, rather than relying on the harder face to do the majority of the work.[59]

The German firm of Deutsche Edelstahlwerke in Krefeld took the lead in pioneering the welding of armour steel and had managed to make it work by the late 1920s, a few years before the problem had been solved in Britain, leading the German panzer manufacturers to make much more expensive use of welding on their vehicles. An example of German ingenuity was the frequent construction of tank hulls as two or three separate welded parts, either top and bottom or as front superstructure, rear superstructure, and bottom. This allowed each component to be built by sub-contractors, and the parts could then be bolted together in a main assembly shop; the parts could also be unbolted quite easily even in field workshops to allow extensive repairs to take place.[60]

However, the Germans suffered problems that the British did not. Firstly, the quality of the welding was often quite poor. In part this was because the Germans did not make extensive use of manipulators to move the components into the best positions to allow gravity welding, probably due to the desire to avoid reliance on large, complicated, and scarce machinery. Not using gravity meant that the welds often failed to join the plates correctly, leading to failures not only when struck by a projectile, but more alarmingly, when subjected to extreme cold – in Russia, for example, although the problem had been identified as early as 1940. Investigations led the Germans to believe that this was due to the use of ferric electrodes, and so from 1942 there was an insistence that only austenitic welds were used, although of course this did not solve the problems caused by non-gravity welding. Another issue was that German techniques demanded that the surfaces (normally the edges) that were to be welded had exceptionally fine finishes. This not only added a lot of time to the process but also led to poor welds where the surface was not prepared sufficiently well.

A War Office Technical Summary in 1944 examined in detail the German preference for welding rather than bolting or riveting armour, and noted that although pre-war Britain, Germany and France had each carried out extensive research into the area as they all recognised the potential advantages to be gained, initially at least only the Germans took it forward with enthusiasm. An innovation adopted by the Germans to simplify and thus speed up their welding on tanks was the use of butt joints and later interlocking mortised plates, both of which supported the whole structure and eliminated 'the need for some of the large manipulators and elaborate jigs'. This may also have been forced upon them as they built ever larger and more thickly-armoured tanks, on which the German welding techniques were not, of themselves, sufficient to ensure structural integrity. Britain, when it finally adopted welding on a large scale, used much better techniques which made the weld joints extremely strong, admittedly on generally thinner armour – the 152mm on the front of the late-war Churchill Mk VII being a notable exception.

One area where the Germans enjoyed a marked superiority over the British for the whole of the war was in the production of optics, particularly those used for the gunner's sights. In general terms, the famous German optical firms such as Carl Zeiss and Leica made the sighting telescopes for German tanks (and other applications), with two major advantages over the British equivalents. Firstly, the quality of the optical glass was maintained at an excellent standard, and secondly they tended to employ much higher powers of magnification that the British equivalents. For example, the gunner's Leica-made TZF5 telescope on the Panzer III used a magnification of x2.5, on the Panther the TFZ12 had selectable magnification of x2.5 or x5, whereas the British tanks for much of the war used only x1 (no magnification), or a maximum of x1.9.[61] Additionally, British crews complained that the aiming markings inscribed within their sights were too thick, so that at 1,000 yards the intended target was completely obscured by the marks, making precise aiming impossible. As late as 1944 British tank crews were still investigating knocked-out German tanks and marveling at the quality of their optics.

The other side of the hill – the RAF

Despite their advantages of priority and manufacture, the RAF did suffer in a similar way to the crisis of 1940, in that there was a temporary suspension of some development work for around nine months, until the spring of 1941. The real difference between the two services in this time was that the MAP was able to turn out large numbers of aircraft that were at least workmanlike and in the case of the Spitfire a world-beater, whereas the army could only increase production of types which were marginal at best, and obsolete at worst. The RAF did not totally suspend all development in the period; some companies were able to continue to prepare prototypes and conduct development of technologies deemed to be of a war-winning nature – the prime example being Frank Whittle's jet engine that was developed in the period, the E28/39 aircraft first flying in May 1941.

We can also state that in the case of the RAF the insistence on quality as the most important consideration was well and truly accepted even before the war started, and aside from one disruption of less than a year, that doctrine was maintained throughout. The technical superiority of RAF officers was much in evidence:

> The MAP and the aircraft industry were fortunate in having to cater for a service so technically minded and so forward-looking as the RAF... the very act of flying and navigating, even when it happened to be non-combatant, provided them with a fund of operational evidence. This alone enabled the RAF even before the war to accumulate more and better experience than was, in the field of land weapons, available to the army... the personnel of the RAF, like that of the Royal Navy but unlike that of the Army was better capable of giving technical expression to its operational experience... Broadly speaking the RAF knew what it wanted... the supply departments at the Air Ministry and the MAP were faced with an easier task than the Ministry of Supply, and this must be borne in mind when the quality of British aircraft is compared with that of the tanks.[62]

The men who were at the top of the RAF were all, without exception, pilots; thus, they all were technically trained, and they all understood the need for quality and reliability. There is no doubt that technical specialists within the army were viewed in a different light and were not seen as having any part to play in the formulation of tactics or on the actual battlefield – they were there simply to support. Where it did exist, the repository of technical expertise within the army was traditionally found in the two supporting arms of the Royal Artillery and the Royal Engineers and their technical colleges. The two traditional 'teeth' arms, the cavalry and the infantry, mostly despised officers who were overly professional and scientific, preferring to rely on good breeding, character, and raw courage. The same army had not regarded staff officers as worthy of formal training until shortly before the First World War. The RTC was thus in effect a completely new type of corps, a scientific teeth arm, and found itself between two camps with few allies in either.

Another advantage that the aircraft firms enjoyed was the much closer level of collaboration between themselves and the officials of the MAP. This included the placement of MAP and RAF officials within the construction firms. The most important of these representatives were the so-called 'Overseers' who, by the end of 1942, were attached to every major aircraft factory: 'The Overseer is the principal representative of the Ministry to whom the firms are entitled to refer all questions requiring immediate decision and to look for advice and assistance in every way possible…'.[63] The other local MAP official was the Resident Technical Officer attached to those firms with design offices. Among the duties of the RTO was the authority to 'grant design concessions to facilitate production'. Both officials therefore required a degree of expertise in order to function, and most importantly were able to make fast local decisions without referring to higher authority. Where they were not in a position to make such a decision, the matter could be referred higher with confidence that a quick judgement would be forthcoming, a system markedly in contrast with the long-winded and bureaucratic MoS arrangement. They were also able to act as a conduit between the company and the Ministry, increasing confidence and (at least in theory) allowing good ideas to be passed around all concerned.

But there were also some similarities with tank production problems, not least the opposition to disrupting production of existing types in favour of newer models:

In general, the [aircraft] industry, or at any rate important sections of the industry, preferred producing the well-established types. It is therefore no wonder that the behaviour of individual firms gave grounds for suspicion that the introduction of new types was delayed in the hope of 'wangling' a continuation order.[64]

The difference was that the MAP was prepared to stand up to the manufacturers when necessary and direct them to do what was necessary, something the MoS did not do until late into the war.

> Whenever obsolete types were 'faded out' and new ones brought in, the flow of production was inevitably interrupted at the very time when all the 'teething' troubles had been overcome and the smooth flow of production could develop. But apart from new types, continuous modifications of the existing types... continually disrupted the work at the factories... The dilemma was well understood and, as a rule, taken for granted... the point of view was also fully accepted in the supply branches of the Air Ministry and in the Ministry of Aircraft Production... [The MAP had laid down that] technical development to achieve superiority in performance was essential to the prosecution of the war; therefore the inevitable effect on production must be accepted... *We have throughout applied one cardinal principle – that quality is more important that quantity* [My emphasis]. Nothing but the best and most up-to-date is good enough... whatever the complications or drawbacks arising from the rapid introduction of improvements and changes, we must introduce these at the earliest practicable moment.[65]

And this was not mere rhetoric; throughout the war the MAP consistently managed to deliver to the RAF sufficient aircraft of the highest quality and performance to enable it to complete its task, while retaining the full confidence of the aircrew who flew them.

Chapter 8

The Late War Tanks

The A24M Cromwell and A24L Centaur

We have seen how the NMA-designed and built A24 Cavalier of 1941/42 was yet another disaster. Fortunately, a similar-looking but vastly better tank was developed at the same time, the A27 Cromwell. What made it so different from the Cavalier was that Rolls-Royce (R-R) were involved, not only in producing the engine but also in developing other aspects of the design. Strangely enough, the idea to involve R-R did not come from them, but from Leyland. The story is one of the high points of British tank design and manufacture, one that David Fletcher described as 'the only truly inspirational moment in the wartime British tank story.'

At the outbreak of war, R-R decided to put all its resources into its flourishing aeroengine business. As a result, the car division found itself somewhat sidelined, despite possessing a large research and design team, complete with experimental manufacturing facilities and a drawing office. Why this team had not been talent-spotted by any of the ministries is not clear, but it is probable that MAP considered the company to be entirely one of theirs, and that the MoS therefore made no attempt to discover if there was anything that could usefully be done by parts of the company not involved in RAF work. The chief executive there was a W.A. Robotham, one of the unsung heroes of the war. As all of the space at the Derby works was needed for aeroengine production, Robotham and his team were moved into a disused iron foundry called Clan Foundry, just outside Belper. The experienced team, with little to do, became involved in salvaging usable parts from recovered Merlin engines.

In October 1940 Robotham was contacted by Henry Spurrier, a top executive of Leyland Motors and an old school friend. Spurrier explained that Leyland was in the process of building a tank for the Mechanization Board but was completely dissatisfied with many elements of the design, and had no confidence in the engine, a Meadows flat 12. This of course was the LMSR-designed Covenanter, and Leyland had been given the poisoned chalice of trying to correct the problems with the cooling system. With remarkable insight, Spurrier had decided that the number of man-hours being spent on the tank was out of all proportion to its likely value to the overall war effort. At a meeting on 29 October, Robotham agreed to set his team to the task of looking at the problems and decided to split the task into three areas: engine and transmission, steering, and track and armour. There was never a suggestion that the Clan Foundry team would design a new tank, but rather to look at the possibilities of making a reliable and powerful engine, as well as improve the transmission, suspension and steering of an existing tank. It was decided to do this with the A15 Crusader.

Rolls-Royce had two aero engines that seemed suitable for the project, the Kestrel and the Merlin. Both would need adapting for use in a tank. The former was smaller, easier to cool and was not supercharged, but it had a serious shortcoming. It had been calculated that running the Kestrel on the low-octane army pool petrol could only produce a maximum of 475bhp, and this was thought to be insufficient. It was decided to concentrate on fitting the Merlin into a Crusader hull without modifying the hull; the gearcase was changed, some accessories had to be repositioned and the propeller reduction gear was removed. The supercharger was removed and replaced by carburettors. The name Meteor was given to the engine and it was thought that it could achieve about 550bhp. It was also decided that the air cleaners should be located inside the engine compartment where they could take relatively clean air that came in via the turret, and that careful consideration had to be given to cooling. On 30 March 1941 the first Meteor was installed in a Crusader hull, with the power reduced to 500bhp for the trial, which took place in the middle of April on Southport sands. Problems encountered were due to the Crusader's ancillaries, particularly the governor, fuel system, cooling and air filtration, but the engine performed well. Leyland, as the lead company, was given an order for 1,200 Meteors in early May, and at that stage it was intended that the Meteor should be installed in the A24 Cavalier, the Crusader derivative, as an alternative to the Liberty. However, just after this, in July, Leyland developed a severe attack of cold feet, ironically down to the potential cooling difficulties that they had been tasked to sort out, and as a result backed out of the partnership. The Rolls-Royce leadership, despite being completely overworked by the need to produce engines for the MAP, took a brave stance and Robotham's boss stated bluntly that 'We'll have to make the blighters ourselves'. R-R would continue to make the majority of the parts for the Meteor, many of them from Merlin components which had failed the very strict quality control mechanisms, but which were still perfectly suitable for tank use. For example, the Glasgow Merlin factory produced a batch of 600 crankshafts that were found to have hairline cracks. These could not be used in a 1200bhp Merlin, but could be employed in a 600bhp Meteor. However, the firm had no spare manufacturing capacity to actually build the engines and a sub-contractor or partner had to be found.[1] This turned out to be Meadows, which started producing Meteors in quantity in 1944, and most importantly, Rootes, which ended up building the majority of the engines.

Cooling remained a problem, but through sheer diligence and a dash of brilliance, new radiators were designed and the cooling fan efficiency in the Crusader hull was improved from under 27 percent to 63 percent; the power used was less than 5.5 percent of the total engine horsepower, compared to the Liberty's nearly 18 percent. Due to Leyland's withdrawal there was an urgent need to find a new partner to work on engine installation, and this was found in the Birmingham Railway Carriage & Wagon Company, whose subsequent work shaved many months off the development time. A huge vote of confidence was given by the MoS to the project on 12 September 1941, when Robotham's team was given open credit to the tune of £1 million, described in the notification telegram as 'a certificate of character and reputation without precedence or equal'. It was fortunate that there were a number of key decision-makers involved who not only had faith in the Meteor, but also backed up their faith with words. Six months later a report noted that the grant had been used to order 686 machine tools, the majority of which were in MAP factories, which was not the original intention of the MoS! Robotham's skills brought him to the attention of Oliver Lucas, Comptroller of Research and Development at the Ministry of Supply. He was persuaded to join Lucas as Chief Engineer of Tank Design, a misnomer if ever there was one as the MoS did not design tanks, but only on the proviso that he could return to his home near Belper at weekends, and continue to work on the Meteor project (for free). The project, naturally, then benefitted from the additional resources that he could access, but the history of the Meteor engine made a defining statement of his time at MoS: 'Having obtained a reasonably clear picture of a very confused situation, [Robotham] would have been glad of some expert help before making any decisions, but DTD were so immersed in current problems that it could scarcely see the wood for the trees.'[2]

At this stage we will leave Robotham and his Meteor for a while to look at the evolution of the tank that it was to be first used in, the A27 Cromwell.

BRCW had been tasked with the overall design for a new heavy cruiser, similar to the A24 Cavalier but preferably lighter and with their own designs for the suspension and tracks, but still mounting the six-pounder gun. It is obvious that the two tanks shared a common ancestry and that BRCW must have communicated closely with NMA in the overall layout, which was very similar. Because BRCW was in close contact with the Clan Foundry team, the installation of the Meteor was straightforward, the rear end of the A27 being designed around it and a new Merritt-Brown transmission known as the Z5. As Lord Nuffield was totally opposed to any suggestion of NMA becoming involved in producing other people's designs, four additional firms were brought into the A27 programme. This was not straightforward, and BRCW became very frustrated with the 'obstinate practices' of some of these, including sub-contractors. Fletcher quotes an example of one north-eastern steelworks that produced armour plates for the front of Cromwells; these proved to be such poor quality that the tanks had to be labelled as unarmoured and put aside for training use only.[3]

In order to cope with the anticipated top speed of 40mph (in a tank weighing 27 tons!), BRCW made the wise decision to double the springs on all roadwheels, and put shock absorbers on all but the middle of the five wheel stations. The suspension arms were also lengthened and there were to be no complaints about the ride that the crew experienced. The early tanks with the six-pounder still retained the old pre-war free elevation system for shooting on the move, but this was now on the way out and the emphasis placed on accurate shooting when static. When the tank received the 75mm gun (and indeed the Close Support versions carrying the 95mm), a geared elevation system was used, controlled by the gunner with a handwheel that also featured the firing switch.

A problem now occurred which led to the unplanned-for development of a variant of the Cromwell. Not enough Meteor engines could be produced to match the output of Cromwell hulls, and rather than leave hundreds of tanks awaiting engines, a practical decision was taken to put the Liberty engine, with all of its known faults, into the Cromwell to allow units to be equipped with the new tank. This led to the designations being altered. The version with the Meteor was now known as the A27M Cromwell, and the Liberty-engined variety became the A27L Centaur. Centaurs were designed in such a way that once Meteors became available, the tank could be re-engined with the minimum of fuss to become a Cromwell. The task of producing the Centaur would be given to Leyland Motors, the firm that had initiated the

Meteor idea, but which had then withdrawn.[4] There were numerous detail differences between the hulls of the Centaur and the Cromwell, but they need not concern us here. Development work started in November 1941, with the first pilot delivered in June 1942 and the first production tanks appearing by the end of the year.

David Fletcher thought that 'with the benefit of hindsight, the entire Centaur project was a complete waste of time and material.'[5] This was a little strong: had the Meteor project met unexpected problems with production, the loss of the anticipated Cromwells would have left Britain going cap-in-hand to the USA for more Shermans or even having to field tanks such as the Crusader or Cavalier in Normandy in 1944. At least the Centaur allowed the crews to gain experience on something very similar to the Cromwell, to conduct field training and firing, and to realise what a fast and reliable tank they had been issued with, once they received their Cromwells.[6]

Back to the Meteor story. As we have seen, Robotham's team was involved in not just the engine, but also other aspects of tank design. One innovation was the introduction of the quill shaft. The gearbox output had to be joined to the final drives. On previous designs removal of the gearbox was a lengthy process, involving dismantling the tracks and final drives. The quill shaft was a keyed piece of hardened steel that linked the final drive to the gearbox, but which could be removed easily by the crew, allowing gearboxes or final drives to be lifted and replaced in the field. By comparison, the much-vaunted German Panther suffered from many transmission problems, including frequent third gear failures caused by alloy shortages making the gears brittle. To replace the gearbox, situated in the front of the hull, the whole front end of the tank needed to be disassembled, which was immensely difficult in the field and took many hours.

Problems of quality control, often from sub-contractors, continued to dog production. The large coil springs used in the A27 suspension were a novelty for the British industrial system and were not widely made. These springs were made of 1in thick wire, made up into coils. They were not easy to make and needed to be of a high build quality, both to fit into the available space and also to work reliably. Ten springs were needed on each tank, so tens of thousands were required. Firms were brought into the programme which were not used to working to fine tolerances, such as those making leaf springs for locomotives. On the face of it they would be viewed as spring specialists, but would be found wanting. Incorrect tempering, poor material and incorrect temperature control caused many to fail only one-hundredth of the way through their expected life. The involvement of the specialists at English Steel, a Vickers subsidiary, was secured and they clarified the specifications and techniques to be followed. Likewise, track links suffered frequent in-service failures due to porosity problems in the manganese steel, traced back to foundries which were used to making only crude grey metal castings. The difference here from previous practice was that Robotham and his team refused to accept such failings and went to great lengths to identify the roof causes of failure and then correct them. As the history of the Meteor project stresses: 'The company never did anything by half-measures'.[7] In May 1942 Robotham commented that 'Supervisory talent is so scarce that we frequently find it easier to do the job ourselves than to guide, from a distance, people who are not always willing to do what we want'.[8] Robotham's frustrations probably mirrored those of many of the parent companies, which felt that they were always being blamed for problems not of their making.

The vehicle acceptance test on Cromwell involved the BRCW-made tank running over 2,000 miles, roughly 50/50 road and cross-country. On 6 December 1942 the chairman of the Tank Board, Micklem, sent the following telegram to the managing director of Rolls-Royce: 'Pilot model completed Acceptance Test in record time, no mechanical failures. Please accept my grateful thanks for all work you and your staff have put in to achieve this successful result'.[9] The Cromwell had done what no other British tank could: it had demonstrated high reliability under testing conditions. The tank was set to go into mass production. In order to assist units which would shortly be receiving the new tanks, R-R decided to create an Instructional School for fitters and instructors, which was set up in the company's car service depot in Willesden, and was ready for its first class in October 1942. In July 1943 Leyland ceased production of the Centaur and started producing Cromwells, as well as taking on the parentage role from BRCW. By October 1944 3,000 Meteors, the initial contract, had been completed.

However, by the time the Cromwell was coming off the production lines in quantities, the gun that it was designed around, the six-pounder, was seen to be poor in many ways, not least in the HE shell that it fired. Used to the American 75mm M48 high-explosive shell, the much smaller six-pounder HE was seen by many tank crews as next to ineffective. However, it had been realised that it was possible, with the minimum of work, to build a British 75mm version of the six-pounder, capable of firing the US ammunition, and this was introduced from autumn 1943. Unfortunately, although this satisfied the high-explosive requirements by using US ammunition, the 75mm was a medium velocity weapon and therefore nowhere near as good a 'hole-puncher' – meaning an anti-tank gun – as the six-pounder. With the development and issue of the outstanding Armour Piercing Discarding Sabot (APDS) ammunition for the six-pounder in 1944, had a proportion of the Cromwells been issued with that weapon and ammunition combination, there may have been less need to equip the Cromwell regiments with seventeen-pounder-armed Sherman Fireflies, or indeed to go to the trouble of developing the A30 Challenger. To prove this point, it is necessary to examine armour penetration tables. The British version of the 75mm gun firing the US-designed (Armour Piercing Capped) APC ammunition at a target 500 yards away could be expected to penetrate about 68mm of armour set at the standard 30 degrees to the vertical. The six-pounder firing British Armour Piercing Capped Ballistic Cap (APCBC) ammunition under the same conditions would do better, with 81 mm, but if APDS ammunition was used, then this would go up to 131mm – theoretically enough to penetrate the front plate of a Tiger I or Panther. The seventeen-pounder and 77mm guns would not surprisingly do better still, and there are other considerations including ammunition supply and the probability of a first-round hit, but it must be listed as an opportunity that could have been investigated further.

Because of a natural desire to mount the excellent seventeen-pounder gun onto British tanks, an investigation found that the turret ring of the standard Cromwell was too narrow, and that the tank would have to be substantially modified, to make it possible. This led to the development of the A30 Challenger starting in January 1942, of which only 200 examples were made.[10] It was estimated that such a tank would weigh about six tons more than the Cromwell which, despite the efforts to allow for additional weight, was more than the standard design could cope with. BRCW was given the task of parentage for the project, with Stothert & Pitt of Bath (a crane-building firm) making the cast and welded turrets, the pilot being completed at the end of July. In February 1943 it was accepted for limited production.

As a result of being ordered to produce both Challenger and Cromwell concurrently (but priority given to Challenger), BRCW designed new adjustable hull assembly machinery that could be used for both. The tank was lengthened (a R-R design) in order to add a sixth wheel station, and although the overall width of the hull was unchanged, the superstructure was widened to allow for a larger turret ring of 70in. The tank made maximum use of existing components to prevent production difficulties, as the tank was required to enter service as quickly as possible; in the end the weight was less than feared, at 32½ tons. At 109in it was ten inches taller than the Cromwell, a frequent cause for criticism, but in fact it was no higher than the M4 Sherman and had 5 degrees more depression than the US tank. Another criticism was that the sides of the turret were too thin, but more armour could have been added with only a slight reduction in overall speed and probably no effect on reliability. It is also questionable whether it needed two loaders in the turret, which could have meant more than forty-eight rounds being carried. In the big scheme of things, the Challenger was a distraction, brought about solely because of the urgent need to mount the new seventeen-pounder on to a tank during 1942. Although some did see service in Europe in 1944, the conversion of Shermans into the seventeen-pounder-armed Firefly made the A30 largely redundant, despite the logistic advantages of using a similar tank to support the Cromwell-equipped formations.

Cromwell ran to eight marks, with a number of different hull variations. Again the details are far from straightforward – the most complex for any British tank in fact – but a couple of points are worth making.[11] Firstly, a re-engined Centaur received a new Cromwell designation; for example, a Centaur I on conversion became a Cromwell III.[12] Secondly, some of the marks featured a 'w' suffix; this indicated the use of a welded hull. At last British tanks were being made by this method, which speeded up production, reduced weight, made the tanks waterproof and added protection. Although turrets were still made by the previous methods of attaching outer armour to a thinner steel skin by the use of large conical bolts, and the vast majority of Cromwells were made using the bolted and rivetted construction method, the all-welded tank was now a possibility. Thirdly, increasing attention was being paid to using appliqué armour panels, particularly on the hull front, to add even more protection. The early design of the Cromwell, in terms of engine power and suspension layout able to cope with more weight as the tank was improved, was paying dividends. Wider tracks were fitted to decrease ground pressure, and an all-round vision cupola was standard, as was power traverse.

Trying to determine exact production numbers for the Cromwell and Centaur is fraught with difficulties, as the available records are often confusing or contradictory; the problems officialdom had with names and marks must be at least part of the reason for this. Orders were placed for 8,550 Centaurs and over 4,500 Cromwells, but nothing like this number was actually made, with many of the contracts either reduced, amended or cancelled as the war was clearly going to reach its conclusion before they could be built.[13] The increasing supply of Meteor engines made the manufacture of so many Centaurs redundant in any case. Although it is impossible – and unwise – to be too dogmatic, it appears that just over 4,800 of both types were built – how many Centaurs ended up as Cromwells is likewise very difficult to say.

In September 1944 General Verney, the commander of the 7th Armoured Division, then fighting in the Low Countries and equipped with Cromwells, took the time to write to the War Office:

> I feel that I must write you a short note to tell you how superb the Cromwell tank has been during our recent activities, and I hope that you will pass on the gist of this letter to the various people responsible for the production of the magnificent machine… At dawn on August 31st we started our advance [and] it has carried us 250 miles in six days. We have lost practically no tanks through mechanical failure (I would guess four or five per regiment). Anyhow, so few that the matter has been no anxiety whatsoever. We have had actions every day [and] there has been no maintenance whatever…The tremendous speed [has] alone made this great advance possible.[14]

Cromwell was not the best tank fielded during the war, nor was it even the best tank that Britain was to produce; that distinction must go to the Comet. But it marked a watershed in the British tank story. Here was a tank that was low, fast, manoeuverable, reasonably well armed and moderately well armoured, made in large numbers and, most importantly, extremely reliable. This made it a balanced design in which the negative features were to a large degree compensated for by positive ones. The involvement of Robotham and his team of Rolls-Royce engineers was what made the difference, and they cannot be praised highly enough for what they achieved.

The A34 Comet

In many respects the Comet was simply a nearly perfect Cromwell. Neither the design features nor the technologies used to build it were novel – it could therefore have been theoretically introduced during 1944 if the will had been there. It featured a much-improved cast and welded turret with an all-round vision cupola for the commander, making fighting from the tank when closed-down a realistic prospect. Rather than using a hydraulic powered traverse, an electrical system was employed instead, deemed to be much safer as there were no pressurised oil lines to fracture. Adding to survivability if hit, the ammunition was placed in steel bins, as by now it had been realised that the biggest cause of fires on tanks was ammunition, not fuel. It had a low silhouette and an improved Christie suspension with hydraulic shock absorbers, wider tracks and, for the first time, top-rollers, and it used the latest Mk III version of the outstanding Rolls-Royce Meteor engine in an all-welded hull. Most of all it mounted the excellent dual-purpose 77mm high-velocity gun with APDS and HE ammunition, and it was exceptionally reliable, having been based upon the Cromwell and adequately tested at the pilot stage – the days of the drawing-board order were over. But it could have been even better: the belly armour was somewhat thin, making it vulnerable to mine damage; the opportunity to fit spaced armour plates on the hull and turret sides was missed; and most importantly it failed to utilise a sloped glacis plate, partly due to insistence by the RAC that it should carry a forward-firing machine-gun in the hull, a carry-over from the pre-war insistence on multiple MGs, and partly due to a desire to make it as similar as possible to Cromwell to facilitate easier production.[15]

The story of the gun the Comet carried is instructive. It was known that the basic hull of the Cromwell was too short and too narrow to carry the seventeen-pounder, hence the A30 Challenger. There had been some suggestions that the British might try to adopt the latest US 76mm gun, but the trials of this were disappointing, with penetration much less than desirable; in part this was due to the American policy of not allowing maximum muzzle velocity in order to lengthen barrel life, whereas the British tended to put in as much propellant as possible. However, Vickers had been developing a new high-velocity 75mm gun, which was somewhat smaller and shorter than the seventeen-pounder. This was redesigned to be able to use seventeen-pounder projectiles, although mated to a 6in shorter cartridge case. The combination of shorter barrel and less propellant meant that the new weapon would not have the same muzzle velocity as the seventeen-pounder, but it would still deliver an effective punch. To avoid confusion with the seventeen-pounder, which was 76.2mm calibre, it was christened the 77mm, and was only ever fitted to the A34 Comet. Despite having less penetrative punch, it could be fitted into a smaller turret and this allowed the A27 hull to be redesigned and mated to a brand-new cast and welded turret specifically for the new gun. Clever redesign of the hull allowed the Comet to adopt a 64in turret ring – this was the largest used up to this point, but it is interesting to note that it was exactly the same as that on the pre-war Panzer IV. The 77mm gun was one of the outstanding tank guns of the war; it was capable of high rates of fire and was an exceptionally accurate and consistent gun, making it much easier for the gunner to achieve a first-round hit than on any other tank. At one stage in 1944 it was considered for inclusion in the A41 Centurion being developed, but the seventeen-pounder was favoured instead. The turret featured another innovation, as a No.38 wireless was mounted along with the usual No.19 set, in order to allow the crew to communicate directly with their accompanying infantry.

Leyland Motors was appointed the parent in February 1943 and had a mock-up ready by September. The first mild steel pilot was delivered in February 1944 and began trials immediately. In March 1944, the company completed production of Cromwell and shifted to building Comets, although the inevitable delays meant that the first production tanks were not completed until September. John Fowler, English Electric and Metro-Cammell were also brought into the programme, although the Fowler tanks do not appear to have been made until after the war ended, and the latter two companies probably did not complete their contracts. Orders were placed for just over 1,800 tanks, but only 1,186 were made, with four regiments using them in action. The only significant criticisms were the relative thinness of the hull floor when attacked by mines, and a minor problem occurred with the early rubber-tyred idler wheels which were based on those used on Cromwells; they tended to disintegrate as they were unable to stand the extra punishment that Comet dished out and at one point threatened to bring the entire operational fleet to a standstill, but the rapid introduction of a cast steel version cured the problem. Despite the limited opportunity to demonstrate its attributes, particularly in a tank versus tank role, the tank performed well, especially bearing in mind that it was only ever intended to be a stop-gap until a much larger tank appeared, the A41. The history of the 15th/19th Hussars, the fourth regiment to receive the Comet, noted that 'The Comet, unlike many previous British cruiser tanks, was reliable and battleworthy from the first – a statement that bodes well for the future but provides a sorry epitaph on British tank production before and during the war'. The future was bright, in the shape of the Centurion.[16]

The A41 Centurion

Although the 'Cent' never saw operational service, it is appropriate to discuss it in its earliest forms, as its heritage makes it a genuine Second World War tank. In October 1943, at a meeting of the Tank Board, the Director Royal Armoured Corps confirmed the specification for a new heavy cruiser, given the GS project title A41. This would be a definitive statement of what the tank required to defeat current and likely future German armour would look like, and sought to utilise all the experience gained over the previous years. In essence, in a tank weighing no more than 45 tons, the hull had to have a turret ring no smaller than that on the Sherman; use the 650bhp Meteor engine coupled to a Merritt-Brown gearbox; have the equivalent of at least 4in of vertical frontal armour with 2½in on the sides (although this could be lessened if required to avoid going over 45 tons); and mount the seventeen-pounder gun. The width, including any skirts/bazooka plates, was to not exceed 10ft 8in, although 10ft 4in was optimum, in order to negotiate Bailey Bridges and be 'readily transportable' by rail. However, later, when the actual width of the new design was known, the in-service Bailey bridge was redesigned and widened by 1ft 9in to accept the new tank – at last, the dog was wagging the tail. The selection of the final size of the turret ring (74in) was one of the major reasons for the increase in width. The Deputy Director General of AFVs, Claude Gibb, stated that:

> Our heavy tank for the future must have a much bigger turret and fighting compartment than anything previously envisaged… it is better to go straight out for the bigger turret and thus leave the way wide open for the next jump in gun size which I feel sure will come at an early stage… neither you nor I want to produce a tank which is only equal to what the Hun is using today, but rather we must take at least one jump ahead.[17]

At last the message had got through. Gibb takes great credit, for he was also largely responsible for the biggest decision taken in relation to the A41, soon to be named Centurion. Rather than entrust its design to any of the commercial companies that had been given the role of parent in the past, the tank would be designed by the experienced staff of DTD; it had been assumed early on that Leyland would get the role once Comet production was complete. The decision to have DTD lead the design was confirmed on 26 November 1943. Additionally, user comments were sought out at an early stage, allowing experienced tank soldiers with recent experience to express opinions and influence the design as it progressed, rather than exposing a completed design to them as a fait accompli, sometimes just before going into action for the first time. This was assisted by making the prototypes in a number of different configurations, allowing the best combination of main and secondary armaments to be confirmed. Critically, this approach led to the dropping of the proposal to mount a 20mm Polsten cannon in a ball mounting alongside the seventeen-pounder. Although the idea had some merits, the crews hated it as it intruded into the turret space a lot and added both complexity and a training bill, and so the trusty co-axial MG was used instead, although most crews expressed a preference for the .30in Browning rather than the Besa, on reliability grounds. Electrical gun control equipment was used, which would in time lead to the development of a genuine two-axis stabiliser system, bringing shooting on the move back into vogue once more. An auxiliary generator engine driven by a small 8bhp Morris engine was fitted, which ensured that the batteries remained charged, even with the Meteor not running, and provided sufficient 'juice' for the increasingly power-hungry systems being fitted. An external mantlet not dissimilar to that on the Panther provided excellent frontal protection,

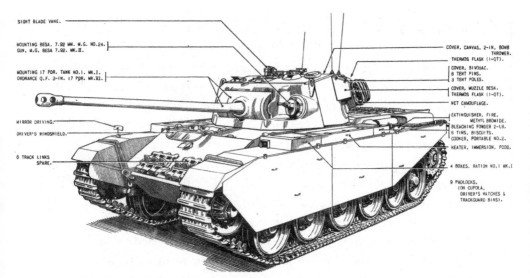

A stowage diagram for the A41 Centurion, shown here with the 7.92mm BESA MG in the turret ball mounting; the post-war A41A design used a more conventional arrangement. The Centurion was the finest all-round tank in the world for the next twenty years and represented the tank that the British crews might have received in 1944 had the DTD team's experience been used earlier.

and the 3in thick glacis plate was sloped at 57 degrees, the first time this had been deliberately incorporated as a feature. To reduce the chance of ammunition fires all ammunition was stowed in armoured bins below the turret ring, subsequently adopted as standard British practice. Consideration was given to the inclusion of a fifth crew member as hull machine-gunner, but this was dropped; the biggest advantage this would have added would have been a fifth pair of hands to help out with the increasingly laborious and time-consuming maintenance tasks. A new all-round vision cupola was fitted, by now an accepted 'must have' on all British tanks.

The Christie suspension was abandoned in favour of a Horstmann design, as the preferred suspension of all British cruisers from the A13 to the Comet had reached its limit and something new was required. Torsion bar suspension was considered – it had successfully been used on German tanks for years – but it was realised that it would encroach into the volume inside the hull, be difficult to repair if damaged, and would raise the overall height of the tank by a few inches. The Horstmann design was therefore selected as not only were the individual units easy to replace – easy always being a relative term when referring to tank maintenance – but they also added a little to the side protection of the lower hull. The Horstmann design could trace its heritage back to the experiments with light tank suspensions conducted in the 1930s, which may be the major contribution made by that line of development. The latest Mk IV version of the Meteor was used, coupled to a Z51 gearbox, developed from that used on Comet. At the user's insistence, this included a high-speed reverse gear, which would have saved many crewmen's lives had it been used during the war. Aside from relatively minor teething problems that any tank, however carefully and cleverly designed, will suffer, the biggest automotive problem was a lack of range, and this continued to dog the tank until the hull was redesigned years later to carry more fuel.

The design parentage of the Centurion remained undefined, allowing DTD to collaborate with a number of firms on elements of the project; this included AEC which produced 'soft-boat' hulls, but as they did not have sufficient capacity in their Southall works, the prototypes were built by hand at ROF Woolwich and Nottingham. The mock-up (entrusted to AEC) took nearly a year to produce, which allowed time for many of the individual sub-systems to be tried and tested before committing them to service. No fewer than twenty prototypes[18] were ordered, using different combinations of armament to ensure that the best balance was found. They were built not by any of the private companies, but at ROFs Woolwich and Nottingham, with construction starting in January 1945.[19] The first few prototypes were completed by April, and were immediately subjected to trials at FVPE, with six being sent to Germany in May, three from each ROF. Despite the war being over, the tanks were manned by crewmen from the Guards Armoured Division and shown to a number of units, although the 5th Royal Inniskilling Dragoon Guards and 5RTR were the two main ones involved. This allowed crews with the very latest experience to comment on the design, which they enthusiastically did. No doubt appreciating the chance to be involved, the overall reaction was extremely positive, and can be summed up as 'This is the tank that we always should have had!'

Design parentage was finally handed over to V-A in mid-1945. The first two contracts had been placed on 26 June 1944 for 500 from ROF, and then on 4 July for another 300 from V-A. These can be considered as tentative orders, and it appears that the intention was not to go into production before trials were complete (as that lesson had been learned), but rather to cue-up the two firms to enable them to begin preparations to build Centurions once their existing contracts had been fulfilled. As it was, full production was not authorised until August 1945, once information from Op Sentry, other reliability trials and users' comments had been explored.[20] Eventually thousands would be built, with many bought by discerning countries in the fifties and sixties who considered the design to be the best available anywhere. At a stroke, the Centurion made all the other British designs obsolescent if not obsolete, and finally gave the crews what the RTC had always wanted in the 1920s – a genuine universal tank.

Chapter 9

Lessons Finally Learned? 1944–1945

In Normandy the baneful influence of this disgrace of tank design would be felt again and again.

Alistair Horne, *The Lonely Leader*

Britain cannot allow a great nation like Germany with its enormous engineering capacity seven years start in the race of tank development and production, and then expect by some miracle unknown to engineering science, to put in the field a force trained and equipped in as many months without paying a heavy price.

Major General Crawford, Deputy Director General Tank Supply

Design and production 1944–1945

By August 1944, a couple of months after the Normandy invasion, and after much tinkering with organisational aspects within the MoS over the preceding four years, the structure looked like this:

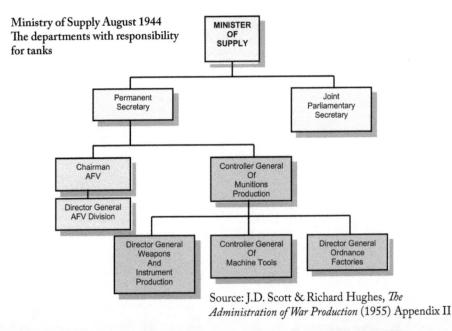

Ministry of Supply August 1944
The departments with responsibility for tanks

Source: J.D. Scott & Richard Hughes, *The Administration of War Production* (1955) Appendix II

It can be seen from the organisation that tanks continued to be considered a weapon apart in terms of structure, while still being considered as a weapon like any other in terms of resource priority. Responsibility for tank production was still separate from the guns and the instruments they mounted which could lead, as before, to bottlenecks in production caused by the lack of a single, key component.

On 2 August 1944 the PM wrote to Sir John Wardlaw-Milne, Chairman of the Select Committee on National Expenditure:

> In 1943 sufficient numbers of US tanks were available, plus after the Tunisian campaign ended, there were less British armoured forces in action, so these two factors removed, for the first time since Dunkirk, the fear of a quantitative deficiency which had previously prevented development of tank design and production *on the lines we should have followed had we been free to do so.* [My emphasis] The situation in 1943 enabled a drastic reshaping of our tank production policy, and this accounts in large measure for the fact that 1943 output fell substantially short of the estimate made at the end of 1942.[1]

Churchill had found himself having to answer questions put to the government in the House of Commons regarding the poor performance of British tanks, and which had led to the Committee being set up. In fact, it produced two reports during the war, both equally damning of production and design, and they had to be graded as Top Secret and kept out of the public view. Throughout the war Richard Stokes, the Labour MP for Ipswich and a First World War gunner officer with a Military Cross, raised the question of British tank inferiority again and again in the House of Commons. He was frequently laughed at, or even accused of a lack of patriotism. His questions were responded to with evasion, inaccuracies, and half-truths. The House of Commons of course is not the government, it is the body of popular representation, but still should be chided for the cavalier and partisan attitude from some of its members to a situation that was daily getting British soldiers killed. If they had taken his statements more seriously, pressure could and should have been applied to the government to improve the situation. As it was, Stokes was an almost lone voice. To be fair to those who had to answer Stokes's questions, there were sometimes issues of national security at stake that precluded straight answers being given, and the morale factor always had to be carefully managed; to admit the true state of affairs publicly would have been disastrous. Montgomery, for example, understood the real issues but publicly always stated that British tanks were the equal of German tanks, a statement he knew to be untrue

According to Ross, by the end of 1944 Britain had produced 24,843 tanks – 'and were still gaining experience.'[2] However, as the end of the war was almost in sight, and barring a miracle, both Germany and Japan were facing certain defeat, a lot of pressure was applied – on both sides of the Atlantic – to scale production back and downscale or cancel new designs. In the USA, the tank manufacturers were huge and successful commercial companies where thoughts naturally turned to the products needed by civilian markets that would be reinvigorated with peace, particularly motor cars. There was also pressure there, as early as September 1942, to cut back tank production in favour of shipbuilding.[3] By late in 1943, and before the first US soldier had even stepped onto the soil of France:

> public opinion in the United States regarded the war in Europe as all but won – and this more than six months before D-Day! This... had repercussions in Detroit where the industrialists, steeped in economic reality, felt the need to reduce the scale of tank production less the market be swamped, knowing that the juggernaut would take a lot of stopping.[4]

Unfortunately, the scaling back in production was to cause a rift between the USA and Britain in 1944, as the latter's monthly requirements for Shermans were not being met. The root of the problem lay in the estimates of the number of reserve tanks required by armoured formations in Europe. By 1944 Britain, with her hard-won experience, insisted on holding high reserve numbers of AFVs, whereas the US thought that fewer would be required, often around 10 percent of the operational tanks in the field force. After the experience of tank casualties in June 1944, when it was clear that the British practice was the more realistic, the US had no choice but to divert Shermans produced for Britain to its own troops in order to create the necessary reserves. This led to strongly worded exchanges between Churchill and Roosevelt, but the shortfall remained. This put even more pressure on British production at exactly the time when it too was just starting to scale back in preparation for peace. In Britain, certain manufacturers had already had their tank contracts cancelled, and were instead given contracts for their previous product types including, as we have seen, some being switched back to locomotive production. There was also US pressure here, as it was felt that Britain's industrial expertise was better suited to locomotive production rather than tanks – on the basis of Britain's record, it was a reasonable supposition.[5]

One of the most common observations made on British production policy was that the sheer number of different types, marks and manufacturers led inevitably to a lack of standardisation. While this is certainly true, it is worthwhile considering just how standardised other nations really were. Germany used a vast number of different types of AFV, many times more in fact than the UK, including not only home-grown types, but also modified captured AFVs: one estimate shows at least fifty different types of captured vehicle in common use. The USA may appear to have managed the issue by the use of just one main type, the M4 Sherman, but this is misleading. In fact, in the Sherman, use was made of: cast and welded armour, riveted and welded construction methods, four major engine types which were not interchangeable, and so on.[6] In fact the nation which made most effective use of standardisation was the USSR, and even then there were many different types of tank that were not interchangeable, including the famous T34. The fact is that different types of tanks were necessary early on because of the circumstances pre-war, but increasingly British generals, designers and soldiers in the field could see the benefits of having a single main tank type, usable for battle but also adaptable for specialised roles.

A company history: English Electric

By way of example, consider a non-designing tank building firm, English Electric, which was based in Stafford. Later to become famous for the EE Lightning and Canberra jet aircraft, the company was founded after the First World War by the amalgamation of five munitions companies, and then became a leading manufacturer of electrical equipment including dynamos and transformers, as well as steam turbines and locomotives. Before the Second World War the company was doing well, and its plant facilities made it suitable to take on tank manufacture, although it was never used as a parent. After the war the company published a booklet describing the part played in the war, and it is this history that provides the figures below. This, in microcosm, is an example of the difficulties of being exact with production figures: whereas EE claim to have built 1,009 Covenanter tanks during the conflict, the official Chilwell census and contract cards have them down as making 1,059!

EEs first involvement with tanks began just before war broke out, on 29 August 1939, building suspension and transmission items for Covenanter tanks as a sub-contractor at its Bradford plant. It was not – unlike some of the other tank building firms, such as Vulcan Foundry – a failing firm. It operated five main sites and was also involved in producing airframes and engines under license for the RAF, an indication of a high-quality, trusted, manufacturer. EE was then awarded further tank-related contracts exactly a month later for the production of 100 Covenanter hulls, suspensions and final drives, and their subsequent assembly (using components from other firms) into gun tanks at the Stafford factory.[7] At the same time authority was given to increase floor space to allow this to happen. On 22 February 1940, the MoS authorised EE to extend the buildings at Stafford and accept new plant and cranes in order to provide production capacity for 500 tanks to be built at the rate of fifteen per week, with a grant of £60,000.[8] On 27 February another 100 Covenanters were ordered. On 28 June 1940 a further order for 200 Covenanters was placed; the company was by now also making the turrets, which before then were being supplied from other firms. The next order for a further 103 Covenanters was placed on 10 December 1940. On 21 March 1941 a further 250 tanks plus 100 turrets (presumably destined for another assembler) were contracted for. Another 166 Covenanters were ordered on 19 November, as well as a contract to complete the assembly of a further ninety from 'another manufacturer', unfortunately unnamed and possibly from two different companies. Testing of hulls and complete tanks was conducted at the company's nearby Cannock Chase site. According to their records, English Electric eventually built 1,009 complete Covenanter tanks (including an unknown number of bridge-layers) of various marks, plus the 100 turrets already mentioned. It was to the firm's credit that it was able to start from scratch and diversify into tank production, despite a lack of experience in the type of work and the competing requirements of all the other items that it was required to build. This included hand grenades and also arc welding equipment of the firm's own design, which was instrumental in allowing welded armour to be adopted subsequently. It was emphatically not EEs fault that the Covenanter tanks it built were so inadequate; there was no indication of quality control issues and the fault lay solely in the poor design that they had not been involved with.

On 26 January 1942 the Stafford factory was contracted to build 1,025 Centaur tanks. This required a further extension to factory space and plant, some of which was not supplied until 24 May the following year.[9] On 28

December 1942 it was noted that a decision was implemented to switch production from the Centaur with the Liberty engine to the similar but much-improved Cromwell using the Meteor engine, 156 of the latter being built; presumably the remaining 869 had been built as Centaurs.[10] The war diary records the Centaur/Cromwell contract as being completed on 16 January 1945, nearly three years after the start date and therefore at an average rate of one tank per day.[11]

On 24 November 1943 English Electric began production of an order for 200 all-welded Comet tanks. The company was already adept at welding armour, having conducted experiments with the process previously and designing and modifying equipment as it went along. Special manipulators were designed and built to allow gravity-flow welding to be used on items as large as complete hulls. Another 300 Comets were ordered on 23 February 1944. The first complete Comet tank was delivered on 18 October 1944, nearly a year after the order was placed, not untypical for a completely new type. Although the total number of Comets required from EE was increased by 100 to 600 on 1 March 1945,[12] not all the contracted tanks were built, as in 1945 the brakes were applied and most contracts amended or cancelled; eventually 276 Comets were built by EE at Stafford. Therefore, in addition to the one or two experimental models built at Stafford, a total of something like 2,310 complete tanks (including bridge-layer tanks) were built there by a company which, five years before, had never had any involvement with AFVs. It was a remarkable achievement.

The capital or universal tank

In 1924, J.F.C. Fuller had noted that 'The Vickers tank is looked upon as a universal machine – that is, one which can be used for all tactical purposes.'[13] The RTC used it as such all through the 1920s, as the artificial distinction of infantry and cruiser was not identified until around 1934, which was to cause many problems for the army throughout the war, not only tactically and in the field of crew training, but also in the supply of spare parts and, not least, in production. However, the use of the phrase universal tank had at least been born; the tank itself would take more than two decades. Until then, the terminology and policy of infantry and cruiser tanks would reign supreme.

Getting the balance right between the production of cruisers and infantry tanks during the Second World War was a constant battle. In the first months, when the opinion of the General Staff was that conditions similar to the First World War would be encountered again, the need for I-tanks seemed paramount. As a result, production contracts placed were in the ratio of around two infantry tanks for every cruiser, although the actual rates of production meant that this ratio tended even more towards I-tank production, partly because the A11 was such a simple tank to build, and partly because the more complicated cruisers were only just coming on-stream for mass production. After Dunkirk, the experience of the BEF had caused a reconsideration of the necessary production ration and in a complete reversal of the previous policy the ratio was set at 2:1 in favour of cruisers. But a change of policy could not be effected overnight, and between August 1940 and February 1941, around 3.25 I-tanks were being built for every cruiser.[14] Later still, after experience in the western desert, the War Office view shifted again, now requiring 2.5 cruisers for every I-tank. However, the reality was that the programme into 1943 would still only yield only 0.9 cruisers per I-tank. It would take many months before production reflected policy, and it was not until 1943 that cruisers were being produced in anything like the required numbers. Statistics like this may well have assisted in turning people's minds to the possibility of designing a tank that could do both roles equally.[15]

Despite this, the need for infantry tanks did not go away completely; at a meeting of the Tank Board on 9 January 1942 it was confirmed that the 'General Staff are clear that there is a requirement for an infantry tank.' It was just as well that this confirmation was forthcoming, as orders for thousands of the latest I-tank, the Churchill, had been given out and the tank was struggling with many problems affecting reliability. However, once the problems were solved – after it coming to within a whisker of being written off as a failure and cancelled – it eventually became a tank that was not only well-liked by its crews for the protection it offered, but was also the basis for a whole range of specialist variants.

But that was in the future. By the end of 1942 large parts of the RAC hierarchy had started to realise that the infantry/cruiser doctrine was flawed. On the very first page of the substantial RAC half-yearly report No.6 of that year, the following statement is made:

There is a very definite trend towards a common use and tactical doctrine for Armoured Brigades – either in Armoured Divisions or co-operating with infantry formations, and the tactical distinction between the employment of Armoured Brigades and Tank Brigades is becoming increasingly nebulous. This trend is naturally reflected in the policy of tank design… the General Staff have definitely stated that their main requirement is for a standard 'all-purpose' medium tank… utilised as the equipment of Armoured Brigades and Tank Brigades… [and] the value of a tank armament firing HE or HE/AP has also been recognised.[16]

Later in the same report, a prediction was made that the days of the separate infantry and cruiser designs were over; that some specialised types of AFV were still required, but only in the form of a proportion of the universal or all-purpose tank being equipped with a seventeen-pounder 'hole-puncher'. Unfortunately, therefore, this partial leap of faith did not go far enough. Had it been taken to its logical conclusion, the General Staff would have realised that *all* frontline tanks required a dual-purpose high-velocity gun capable both of knocking out German tanks at long ranges and of firing a capable HE round for use against transport, anti-tank guns and infantry. This muddled thinking was not rectified until the introduction of the Comet – which, even when it came into service in early 1945, was still classed as a cruiser.

It is worth noting at this juncture that the term universal tank could be applied in two different ways. Firstly, in its simplest form it could be used synonymously with capital tank, to describe a tank capable of fulfilling the roles of cruiser and infantry tank. However, and increasingly in the post-war period, it came to be applied to the concept of building a base gun tank that would form the basis for a whole family of specialised tanks using the common chassis and wherever possible, common components. These would include such vehicles as armoured recovery vehicles, bridge-layers, , heavily armoured assault tanks, duplex drive amphibious tanks, and even armoured personnel carriers. But that story lies outside the scope of this work, and it is the former, simpler, definition that will be applied here.[17]

Through 1943 and certainly by 1944, as the infantry tank was oh-so-slowly overtaken in production numbers by the cruisers, it continued to dawn on many other observers, even outside the RAC, that the dichotomy of the two types was an artificiality, and that tanks needed, at different times and outside of the user's control, to be able to support the infantry *and* to destroy enemy armour *and* to conduct fast, mobile operations to exploit opportunities. What was needed to fulfill the requirement was a tank with the right blend of armour, firepower and mobility (not to mention reliability) in order to achieve all of these tasks at least acceptably; with the issue of getting the right balance between the competing elements being the key. Luckily, the concept had one important supporter, a commander who believed in the doctrine of 'balance', who had refused the offer of more infantry tanks in 1943, and who preferred the term Medium to Cruiser, reflecting the old pre-war use of Medium tanks as a dual-purpose workhorse: 'Significantly the concept of an all purposes main battle tank – the Capital tank – found strong favour with General Montgomery.'[18]

It is fair to say that Montgomery both helped and hindered the search for the all-round tank. On the one hand he believed in the concept, but on the other he thought that the Sherman, with which he had achieved so much in North Africa and Italy, was adequate to fulfill the role. Unfortunately, he failed to realise how dated the Sherman was, and how much better the new British tanks were about to become. However, in December 1944 his experience had grown and he realised that the ideal tank would have to be a new design. He wrote that:

the tank must have a really good gun (dual purpose), and mechanical reliability is a necessity. The term capital tank means a dual-purpose tank, suitable for working with infantry and also for operating in an armoured division. It is undesirable to have special function tanks, eg close support tanks, because they can only be used for special purposes at intermittent stages of the battle. The weight of any tank should not exceed about 45 tons... armour should be fitted up to the maximum weight allowed.[19]

By 1944 Britain was getting close to building if not excellent then certainly workmanlike all-round designs, even if in certain areas they continued to under-perform, particularly in the critical areas of size of gun and (the Mk VII Churchill aside) in weight of armour. But in terms of reliability, speed, flexibility, and balance – and very importantly in sheer numbers available, including immediately available battle replacements – they were now better than their German opponents. And even the much-vaunted Sherman was starting to lose its appeal as a result:

When 3rd and 4th County of London Yeomanry amalgamated [in August 1944], officers from the latter reckoned that the Cromwells they had just given up were in every way superior to the Shermans they would now have to work with... Major General Verney, commanding 7th Armoured Division... praised the Cromwell as 'superb' and claimed that mechanical breakdowns had been so few as to be negligible...[20]

In contrast, the Sherman design was tired, it was too thinly armoured, and the US were struggling to update it. Its reliability was also suffering; in 1944:

4th Armoured Brigade was extremely critical of the M4 and M4A1 (Shermans). The engines seem to have required replacement on average every 600 to 700 miles. Brigade workshops had already changed thirty and expected to deal with another one hundred in the near future...[21]

The earlier decision by the British government to continue to produce their own tank designs rather than rely on American production (despite some considerable pressure from the Americans to do so in the interests of standardisation) was about to bear fruit. A better tank even than the Cromwell was about to enter service in early 1945, and which was to be the last – and by far and away the best – British-designed tank to see significant operational service during the Second World War. The Comet was a derivative of the Cromwell; it benefited hugely from that lineage, and its evolutionary design was immediately successful. It only appeared in January 1945; in its short period of service it was to achieve a level of popularity among its crews that all other British wartime designs failed to match. However, the peak in British tank design was to enter service in prototype form just as the war ended, in the shape of the Centurion; unfortunately, it never saw active service in the Second World War. This tank came to be widely regarded as *the* best tank in the world for the next two decades, with balanced mobility, firepower, reliability and protection; it was able to be continuously upgraded through thirteen marks and is still in widespread service today. Unlike all the other tanks designed and produced in Britain during the Second World War, the Centurion was not designed by industry, but by the War Office's own team of experts, the Department of Tank Design led by Claude Gibb. During most of the conflict, the DTD did not have a remit to actually design tanks, but was there to support and assist industrial manufacturers, and supervise modifications. It can be convincingly argued that the success of the Centurion proved that the mis-employment of the DTD, with its acquired expertise and experience from 1940–1943, was a major contributory factor in the poor designs actually used in that period. Indeed, the decision to entrust the Centurion project to DTD appears to have been (at least in part) in reaction to increasingly public criticism in Parliament of the commercially-led designs.[22]

This was an interesting organisational decision. On the one hand, the DTD was able to amass a range of experience across the board in all elements of design, development and production and relating to all the types and marks of tanks being worked on, and this was to prove invaluable when it came to (finally) tasking the DTD to design its own tank in the shape of the Centurion.[23] On the other hand, it is fair to ask why it took so long to realise that enormous expertise resided within DTD? This expertise was underused in merely using it to rectify faults and suggest modifications. As Postan underlined:

> The Department of Tank Design was growing steadily and, as the ONLY body of technicians concerned with the whole of the tank programme, acquired by mere experience an ever more commanding voice in tank development... Undoubtedly the DTD was the main source of new design strength in the later years of the war.[24]

Moreover, DTD was able to profit from its easy access to official channels, including secret reports on tank developments in other countries, and of course, crucially, was not hampered by having to adhere to particular company practices and preferences, as the commercial companies were. In other words, it was the only organisation involved in the design and construction of tanks that not only had the whole picture, but also had the expertise – and time – to evaluate what best practice looked like. Thus one of the major, if not *the* major, missed opportunities was in not using DTD much earlier to design and develop a true universal tank, concurrently with (but independent of) the commercial companies, before passing on the resultant design to the best of the manufacturers who could then simply concentrate on producing them efficiently and to the highest build standard. The eventual success of the Centurion was proof positive that the lessons of the previous years had been learned, and that a reliable, well-armed and well-protected tank capable of destroying enemy tanks and supporting the infantry could be made in Britain – but only if designed and built by the right people.

British tank production 1939–1945

How many tanks did Britain produce during the war? This is not a simple question to answer. Firstly, even the official versions of the war history give different figures. As we have seen, the methods used to measure production changed as the war progressed, and some versions only refer to tanks by the main types – cruiser, infantry, and light – while others use names. And what do we mean by 'during'? Many of the tanks used in the first year or so of the war were contracted for and produced before 3 September 1939, so should those be counted? And fast forward to the end of the war; do we stop counting on 15 September 1945, VJ Day?

In many cases, it is also clear that confusion over the complicated nomenclature that developed and changed during the conflict has caused mistakes. For example, in at least one case Valentine infantry tanks – being used in lieu of cruisers in 1941 – were accounted for as cruisers. It is no surprise that people were puzzled by the fact that a Covenanter Mk II was the same as the Cruiser Mk V, or indeed the A13 Mk III. The rework programmes, particularly for Churchill and to a lesser extent Centaur/ Cromwell, muddy the waters still further, as do the number of cancelled and incomplete contracts, particularly towards the end of the war. In some cases, armoured cars and self-propelled guns or other types of AFV may have been labelled as tanks, with the Guy armoured car being officially called the Guy wheeled tank, which was not helpful! The issue of Canadian Valentine production adds yet more uncertainty, as does the building of tank hulls for other manufacturers to complete by adding someone else's turret. And Vauxhall, the design parent for Churchill, seems to have been awarded the master contracts for all Churchills, with the other companies in the programme being giving sub-contracts for the same tanks but using different contract numbers. There is also a suspicion that as the war began to draw toward an inevitably successful conclusion, there was a waning of interest in the whole issue of quantities being built, certainly in comparison to the dark days of 1940–1942. Nevertheless, it is important to try to summarise the production position in regard to quantity, fraught with difficulties as it is. The official *Statistical Digest of the War* breaks tank production down into quarters as follows:

Tank production 1938–1944

Year	Q1	Q2	Q3	Q4	Total
1938	Nil	75	146	198	419
1939	145	394	116 (Jul–August)	314 (September–December)	939
1940	218	340	392	449	1,399
1941	653	943	1,368	1,877	4,841
1942	2,118	2,220	2,200	2,073	8,611
1943	2,041	2,147	1,878	1,410	7,476
1944	1,400	1,074			2,474 (First 2 Quarters only)

Source: *Statistical Digest of the War*, Table 126

This gives a total from September 1939 until June 1944 of 25,115. However, these figures also include an unspecified number of 'special purpose tanks and self-propelled artillery on tank chassis.' If the special purpose tanks are, for example, Crocodile flamethrowers or Valentine duplex drive tanks, then we can confidently include them. If, however, they are Archer or Bishop self-propelled guns, or anti-aircraft guns, or gun tractors or armoured bridge-layers, then they are not gun tanks and should be excluded. They may of course be in yet another category: a vehicle initially built as a gun tank and then converted to another purpose, for example into an ARV. Back to the numbers: according to Harrison,[25] during the war Britain produced the following tanks and SPGs:

Second World War British tank and SPG production

1939	1940	1941	1942	1943	1944	1945	TOTAL
300	1400	4800	8600	7500	4600	2100	29300

Source: Mark Harrison *Economics of World War 2* (1998) p15, Table 1.6

These figures are clearly rounded up or down to the nearest hundred, and are not specific – do they also include armoured cars, experimental models, conversions, and rebuilds? The figure for 1939 almost certainly only indicates production from 3 September on. When the figures from the *Statistical Digest of the War* are compared, we can see a trend emerging:

1939	1940	1941	1942	1943	1944	1945	TOTAL
300	1,400	4,800	8,600	7,500	4,600	2,100	29,300
314	1,399	4,841	8,611	7,476	2,474 (to June)		

It appears that Harrison took the statistical digest figures and rounded up or down. What they do indicate is that, as expected, output rose quite rapidly (albeit never fast enough to meet demand) in the early years, peaking in mid-1942 and then declining, partly as the dependence on US supplied models took hold. As soon as Britain adopted a policy of reliance on the Sherman and its stablemates, a degree of impetus was lost in the battle to produce a truly battle-worthy British tank. The procurers could cite Allied standardisation as a major reason for the policy, or alternatively that many British crews preferred the Sherman. Many did, but only for want of something better.

Jane's gives the following table, which serves as a useful comparator between the four major tank building countries:

Tank production by nation 1939–1944

	1939	1940	1941	1942	1943	1944	Total
UK	752	1,382	4,851	8,190	7,329	4,057	26,561
USA	18	365	4,021	26,608	37,198	20,357	88,567
USSR	2,988	2,669	6,449	24,713	24,227	29,029	90,075
GERMANY	743	1,479	3,057	3,463	12,780	16,832	38,354

Source: *Jane's World War II Tanks and Fighting Vehicles* p13

Finally, H. Duncan Hall noted the following totals for British (tank only) production from September 1939 to June 1944:[26]

- Infantry Tanks   13,604
- Cruisers   11,013
- Light Tanks   498
- Total   25,115

We can summarise these as follows:

UK tank production totals 1939–1945

Work	Total Production	Period	Remarks
Statistical Digest of the War	26,189	September 1939 to May 1944	Includes special purpose tanks and SPG
Economics of World War 2	29,300	September 1939 to 1945	Includes SPG
Jane's World War II Tanks and Fighting Vehicles	26,561	September 1939 to December 1944	
North American Supply	25,115	September 1939 to June 1944	Tanks only

Therefore, at this stage we can state with reasonable certainty that British tank production during the war totalled somewhere between 25,000 and 29,000 tanks. With this as our start point, we can look carefully at the census cards held by the Bovington Tank Museum and other reliable sources, and attempt to work out, as best we can, the totals made by each manufacturer, and for each type of tank. This gives us the following:

UK tank production by type 1936–1945

Type	Qty built	Manufacturers (Parent shown first)	Remarks
LIGHT TANKS			
Light Mk VIB	979	V-A. JF, NBL, Thornycroft, RH, VF.	Includes Indian Pattern and AA tanks. Unknown number of these built pre-war.
Light Mk VIC	168	V-A. JF, RH, VF.	Unknown number of these built pre-war.
VII A17 Tetrarch	177	V-A	Limited operational use.
VIII Harry Hopkins	100	M-C.	No operational use.
Total Light Tanks: 1424			
INFANTRY TANKS			
A11 Matilda I	139	V-A.	
A12 Matilda II	2905	VF. RH, NBL, LMSR, JF, HW.	5 marks.
Valentine	5895	V-A, MC, BRCW.	11 marks. 76% built with two-pounder, remainder with six-pounder or 75mm. Total includes 647 DD tanks, but excludes all other variants (Bridge-layer, Bishop, Archer). 1,420 also built in Canada by CPR, not included here.
A22 Churchill	5589 (estimate)	Vauxhall, BRCW, MC, Leyland, Dennis, BW, NC, H&W, GRCW, BP.	8+ marks.[27] Excludes pilots and variants not originally built as gun tanks (49 or 50 Gun Carrier Tanks).
Total Infantry Tanks: 14528			

CRUISER TANKS			
Type	Qty built	Manufacturers (Parent shown first)	Remarks
A9 Cruiser Mk I	125	V-A. H&W.	First British tank with two-pounder gun, powered traverse. Some built as CS tanks.
A10 Cruiser MK II/IIA	170	V-A. BRCW, NMA, Crabtree.[28]	First British tank with composite armour. 30 built as CS tanks.
A13 Cruiser Mk III/IV/IVA	345	NMA. LMSR.	3 marks. First British tank with stand-off armour.
A13 Covenanter Cruiser Mk V	1768	LMSR. EE, Leyland.	4 marks. Does not includes 3 pilots. Unknown number of bridgelayers may be included.
A15 Crusader Cruiser Mk VI	4286	NMA, Foden, WG, MC, Lysaght, Milner's, RB, MG Cars, MIE	3 marks. Includes 668 OP tanks but does not include Pilot A15E1 or 685 AA tanks. Contract cards refer to MCC, assumed to mean Metro-Cammell Carriage and listed here as MC.
A24 Cavalier Cruiser Mk VII	500	NMA.	1 mark. Does not include the single pilot. 340 completed/converted as OP tanks.
A24L Centaur Cruiser Mk VIII	4827 (estimate)	Leyland, EE, HW, JF, LMSR, Morris, NMA, RB.	5 marks plus sub-types. Total includes pilots.
A24M Cromwell Cruiser Mk VIII		BRCW, EE, JF, Leyland, M-C, LMSR.	8 marks plus sub-types. Total includes pilots. Some built with welded hulls.
A30 Challenger	200	BRCW.	1 mark.
A34 Comet	600 (estimate)	Leyland, JF, EE, MC.	1 mark. Excludes pilot. 1186 in total built, but possibly only around 600 made before the end of the war, hence figure used. Cast and welded construction.
A41 Centurion	12 (estimate)	ROF	Prototypes only were produced during the Second World War. 20 prototypes were ordered but only 16 were completed, with 12 being completed by 1946 (possibly all by end of 1945). Sloping glacis plate, Horstmann suspension, generating engine, electrical power traverse. Fully welded with cast turret components. First series production ordered Aug 45 (800).
Total Cruiser Tanks: 12,833			
Total All Tanks: 28,785			

Some of these figures can be treated with a degree of certainty. However, there are some where there is more than a reasonable amount of uncertainty; this mainly applies to Churchill production, but also to Cromwell/Centaur, and also to Valentine to a lesser degree.

Listed below are the main tank manufacturers; it should be noted that some of these were purely assemblers and did not manufacture any of the component parts themselves.

British tank manufacturers and builders 1934–1945

- Beyer Peacock (BP). Gorton, Manchester.
- Birmingham Railway Carriage & Wagon Company (BRCW). Smethwick.
- Broom & Wade (BW). High Wycombe.
- RW Crabtree. Huddersfield.
- Dennis Bros. Guildford.
- English Electric (EE). Stafford.
- Foden. Sandbach.
- John Fowler (JF). Leeds.
- Gloucester Railway Carriage & Wagon Company (GRCW). Gloucester.
- Harland & Wolff (H&W). Belfast.
- Leyland Motors. Kingston upon Thames and Lancashire.
- London Midland & Scottish Railway (LMSR). Horwich, Cheshire.
- John Lysaght. Newport and Scunthorpe.
- Metro-Cammell (MC). Saltley, Birmingham.
- MG Cars. Abingdon.
- Morris Industries Exports (MIE). Cowley.
- Milner's Safe. Liverpool.
- Newton Chambers (NC). Sheffield.
- North British Locomotive (NBL). Glasgow.
- Nuffield Mechanizations & Aero (NMA). Birmingham. Includes Wolseley Motors.
- Charles Roberts. Wakefield.
- Royal Ordnance Factory (ROF). Woolwich & Nottingham
- Ruston Hornsby (RH). Lincoln. Includes Ruston Bucyrus (RB)
- Thornycroft. Basingstoke.
- Vauxhall Motors. Luton.
- Vickers-Armstrongs (V-A). Leeds. Includes some subsidiary firms, eg Armstrong-Whitworth, Vickers-Carden-Loyd.
- Vulcan Foundry (VF). Newton-le-Willows.
- West's Gas Improvements (WG). Manchester.

Major British tank component manufacturers 1934–1945

Although this cannot claim to be a comprehensive list of all the sub-contractors who supplied parts for British tanks, it is an attempt to list at least some of the major contributors.

- AEC: Gearboxes.
- Aircrew Company: Fan drives.
- Avon India: Tyres.
- Babcock & Wilcox. Welding, armour.
- Borg & Beck: Clutches
- CAV: Lighting, electrical equipment, fuel injection pumps
- David Brown: Gearboxes.
- Dunlop: Tyres.
- Ferodo: Brake linings, fan belts.
- Hadfields: Armour.
- Horstmann/Slow Motion Company: Suspensions.
- Henry Meadows: Engines and gearboxes.
- Lockheed: Controls.
- Newton & Bennett: Shock absorbers.
- Pye: Radios and ancillaries.
- ROF: Guns, ammunition
- Rolls-Royce: Engines.
- Rootes: Engines.
- Smiths: Electrical equipment, instruments.
- Stothert & Pitt: Turrets.
- Whessoe Foundry: Hulls.
- Zenith: Carburettors.

Conclusion

It cannot be too strongly stressed that among military equipment the tracked and armoured vehicle had no antecedents prior to 1916, and that commercial tracked vehicles during the interwar years offered little experience relevant to the later evolution of the tank.

Postan, *Design and Development of Weapons*

The story of Britain's tank inferiority all through the Second World War is one of the great disgraces of her military history. The blame has never been properly apportioned or the 'guilty men' named.

Alistair Horne, *The Lonely Leader*

If one looks for scapegoats they might be found in many places – in a government that always skimped on tank production... or a War Office that still did not understand the importance of armoured fighting vehicles in modern war, and an industrial regime that could not get its act together.

David Fletcher *The Great Tank Scandal*

Guilty men?

The intention of this work was not to produce an apology for the appalling inadequacy of British tank production during the Second World War, but rather to examine in detail the context in which production took place and to explain the root causes of any failure. In looking for the reasons we must first recall the context in which rearmament took place. Partly as a reaction to the appalling loss of life of the First World War, partly due to the world financial crises of the early 1930s, and not least partly because of the historical resistance to a large standing army, there was no desire within Britain to rearm the services. The army had no continental commitment role and was primarily the instrument of imperial policing. The government sponsored Ten Year Rule prevented any real rearmament while it remained in place. It was only from around 1934 that Germany was once again identified as likely to upset the European balance of power, forcing an unwilling National Coalition government to start the process of rebuilding Britain's armed forces.

When rearmament did begin, the vision of air power as the weapon that could win wars without the horrendous cost in manpower was too attractive to be ignored; Baldwin's hopelessly inaccurate 'the bomber will always get through' speech summarised what would become policy, the building-up of the RAF fighter and bomber fleets to the detriment of the other two services. Allied to this, where money was allocated to the army, it was directed to be used primarily to build up the Air Defence of Great Britain, meaning anti-aircraft guns and searchlights. Not only did this prevent money being used elsewhere within the army, it also focused the limited gun design capacity firmly on AA guns to the detriment of all other types, including tank-mounted guns.

While this was going on, the sums allocated to the army for tank development were kept tiny, restricting research and development and preventing any effective preparation for future expansion. Even the paltry amounts often could not be spent within the time specified by law and were lost. The army's specialist tank design department was dismantled, and the few technical officers specialising in tank development were decried by the senior leadership as fanatics. We must not forget that much of the damage to the vision to mechanise the army as a whole was done by over-enthusiastic RTC officers, whose vocal intellectualism so frightened the establishment that they were deliberately sidelined; a more considered and persuasive approach may have produced better results. The ill-conceived division of tanks into the infantry and cruiser types with widely different roles was an artificiality brought about by some of the same experts within the RTC, and which had serious repercussions before a universal type was introduced at the war's end.

When the army finally regained a continental commitment, in March 1939, the Ministry of Aircraft Production had already taken control of many of the resources that would be needed for an expansion of tank production: not only factories and plant, but also skilled manpower. The MAP had also had the foresight to put into place the Shadow Scheme, which would pay huge dividends as aircraft manufacture increased many-fold, and was never replicated for tank production. It is worthy of note that even in 1944, more factory space and skilled labour was allocated to production associated with RAF Bomber Command alone than to the whole of the army.[1]

The belated formation of the Ministry of Supply in autumn 1939 was intended to solve the problems of weapon and equipment supply for the army, but it did little to assist in tank production. It was always a junior partner to the well-established, efficient and more astute MAP, and always lost the battles for priority. It also lacked a functional organisational structure, continually reorganising itself and forming boards and committees with little effect. It ignored pleas from the customer, the tank crews, for better and more reliable tanks, preferring to sacrifice quality for quantity, and was still unable to stimulate the manufacturers to provide the numbers required fast enough, forcing Britain to rely heavily on US tanks. There was a failure to notice the point at which the immediate danger of the Great Tank Crisis had passed, and quantity ceased to be the main priority, allowing a switch over to quality instead. That opportunity certainly occurred by late 1942 once US tanks were available in sufficient numbers to supply the 'active' theatre of operations, the Middle East; it can also be argued that in fact it came much earlier, as soon as the threat of invasion had passed in 1941.

The companies that built the tanks were, with the solitary exception of Vickers-Armstrongs, totally inexperienced in the type of techniques required to design or build tanks. This was not their fault; the responsibility lay within government, with those officials who believed that tanks were simply large vehicles, akin to locomotives or lorries. However, the lack of anything resembling a modern production line slowed down production and also prevented the easy introduction of the necessary modifications and new models. Many of the companies, to their discredit, fought hard to prevent any alterations to the design once production was underway, and pushed back hard against technological innovations, for example welding. They also begrudged providing the required spare parts needed by the army in the field.

The British craftsmanship tradition employed within the firms was a major handicap in a number of ways. It required skilled manpower which was often lacking, as the MAP could and did claim priority. The system should at least have produced consistently high-quality products, but instead slowed production down without any benefit of excellence. In part this was because of a lack of quality control mechanisms, with skilled workers being responsible for their own standards of work. When dilution of the skill-base occurred, standards slipped, often disastrously, and the MoS was both weak and slow in insisting on thorough regimes of testing. There were undoubtedly systemic failures in British industry. These included: lack of modern plant and factories; outdated machine tools; poor rates of apprenticeship and technical training; antiquated methods of production; over-reliance on skilled workers; resistance to trade dilution by the unions; and an almost complete lack of quality control. These applied to almost all industries, not solely to the tank builders. So how culpable could the companies be held to be? They were contracted, sometimes under pressure (although never duress) to speedily produce a particularly specialised product that they had no previous experience of. Having been thus contracted, they were given little guidance and assistance beyond a general specification that in many cases was so sketchy as to be almost laughable. Where government funds were released to invest in new facilities this was done almost grudgingly.

It was emphatically not the fault of the companies that British tanks were generally under-gunned. They had absolutely no say in which gun their tank would mount, as this was laid down in the specification. Indeed, the guns themselves were developed under the control of the Royal Artillery, and then supplied as complete sub-components to the assemblers. In many cases, the guns were never even seen by the tank builders, instead being mounted by army ordnance personnel in the storage and distribution depots prior to issue, or even by the units themselves. The failure to introduce the six-pounder gun in 1940 was the major failing, leading to British tanks being constantly outgunned for the next four years. Ironically, the guns themselves – and the ammunition they fired – were often excellent, but invariably introduced too late.

Before 1940, despite the handicaps already noted, the tanks that Britain produced, the A9 and A13 cruisers, and the A12 Matilda II infantry tank, were, despite their many flaws, at least as good as the German equivalents and in some respects better. The gun they carried was the best in the world. But when the financial shackles were released and tank rearmament became the order of the day in 1939, the loss of the experienced military design department both forced the MoS to pass on the responsibilities for design of the tanks to the same inexperienced firms, and prevented the MoS from close and critical supervision of the projected tanks. At the same time, partly because of the tank crisis of 1940, the firms were frequently instructed not to build pilot models, but were awarded, by the MoS, contracts 'off the drawing board'. It was a recipe for disaster. This directly led to the fallow and fatal period, from 1940 until 1943, when the tanks being produced could rightly be labelled as 'mechanical abortions.' It was only when Rolls-Royce intervened to produce the Meteor for the Cromwell, when the Comet was produced in late 1944, and particularly when the Department of Tank Design was finally authorised to use its collective experience to design a new universal tank, the Centurion, and have it built not by private industry but by the ROFs, that Britain regained her position and pride in tank design. If there was one single area where Britain got it wrong above all others, it was this. Had DTD been authorised to be more closely involved in the design of tanks, and then test the pilot models thoroughly, putting in place a plan to incorporate the necessary modifications, then the task of manufacture could have been left with more confidence in the hands of the builders.

If there were (largely unnamed) guilty men then there were also heroes: we should praise the likes of Carden, Martel, Pope, Gibb, Stokes and Robotham for their personal and direct contributions to the positive development of British tanks. There are doubtless many other unnamed and unknown heroes to be found within the civil service and the companies that made the tanks and their components, but their efforts have not been well recorded, and they will probably have to remain anonymous. It should also be noted that the British gun and ammunition designers were of the highest quality, and it was not their fault that each of the tank guns that they produced to replace the (in its day world-beating) two-pounder, in the shape of the six-pounder and then the seventeen-pounder, were both introduced into service somewhat later than they might have been, and which would have gone a long way to reducing the quality gap between British and German tanks.[2] And of course, let us not forget all the unwilling heroes: the tank crews condemned by a whole series of bad decisions to go to war in tanks that brought shame upon the nation. All too many of them became victims.

To conclude, let us firstly quote Hancock, such an important primary source in this work, and who, as so often, puts his finger right on the bottom line:

The Ministry of Supply technical departments must share with the General Staff the responsibility for the success or failure of British equipment in the field.[3]

With regard to tanks, the result was mostly failure. The final voice is rightly Churchill's, who was both a champion for tank development and, at times, a positive hindrance. He offers us a comment on the past, but also a warning for the future:

I have no doubt there can be made plenty of explanations for such a failure, but failure it remains none the less. Pray do not let it be thought that you are satisfied with such a result. If you simply take up the attitude of defending it there will be no hope of improvement.[4]

Appendix

A diary of British tank development

1919
- August. Ten-Year rule introduced.

1923
- March. Medium I tank introduced into service.

1925
- Martel works on first one-man tank design.

1926
- Carden-Loyd formed.

1927
- (To 1930) Armour welding experiments at ROF Woolwich.
- September. A6E1 and E2 completed.

1928
- MWEE formed.
- Post of Director of Mechanization created.
- V-A absorb C-L to form Vickers-Carden-Loyd.
- Ten-Year rule becomes permanent (rolling).
- October. A6E3 completed.

1929
- May. Medium III E1 and E2 completed.

1931
- February. Medium III E3 completed.

1932

- 23 March. Ten-Year rule rescinded.
- 7 November. Provisional specification for three-man light tank issued.
- 16 December. Sir John Carden presents initial design for three-man light tank to WO.

1934

- MWEE becomes MEE.
- ROF Woolwich identified a functional armour welding technique.
- May. A10 specified.
- 15 June. A9E1 contract awarded.
- October. First A10 contract awarded.

1935

- October. Carden proposed A11.
- 10 December. Death of Sir John Carden.

1936

- Post of Director General of Munitions Production created.
- A7E3 completed.
- Light Tank Mk VIB entered service.
- 25 January. A11E1 contract awarded.
- April. A9E1 completed.
- September. Martel (with Wavell) attended Red Army tank manoeuvres in USSR. A11E1 delivered to MEE.
- October. Martel unsuccessfully attempted to purchase a Napier Lion engine. Outline proposal for A12.
- November. VF become A12 parent. Work started on A12.

1937

- Light Tank Mk VIC entered service.
- January. A13E2 and E3 contract awarded.
- April. A9E1 refitted with AEC engine.
- 25 May. Two A12 pilots (A12E1 and E2) ordered.
- Late. A13E2 completed.

1938

- Post of MGO abolished.
- Early. A13E3 completed.

- 22 January. First A13 contract awarded.
- 10 February. Valentine design unveiled to WO.
- 24 March. Valentine mock-up completed.
- 29 April. First A11 contract awarded.
- 11 June. First A12 Matilda II contract awarded.
- August. First A11 Matilda completed.

1939

- Early. LMSR becomes A13 Covenanter parent. NMA becomes A15 Crusader parent.
- February. First A9 completed.
- April. First Valentine contract awarded.
- 13 April. A13 Covenanter mock-up completed.
- 17 April. First A13 Covenanter contract awarded (The first Drawing Board order).
- 27 June. First A15 Crusader contract awarded (Drawing Board order).
- August. Ministry of Supply created.
- October. LMSR reject use of welding for A13 Covenanter.

1940

- Final A9 completed.
- 9 April. A15E1 Crusader pilot delivered to MEE.
- May. Valentine pilot to MEE.
- 23 May. First A13 Covenanter pilot to MEE.
- 26 May. General Pope's 'BEF Lessons' letter sent to WO.
- June. First Valentine produced.
- July. Department of Tank Design created. The PM demands 500 A22 Churchill to be in service by Mar 41. Vauxhall appointed as A22 Churchill parent.
- 2 August. Final A11 Matilda completed.
- September. A22 Churchill mock-up completed.
- 9 September. 6 Pounder approved.
- 5 October. First A22 Churchill contracts awarded (Drawing Board order).
- 29 October. Leyland contact Rolls-Royce to discuss poor engine performance on A13 Covenanter (start of Meteor project).
- December. First A22 Churchill pilot completed.

1941

- January. Final A13 completed. A24 Cavalier proposal by NMA accepted.
- 31 January. 3 x A24 Cavalier pilots ordered.
- 30 March. First Meteor delivered, installed in A15 Crusader.
- April. Meteor-engined A15 Crusader trials on Southport sands and Sandbach.
- May. First contract for 6 Pounder guns awarded. Babcock & Wilcox construct welded turret for firing trials. Leyland receives first order for Meteors (1200).
- 20 June. A24 Challenger contract awarded (Drawing Board order).
- July. Leyland renege on Meteor production; Rolls-Royce take over responsibility.
- August. Babcock & Wilcox given contract for 100 welded turrets.
- 15–28 August. Trials of Meteor-powered A15 Crusader at Farnborough.
- September. Development starts on A15 Crusader III.
- November. Development starts on A27L Centaur.

1942

- Fighting Vehicles Proving Establishment (FVPE) founded.
- February. Pilot A27M Cromwell completed by Rolls-Royce, to MEE. First A27 contracts awarded.
- April. Re-work scheme for A13 Covenanter initiated.
- 21 May. Vauxhall agree to start A27M Cromwell production once A22 Churchill programme complete.
- 29 June. First A27L Centaur pilot completed.
- July. Pilot A30 Challenger completed, to MEE.
- 28 August. Cromwell I/II/III renamed as A24 Cavalier, A27L Centaur, and A27M Cromwell.
- August. First tanks fitted with 6 Pounder gun.
- October. MoS order that in future at least six pilots are made and tested before orders placed (End of Drawing Board orders). Rolls-Royce open Meteor instruction school at Willesden.
- End. First production A27L Centaur completed.

1943

- January. BRCW commence A27M Cromwell production.
- 30 January. Last A13 Covenanter completed.
- February. A30 Challenger accepted for limited production. Leyland becomes A34 Comet parents.

- 22 February. GS Policy is to concentrate on one type of cruiser.
- 25 February. First production A24 Cavalier completed.
- 5 March. A30 Challengers ordered (200).
- July. Leyland complete final A27L Centaur and start producing A27M Cromwell. Leyland take over parentage of A27M Cromwell from BRCW.
- 8 September. GS long-term policy on the role of tanks published.
- September. A34 Comet mock-up completed.
- 7 October. Draft specification for A41 Centurion agreed.
- 26 November. DTD confirmed as design lead for A41 Centurion.

1944

- 1 January. Rover take over parentage of Meteor.
- 16 January. EE complete A27M Cromwell production.
- 23 February. Final specification for A41 Centurion agreed.
- February. First mild steel A34 Comet pilot completed.
- March. Leyland complete final A27M Cromwell and start producing A34 Comet.
- April. First A41 Centurion pilot completed and sent to FVPE.
- 20 June. EE complete manufacture of first A27M Cromwell with F Type hull.
- 26 June. First tentative order for 500 A41 Centurion from ROF.
- September. First production A34 Comet completed.
- 18 October. EE complete first A34 Comet.
- December. First Comets issued to troops (Belgium).

1945

- February. Rover start work on Meteor Mk IV for A41 Centurion.
- Late May. Op Sentry: six A41 Centurion prototypes arrive in Germany for trials.
- August. Full Centurion production authorised.

Abbreviations

AA	Anti-Aircraft
ACIGS	Assistant Chief of the Imperial General Staff
ADGB	Air Defence of Great Britain
AFV	Armoured Fighting Vehicle
AP	Armour Piercing
APC	Armour Piercing Capped
APCBC	Armour Piercing Capped Ballistic Cap
APDS	Armour Piercing Discarding Sabot
ARV	Armoured Recovery Vehicle
AVRE	Armoured Vehicle Royal Engineers
A/T	Anti-Tank
BAOR	British Army of the Rhine
BEF	British Expeditionary Force
bhp	Brake Horsepower
BP	Beyer Peacock
BRCW	Birmingham Railway Carriage and Wagon Company
BW	Broom and Wade
CIGS	Chief of the Imperial General Staff
CinC	Commander in Chief
CS	Close Support
CTA	Cemented Tank Armour
DAFV	Director (and Directorate) Armoured Fighting Vehicles (from June 1940)
DCIGS	Deputy Chief of the Imperial General Staff
DD	Duplex Drive
DGMP	Director General of Munitions Production
DGTT	Director General of Tanks and Transport
DSO	Distinguished Service Order
E1 etc	Experimental model
EE	English Electric
ESC	English Steel Company
FVPE	Fighting Vehicles Proving Establishment
GS	General Staff
GRCW	Gloucester Railway Carriage and Wagon Company

I-Tank	Infantry Tank
JF	John Fowler
HE	High Explosive
HMSO	His Majesty's Stationery Office
H&W	Harland and Wolff
LMSR	London Midland and Scottish Railway
MAP	Ministry of Aircraft Production
MC	Metropolitan-Cammell
MEE	Mechanization Experimental Establishment
MG	Machine Gun
MGO	Master General of the Ordnance
MIE	Morris Industries Exports
Mk	Mark
MMG	Medium Machine Gun
MoS	Ministry of Supply
MWEE	Mechanical Warfare Experimental Establishment
NBL	North British Locomotive
NMA	Nuffield Mechanization & Aero
OP	Observation Post
Pdr	Pounder
PSOC	Principal Supply Officer's Committee
RA	Royal Artillery
RAC	Royal Armoured Corps
RAE	Royal Aeronautical Establishment
RAOC	Royal Army Ordnance Corps
RB	Ruston-Bucyrus
RH	Ruston-Hornsby
RHA	Rolled Homogenous Armour
ROF	Royal Ordnance Factory
R-R	Rolls-Royce
RTC	Royal Tank Corps
RTR	Royal Tank Regiment
SCC	Standard Camouflage Colour
SCNE	Select Committee on National Expenditure
SPG	Self-Propelled Gun
TC	Tank Corps
V-A	Vickers-Armstrongs
VCL	Vickers Carden Loyd
VF	Vulcan Foundry
WG	West's Gas
WO	War Office

Notes

Introduction

1. W.K. Hancock, (Ed) *The Design & Development of Weapons (1964)* p.368 *and David Fletcher, The Universal Tank* (1993) p.111.

Chapter 1

1. Maj Gen N. Duncan in Duncan Crow, *British Armoured Fighting Vehicles 1919/1940* (1970) p.1.
2. The weight method was still being used in documents written in autumn 1943 as a general indicator of a new project's likely size.
3. Kenneth Macksey, *The Tank Pioneers* (1981) pp.97-98.
4. *Ibid.* p.103.
5. *Ibid.* p.97.
6. The intention to build a better armoured version as a land 'battlecruiser' with 30mm of armour was rendered unnecessary in 1939 when it was realised that all cruisers needed at least this level of protection. See David Fletcher, *The Great Tank Scandal* (1989) p.6.
7. The suffix E (for Experimental) followed by a number indicated each distinct trials version, e.g. A6E3.
8. Churchill had become completely exasperated by the confusion caused by the unwieldy official system, even noting that some documents had confused the reader as to whether the 'Mk III' tank being referred to was British, German, or American! In the face of much bureaucratic intransigence, he eventually got his way.
9. That tanks should carry a gun was a Royal Artillery, not a Tank Corps, decision; it was confirmed in March 1922. See David Fletcher, *Mechanised Force* (1991) p.7.
10. Macksey, *Pioneers* p.65.
11. *Ibid.* p.75.
12. Peter Chamberlain & Chris Ellis *Tanks of the World 1915-45* (1972) pp.36-80.
13. A.J. Smithers, *A New Excalibur* (1986) p.238.
14. Hancock, *Design* p.310.
15. *Ibid.* p.305.
16. *Ibid.* p.343.
17. David Fletcher, *Matilda Infantry Tank* (2003) p.6.
18. Hancock, *Design* p.343.
19. A.R. Smart, 'The Churchill Tank – Its Development and Manufacture.' *Journal of the JIE* (October 1946) p.1.
20. Macksey, *Pioneers.* p.106.

21. Roman Jarymowycz, *Tank Tactics* (2001) p.43.
22. In this book manpower refers to the entire workforce and acknowledges the increasing role that women played in the overall industrial effort.
23. A.J. Smithers, *Rude Mechanicals* (1987) p.37.
24. The War Office did discuss the possibility of relaxation of the gauge by adopting the continental version, which would have allowed a width increase of about ten inches, but this was turned down as there was not, at that time, any official continental commitment for the army.
25. The desire to keep the overall weight down also played into the formula, again prompting designers to make the tanks as small as possible, and therefore smaller than purely military logic would have dictated.

Chapter 2

1. The designation Medium replaced the proposed name of Vickers Light Tank Mk I around 1923.
2. ROF
3. Sometimes spelt mechanisation; the two spellings were interchangeable.
4. The small design section at Woolwich was formed in 1931. See G.M. Ross, *The Business of Tanks* (1976) p.83.
5. Postan noted that they were not equal partners: 'The Mechanization Board never had the resources, the experience or the status of the Ordnance Board.' Hancock *Design* p.366. This comment was echoed by J.D. Scott: 'The Director of Mechanization was and remained the junior partner.' J.D. Scott & Richard Hughes, *Administration of War Production* (1955) p.20.
6. Hancock *Design* p.243.
7. Scott & Hughes, *Administration* p.21.
8. Ross, *Business* p.157.
9. *Ibid.* p.161.
10. Hancock, *Design* p.305.
11. The company was the result of a merger in 1927 of Vickers with Armstrongs-Whitworth
12. Macksey, *Pioneers* p.90.
13. Christopher Foss & Peter McKenzie, *Vickers Tanks* (1995) p.37.
14. Smithers, *Mechanicals* p.32.
15. A staggering cost of £150,000 per tank had been forecast – around 0.4% of the whole 1930 army estimates! General Duncan reckoned that the total cost of the project was £77,400. See Crow, *AFV* p.24.
16. Smithers, *Mechanicals.* p.27.
17. A.J. Smithers *A New Excalibur* (1986) p.242.
18. *Ibid.* p.255.
19. Smithers, *Mechanicals* p.33. Macksey, *Pioneers* p.103.
20. *Ibid.* The rough calculation of £1,000 per ton was a remarkably accurate yardstick.
21. Foss & McKenzie, *Vickers.* p.59. Carden was primarily a designer of light vehicles. His prowess with larger types was unproven, although his *Valentine* design showed promise.

22. Smithers, *Mechanicals*. p.35.
23. This means 'delete Britain insert Vickers'; at the official level there was little to brag about.
24. Ironically the undelivered final six of a Finnish order ended up being used by the British army in 1939 as training machines! Smithers, *Excalibur* p.240.
25. CAB 102/851 *Design and Production of British Tanks 1935-1943*
26. The award of Cruiser tank contracts to Nuffield Mechanizations and Aero Ltd followed an unusual pattern, in that the company was a specialist division of Nuffield's created to build cruiser tanks. As the Christie suspension was widely believed to be the best option for future cruiser tank chassis, the company was created in order to acquire the licence to manufacture tanks based on that suspension. However, the Christie suspension proved to be troublesome in practice, and significant effort had to be expended on making it suitable for use on a battle tank. Partly as a result, the A13, the Covenanter, the Crusader and even the early Cromwells were all very unreliable. Furthermore, the company suffered from the malaise that affected the other newcomers, a lack of knowledgeable designers and inexperience in construction.
27. CAB 16/148 *War Office Production*
28. *Ibid.*
29. Macksey, *Pioneers*. pp.46-47.
30. That much of the army was reactionary is not at issue. It may surprise the reader to discover that the lance was not formally abolished as a weapon of war until 1927. (Hancock, *Design* p.264).
31. Hancock, *Design* p.240 & p.257.
32. *Ibid.*
33. Macksey, *Pioneers*. p.81
34. *Ibid.* p.139.
35. Smithers, *Mechanicals* pp.33-39.
36. Macksey, *Pioneers*. pp.104-105.
37. Army Doctrine Publication 'Land Operations' Introduction.
38. Richard Ogorkiewicz, *Design & Development of Fighting Vehicles* (1967) p.31.
39. Smithers, *Mechanicals* p.40.
40. *Ibid.* p.42.
41. Michael Carver, *Dilemmas of the Desert War* (1986) p.13.

Chapter 3

1. N.H. Gibbs, *Rearmament Policy (1976)* p.57.
2. *Ibid.* p.80.
3. Tuvia Ben-Moshe, *Churchill: Strategy & History* (1992) p.87.
4. Hancock, *Design* p.240 & p.256.
5. Christopher Price, *The Cost of Failure (2001)* p.187.
6. Robert Shay, *British Rearmament in the Thirties (1977)* p.194.
7. Gibbs, *Rearmament* pp.308-309.
8. Shay, *Rearmament* p.190.
9. Richard Croucher, *Engineers at War 1939–1945* (1982) p.6.
10. Shay, *Rearmament* p.162.

11. Price, *Failure*. p.154.
12. George Peden, *British Rearmament and the Treasury* (1979) p.102.
13. Hancock, *Design* p.308.
14. CAB 102/851
15. Fletcher, *Scandal* p.4.
16. Fletcher, *Scandal* p.4.
17. Price, *Treasury*. p.165.
18. Costs were to drop below this figure during the conflict.
19. Hancock, *Design* p.304.
20. William Ashworth, *Contracts and Finance* (1953) p.123.
21. http://www.crossley-motors.org.uk/history
22. http://www.localhistory.scit.wlv.ac.uk/Museum/Transport/Cars/Sunbeam/
    Speed.htm
23. Scott & Hughes, *Administration* p.281.
24. Smithers, *Mechanicals* p.37.
25. Hancock, *Design* p.241.
26. Gibbs, *Rearmament* p.447. Chamberlain often used letters to his sisters to
    explain his motivations.
27. Aircraft production used an enormous amount of resources that otherwise
    might have been employed building tanks. Aircraft production (calculated by
    number of aircraft x weight) increased by a factor of over 21 between 1938 and
    1944. Mark Harrison (Ed), *The Economics of World War II* (1998) p.58.
28. Shay, *Rearmament* p.218.
29. Gibbs, *Rearmament* p.261.
30. *Ibid.* p.458.
31. *Ibid.* p.469.
32. *Ibid.* p.467-469.
33. *Ibid.* p.467-473.
34. *Ibid.* p.467.
35. *Ibid.* p.308.
36. *Ibid.* p.478.
37. Shay *Rearmament* p.200.
38. Hancock, *Design* p.285.
39. Gibbs, *Rearmament* p.481.
40. *Ibid.* p.491-492.
41. Hancock, *Design* p.260.
42. *British War Production 1939–1945: A Record* (1945) p.103.
43. Macksey, *Pioneers* p.140.
44. Hancock, *Design* p.349.
45. WO185/119 *Fighting Vehicles: Development and Production*
46. Fletcher, *Scandal* p.88.
47. Luyks was apparently easy to work with, Nuffield being the difficult one.
    Ross, *Business* p.149.
48. Fletcher, *Universal* p.36.
49. Fletcher, *Scandal* p.5.
50. Michael Dintenfass *The Decline of Industrial Britain* (1992) p.22.

51. Dintenfass *Decline* pp.28-29.
52. Smithers, *Excalibur* p.241.
53. Hancock, *Design* p.363.
54. Croucher *Engineers* pp.7-8.
55. Ross, *Business* p.71.
56. *Ibid.* pp.258-259.
57. Smart, *Churchill* pp.8-12.
58. Terence Cuneo's oil painting 'Churchill Tank' (1941) shows a workman bolting armoured plates on a tank's hull. The scene which was painted at the Vauxhall works in Luton is not one depicting mass production, but rather looks like a back-street workshop, with tank components lying around in a very random and disorganised way.
59. In 1938 these were among the smaller car companies, 92% of the market being serviced by Morris, Austin, Ford, Vauxhall, Rootes and Standard. See Croucher, *Engineers* p.6.
60. Dintenfass, *Decline* p.14.
61. H.M.D. Parker, *Manpower* (1957) p.103.
62. P. Inman, *Labour in the Munitions Industries* (1957) p.198.
63. Croucher *Engineers.* p.76.
64. Hancock, *Design.* p.169.
65. Hancock, *Design.* p.239.
66. *Ibid.*
67. Fletcher, *Universal* p.118.
68. Scott & Hughes, *Administration* p.282.
69. Ross, *Business* p.157.
70. Hancock, *Design* pp.318-319.
71. *Ibid.* p.242.
72. Mechanization Experimental Establishment
73. CAB 21/1544 *Production Council and Production Executive: Priority for Tank Production*
74. *Hancock,* Design<I> p.317.
75. *Ibid.* p.41.
76. Ross *Business* p.106.
77. Clive Law, *Making Tracks* (2001) p.10.
78. Hancock, *Design.* p.37.
79. *Ibid.* p.44.
80. Fletcher, *Scandal* p.5.
81. Hancock, *Design* p.244.
82. David Birch (Ed), *Rolls Royce Meteor* p.11.
83. Hancock, *Design* p.238.
84. The creation of the MoS had been delayed until the last moment; letting it loose on the very eve of war was not guaranteed to make its task any easier, and it struggled to cope with the demands placed on it. It was forced to reorganise many times during the war in efforts to improve efficiency, and this particularly applied to the area of tank production, which constantly changed masters and titles.

85. *Ibid.* pp.243 & 308.
86. *Ibid.* p.243.
87. *Ibid.* p.356.
88. Later the RAC Gunnery Wing/School.
89. Fletcher, *Scandal* p.4.
90. Birch, *Meteor* p.11.
91. Ashworth, *Contracts* pp.123-124.
92. *Ibid.* p.1.
93. *Ibid.* p.125.
94. A contract card for A9 purchase in 1939 gives the price as £11,280 per machine; the higher figure may represent the all-up cost including ancillaries. Bovington Tank Museum Contract Card T.4571.
95. Ashworth *Contracts* p.157.
96. *Ibid.* p.124.
97. Bovington Tank Museum Census Cards and Registers.
98. Price, *Failure* pp. 215-216.
99. H. Duncan Hall, *North American Supply* (1955) p.9.
100. *Ibid.* p.221.
101. *Ibid.* p.423. See also Fletcher, *Universal* p.77.
102. Gibbs, *Rearmament*. p.525.
103. Ogorkiewicz, *Development* p.38.
104. The Mediums employed flat armour plates bolted and rivetted onto a metal frame, so in theory at least replacing plates could be done quite easily.
105. CAB 21/1160 *Production of Tanks 1936–1940*
106. Interestingly, the only home-designed tank ever produced by Australia, the AC1 Sentinel, featured large and complex cast components, including the turret and much of the hull.
107. Fletcher *Matilda* p.7.
108. Fletcher, *Scandal* p.5. There is a suggestion that this plate was being ordered pre-cut to size and shape, which would seem a terrible breach of security.
109. Hancock, *Design* p.307.
110. Macksey, *Tank Force* (1970) p.113.
111. *War Production* p.65.
112. Macksey, *Pioneers* p.107.
113. Of course, the USA adapted aeroplane engines successfully for use in tanks, including the Wright Cyclone and Guiberson T1020 radial engines.
114. Even the air cleaners were not adequate for the fine dust of the desert and caused many avoidable breakdowns.
115. David Fletcher, *Crusader & Covenanter Cruiser Tanks* (2005) pp.4-11.
116. Hancock, *Design* p.242.
117. *Ibid.* pp.3-4.
118. Fletcher, *Scandal* p.18.
119. Thomas L. Jentz and Hilary L. Doyle, *Germany's Panzers in World War II* (2001) p.6.
120. Panzer Kampf Wagen, or Armoured Battle Vehicle.
121. Ogorkiewicz, *Development* p.35.

122. Terry Copp (Ed), *Montgomery's Scientists* (2000) p.396.
123. Peter Chamberlain, *Encyclopedia of German Tanks of WWII* (1978) pp.58-69 & 88-99.
124. *Ibid.* p.83.
125. *Ibid.* p.162.
126. Macksey, *Pioneers.* p.142.
127. Fletcher, *Scandal* p.32.
128. Ogorkiewicz, *Development.* p.35.
129. Hancock, *Design* p.2.
130. *Ibid.* pp.36-37.
131. *Ibid.* pp.32-34.
132. Ross, *Business* p.159.
133. Hancock, *Design.* p.37.
134. *Ibid.* p.10.
135. *Ibid.* p.11.

Chapter 4

1. Plus one Depot Bn and a Workshop Bn.
2. The original estimate for the Medium Type D had been an eye-watering £4,500 per tank, but in mid-1919 a new estimate nearly trebled it, to £12,250 each. There was no way that this would be sanctioned, particularly as seventy-five were required, totalling nearly £1 million.
3. Probably to assist V-A by demonstrating the techniques and procedures for building tanks – by hand of course, not as a production line.
4. The ratio was usually ⅔ smoke to ⅓ HE.
5. This conjecture is supported by the fact that the first two were built at ROF Woolwich, with the third made by V-A, which was undoubtedly hoping that it would be the first of many dozens of the type.
6. Fletcher, *Mechanised Force*, p.19.
7. An A8 was specified and a mock-up made but was not proceeded with.
8. Subsequently the Royal Artillery was to stop using tracked tractors, as it was found that they could move across country much faster than the guns and limbers they towed and tended to damage them, and they were both mechanically complicated and expensive. A series of simpler unarmoured 4 x 4 wheeled tractors called Quads were used instead.
9. These were the only tanks that Thornycroft of Basingstoke built, probably only fourteen in total, although the company produced many thousands of carriers during the Second World War.
10. Subsequently becoming known as Matilda I when the A12, Matilda II, was developed.
11. The same design was later used successfully on the heavier and slower Valentine.
12. It is unclear just how reliable the tank was in service, as many tanks abandoned out of combat were as the result of either shed tracks or through running out of fuel. As the design was clearly obsolete by 1940, not much effort seems to have been put into investigating its automotive performance in action.

13. Crisp's three tanks were named COOL, Calm and collected. His memory is possibly playing him false here, as he refers to the commander being the troop sergeant, which would make the tank CALM – see photograph.
14. Fletcher *Mechanised Force* p.119.
15. While Christie's tank cost the War Office over £10,000 pounds, one Lion engine could have been acquired for trial purposes at the paltry sum of £500 – and which would have remained in Britain. Such parsimony beggars belief.

Chapter 5
1. Hancock, *Design* p.242.
2. Egbert Kieser, *Sea Lion* (1997) p.20.
3. Hancock, *Design* p.241.
4. Ronald Lewin, *Man of Armour* (1976) p.119.
5. Other sources reckons less than this: Fletcher gives figures as six light tanks and seven cruisers: *Scandal* p.34. Ross believed only 704 tanks went to France, with 25 returning: *Business* p.40.
6. Peter Fleming, *Operation Sea Lion* (1975) p.93.
7. Winston Churchill, *Their Finest Hour* (1949) p.146.
8. Inman *Labour* pp.294-296.
9. Patrick Delaforce, *Churchill's Secret Weapons* (1998) p.27.
10. Macksey, *Pioneers* p.170.
11. *Ibid.* p.162.
12. Lewin, *Armour* p.124.
13. Fletcher, *Scandal* p.32.
14. Basil Collier, *The Defence of the United Kingdom* (1957) p.124.
15. Ben-Moshe, *Churchill* p.117.
16. PREM 3/426/16 *Tanks: Production*; CAB 120/356 *Tanks: Periodical Returns of Production Figures*
17. *Churchill* Finest Hour<I> p.147.
18. Macksey, *Force* p.59.
19. *Ibid.* p.60.
20. Hancock, *Design* p.241.
21. *Ibid.* p.322.
22. Hancock, *Design* p.321.
23. *Ibid.* p.148.
24. Plant, *Anti-tank.* p.206.
25. Fletcher, *Scandal* p.57.
26. Hancock, *Design.* p.357. My emphasis.
27. An interested outsider might have noticed that the specifications for infantry tanks and cruisers were even then drawing ever closer.
28. Macksey, *Force* pp.57-59.
29. Hancock, *Design* p.335.
30. *Ibid.* p.264.
31. Smithers, *Mechanicals* p.74.
32. Crow *British AFV* p.51.
33. Parker, *Manpower* pp.97-98.

34. They were previously Priority 1B; this increase in priority was first suggested in July and rejected in August 1940 because of concerns over the competition for drop forgings and alloy steel: PREM 3/426/8

35. These included armour plates and drop forgings for engines.

36. PREM3/426/9

37. PREM 3/425/3 *Tanks: Periodical Returns August 1940–March 1945*

38. Hancock, *Design* p.25.

39. Hancock, *Design* p.335.

40. PREM 3/426/8

41. August was in production terms a five-week month, hence the higher figures.

42. PREM 3/426/8

43. CAB 120/356

44. Figures often refer to Z+, where September 1939 was Z. Thus Z+5 was January 1940.

45. Excludes Canadian production figures.

46. Smithers, *Mechanicals* p.40.

47. CAB 21/1161

48. Macksey, *Force* pp.88-89.

49. PREM 3/426/8

50. *Ibid.*

51. *Ibid.*

52. CAB 120/357 *Tanks: Production and Allocation*

53. Inman, *Labour* p.163.

54. PREM 3/425

55. CAB 21/1161

56. PREM 3/426/15

57. *Ibid.*

58. *Ibid.*

59. PREM 3/425

60. PREM 3/425

61. PREM 3/426/16

62. PREM 3/425

63. Hancock, *Design* p.152.

64. W.K. Hancock (Ed), *Statistical Digest of the War* (1951) Table 189.

65. *Ibid.* Table 188.

66. Hancock, *Design* p.151.

67. Inman, *Labour* pp.420-421.

68. Fletcher, *Scandal* p.77.

Chapter 6

1. Each company involved in the Covenanter programme built one mild steel pilot – this was laudable and while it may have assisted in setting up the production facilities, it did not help the development of the tank as they were not tested before production began.

2. The replacement of the original aluminium wheels with pressed steel versions, due to MAP claiming almost total priority over the scarce metal, added

another 170lb – in itself quite insignificant, but all such modifications added up to more weight overall.

3. 2in wider tracks were later added, but even these caused problems, as the switch from welded to rivetted and bolted construction meant that many hex screw heads on the hull sides had to be countersunk to prevent the track contacting them; this would have been avoided with a welded hull.

4. Nonetheless, the tank would grow even heavier over time.

5. Fletcher, *Scandal* p.67.

6. Birch (Ed), *Meteor*, p.41

7. Morris Industries Exports.

8. Fletcher, *Churchill's Tank*, p.12

9. On 9 November 1943 GRCW were awarded a contract to build ninety-five welded hulls; unfortunately, it is not clear if this was the first such contract.

10. When many Churchills were captured following the Dieppe raid of August 1942, the German assessed that the Churchills, which they had not encountered before, must be obsolete types that the British could afford to throw away in the raid.

11. Reliability was terrible; in mid-January 1942 no fewer than 42% of all Churchills were 'off the road.' Fletcher, *Churchill's Tank*, p.56.

12. The records at the Bovington Tank Museum archive have details of four companies involved in converting tank hulls to bridge-layers. These are: Ruston Bucyrus (49), Robert Boby of Bury St Edmunds (30), Wellman Smith Owen of Darlaston (34), and F.C. Hibberd of London (35), giving a total of 148, although this may not be the complete number.

13. Whenever Vauxhall was asked to design a new tank, it simply produced a scaled-up or scaled-down version of the Churchill, which must have been immensely frustrating for DTD!

1. The phrase is unfortunately not mine. It was first used by Hancock, *Design* p.363.

Chapter 7

2. Tank Board Notes, Bovington Tank Museum.

3. Hancock, *Design* p.337.

4. The initials were R.B., so it was probably Major General Raymond Briggs, commander of 1st Armoured Division.

5. Hancock, *Design* p.363.

6. Fletcher, *Scandal* p.31.

7. RAC Half-Yearly Report No.6

8. CAB 120/357

9. Hancock, *Design*. p.337.

10. PREM 3/426/15

11. Hancock, *Design*. p.325.

12. Tank Board Notes.

13. Hancock, *Design* p.325.

14. *Ibid.*

15. CAB 120/356

16. Hancock, *Design* p.362.
17. This figure did not include those unfit due to deficiencies in equipment, nor those awaiting short-term repairs.
18. PREM 3/426/16
19. PREM 3/426/3
20. PREM3/426/4
21. PREM3/426/4
22. *Ibid.*
23. PREM 3/426/12. Margesson was replaced three days after this letter was written.
24. PREM 3/426/15
25. *British Tank History 1938–1943* Tank Board Notes.
26. Hancock, *Design* pp.244-245.
27. *Ibid.* p.245.
28. Tank Board Notes.
29. There are many references in this period to confirm the desire to stop Churchill production as it was initially seen as a complete failure. Luckily, it was made reliable and proved to be a successful tank, well-armoured with a legendary cross-country mobility, and was able to be adapted to fulfil specialist roles.
30. CAB 21/935 *The Memorandum on Tank Production by the Select Committee on National Expenditure 'Weapons for the Army'.*
31. The increased emphasis on Cruiser production over 'I' Tanks led to a requirement for 3,700 Cruisers in 1942-43: Fletcher *Universal* p.36.
32. Hancock, *Design* p.323.
33. *Ibid.*
34. *Ibid.* p.322.
35. *Ibid.* p.325.
36. *Ibid.* p.351.
37. Fighting Vehicle Proving Establishment, formed in 1942 at Farnborough.
38. *Ibid.* p.335.
39. *Ibid.* p.246.
40. These figures reflect actual output to 31 October 1942, and the estimated output for the two remaining months.
41. This figure appears to include Canadian production.
42. PREM 3/426/16
43. PREM 3/425
44. Tank Board Notes.
45. Fletcher, *Universal* p.70.
46. CAB 21/935
47. Hancock, *Design.* p.307.
48. *Ibid.* p.345.
49. The B&W design became the turret for the six-pounder-armed Mk III.
50. http://www.royaltankregiment.com/9th_RTR/tech/welded%20churchill/
51. Birch, *Meteor.*
52. Fletcher, *Universal* p.83.
53. Richard Overy, *Why the Allies Won* (1995) pp.217-218.

54. Jarymowycz, *Tactics* p.268. Page 282 includes a table assessing the causes of German tank losses in a more scientific manner, indicating a similar 43% rate for mechanical failure.
55. *Ibid.* p.276.
56. Hancock, *Design* p.369.
57. Over the course of the war during air attacks on the UK the Germans managed to drop about 45,000 tons of bombs, whereas the Allied air forces dropped around 1.6 million tons of bombs on Germany, thirty-six times more. Deaths were around 300,000 (German) and 60,000 (British).
58. Armour Piercing Cap, Ballistic Cap
59. During tests the British found typical FH armour to have a Brinell hardness of 430 on the surface, 570 just under the surface, but only 335 at a depth of 6mm. If the face could be penetrated using ammunition specially designed for the job (e.g. APCBC), penetrating the remaining depth of weaker armour would be much easier.
60. Appendix E to *War Office Technical Summary 129* dated 15 May 1944.
61. On the Panzer III, even the hull machine-gunner was provided with a x1.8 sight.
62. Hancock, *Design* pp.51-52.
63. *Ibid.* p.63.
64. *Ibid.* p.15.
65. *Ibid.* p.2. Teething was a recognised term; Ross considered that teething a new tank pre-war normally took three years for a Light, and five for a Medium: Ross *Business* p.113.

Chapter 8

1. The team at Clan Foundry even found that there was a nearby scrap merchant who was buying Category E (write-off) Merlin engines from the MAP, but which contained many parts suitable for salvage and reuse on Meteors. Birch (Ed), *Meteor*, p.47.
2. Birch (Ed), *Meteor*, p.52.
3. Fletcher, *Cromwell*, p.10.
4. It is worth re-emphasising the name changes for the three tanks: originally known as Cromwell I, II and III, on 28 August 1942 the A24 Cromwell I became the A24 Cavalier, the A27 Cromwell II became the A27L Centaur, and the A27 Cromwell III became the A27M Cromwell.
5. Fletcher, *Cromwell*, p.12.
6. The first Centaurs and Cromwells started to replace the useless Covenanters in 9th Armoured Division in April 1943. Ibid., p.20.
7. Birch (Ed), *Meteor*, p.63.
8. *Ibid.*, p.69.
9. *Ibid.*, p.74.
10. There is a suggestion that the Challenger was going to be named Centurion, but this famous name was used on the A41 project instead.
11. Hull development included better arrangements being made for the two hull crew men to be able to escape if the gun was positioned over their hatches,

which must have saved many lives. One cannot help but think that such a proposal offered in 1941 would have been discarded on the basis of slowing down production.

12. And even this was made more complex: originally such a conversion was called Cromwell X.

13. For example, there is no photographic or documentary evidence of Contract T11243 for 2350 Centaurs being fulfilled by NMA. Given Nuffield's opposition to building other designs, this would make sense.

14. Birch (Ed), *Meteor*, p.82.

15. This was not beyond the wit of man to solve – both the T34 and the *Panther* were able to combine these features.

16. Birch (Ed), *Meteor*, p.104.

17. WO185/119

18. It seems that unlike previous practice, they were referred to as such and not as pilots. The terms seem to have been used interchangeably, but strictly speaking, prototypes should come first, and then be developed into pilots.

19. Simon Dunstan, *Centurion* (1980) pp.10-11.

20. The timescale fits nicely with the received wisdom at the time that to field a new tank should take at least two years from specification to production, and anything shorter would lead to mistakes.

Chapter 9

1. CAB 21/935

2. By late 1945, they had received more than that from the USA: 25,600. Ross, *Business* p.153.

3. *Ibid.* p.257.

4. Fletcher, *Universal* p.70.

5. *Ibid.* p.70.

6. *Ibid.*

7. *English Electric War Diary* pp.43-46.

8. *Ibid.* p.65.

9. *Ibid.* p.132.

10. *Ibid.* p.158.

11. *Ibid.* p.211.

12. *Ibid.* p.214.

13. Fletcher, *Force* p.9.

14. CAB 21/1161 *Production of Tanks 1941–1945*

15. Fletcher, *Scandal* p.66.

16. RAC Half-Yearly Report No.6. My emphasis.

17. The term Main Battle Tank or MBT is a NATO term that was not used until the mid to late 1950s, and which in any case referred to tanks used in the main defensive battle, rather than in the covering force. See David Lister's *The Dark Age of Tanks* for more details of British development work in the area post-war.

18. Macksey, *Force* p.129.

19. Beale, *Design* p.72.

20. Fletcher, *Universal* p.100.

21. *Ibid.* p.102.
22. Dunstan, *Centurion* p.8.
23. From 1945 the production of tanks was once again accepted to be the business of the public sector, not the private.
24. Hancock, *Design* p.352.
25. Harrison, *Economics* p.15 Table 1.6.
26. Hall, *Supply* p.426.
27. There were eight main marks, but different combinations of turret and hulls led to other mark designations being used.
28. The ten A10s built by R.W. Crabtree of Huddersfield appear to be the only tanks built by that firm; presumably the experiment was not successful.

Conclusion
1. Smithers, *Mechanicals* p.220.
2. The six-pounder could have started mass production in late 1940, and the seventeen-pounder could have been ready to mount onto a tank – if a suitable one was available – in 1942.
3. Hancock, *Design* p.367.
4. PREM 3/428/4.

Bibliography

Primary sources – National Archive War Office files

WO 106/4360 21 Army Group: Armoured fighting vehicles technical report by Lt Col G.C. Reeves, June 1944

WO 185/119 Fighting vehicles: development and production, 1943–44

WO 185/158 Reorganization of tank supply department: new fighting vehicle supply department, 1942

WO 185/160 Vehicle repair scheme, 1940–1952

WO 185/186 Armoured fighting vehicles and their guns: enquiry by committee on national expenditure, 1943–1944

WO 185/7 Armoured fighting vehicles: minutes of meetings of liaison committee, 1942–1944

WO 188/1146 Vehicles and tanks, 1941–1949

WO 190/783 Note on German armoured fighting vehicle strengths, etc., 1939

WO 193/944 Armoured fighting vehicles and tanks, December 1940–February 1942

WO 195/5433 Fighting Vehicle Armament Research and Development Committee: A.F.V. sighting systems, 1943

WO 216/23 Shipment of mechanical vehicles, July 1942–June 1943

WO 222/82 Vision devices in armoured fighting vehicles, 1942

WO 232/36 Armoured fighting vehicles: general staff policy and requirements; technical development; design and equipment, January 1942–July 1948

WO 32/10422 Army organisation: Royal Armoured Corps (code 14(r)): directoral equipment for armoured fighting vehicles, 1942–1945

WO 32/10522 General and warlike stores: tanks (code 45(e)): shipment of vehicles from America, 1942– 1944

WO 32/10525 General and warlike stores: tanks (code 45(e)): armoured fighting vehicle gunnery policy, 1943

WO 32/10527 General and warlike stores: vehicles (code 45(f)): vehicle provision and maintenance for the army as a whole, 1942

WO 32/11036 General and warlike stores: vehicles (code 45(f)): armoured fighting vehicles, south east Asia command 11th Army Group, technical staff field force reports, 1944–1945

WO 32/11036 Operations (narratives of): general (code 46(a)): armoured fighting vehicles, south east Asia command, 11th Army Group, field force reports, 1944–1945

WO 32/11039 General and warlike stores: vehicles (code 45(f)): armoured fighting vehicle bulletin GHQ India, 1944

WO 32/11039 Operations (narratives of): general (code 46(a)): armoured fighting vehicle bulletin GHQ India, 1944

Primary sources – National Archive Prime Ministerial files
PREM 3/412/2 Steel: Loss of production due to air raids, September 1940
PREM 3/412/3 Steel: drop forgings, December 1940–January 1941
PREM 3/424 Tanks: availability of, and requirements armoured formations, October 1941–November 1941
PREM 3/425 Tanks: Periodical returns, August 1940–March 1945
PREM 3/426 Tanks: Production, 1940–1942
PREM 3/427 Tanks: Production, 1943–1945
PREM 3/428 Anti-Tank Weapons, March–April 1942
PREM 3/284 Middle East: Armoured and other reinforcements, 1941–1945

Primary sources – National Archive Cabinet files
CAB 16/148 War Office Production
CAB 21/935 The memorandum on Tank Production by the Select Committee on National Expenditure 'Weapons For The Army', 1946
CAB 21/1160 Production of tanks, 1936–1940
CAB 21/1161 Production of tanks, 1941–1945
CAB 21/1544 Production Council and Production Executive: priority for tank production, 1940–1941
CAB 102/851 Design and production of British tanks 1935–1943, 1943
CAB 120/56 Enquiry by Lord Privy Seal, Sir Stafford Cripps, into the condition of Valentine tanks on arrival in the Middle East, July–September 1942
CAB 120/356 Tanks: periodical returns of production figures, January 1944–April 1945
CAB 120/357 Tanks: production and allocation, June 1940–December 1944

Primary sources – National Archive Air Ministry files
AVIA 22/469 Armoured fighting vehicles: monthly returns of deliveries, 1939–1941

Primary sources – Bovington Tank Museum
RAC Half-Yearly Reports
RAC Journal articles
• Vol I No2 Problems of Tank Production plus Editorial
• Vol III No1 Where Tanks Are Tested
• Vol VII No1 Tank Policy 1939-45

Tank Board Notes
Bovington Tank Museum Vehicle Census Contract Cards and Registers

Secondary sources - Published
War Office Technical Summary 129, 1944
War Office, British War Production 1939–1945: A Record, 1945, The *Times*
War Diary of the English Electric Company Ltd, 1946

German Tank Industry Report (Second Edition), 1947, United States Strategic
    Bombing Survey, Bellona Prints No.73 Infantry Tank A22 Churchill, 1969,
    Bellona
Bellona Prints No.79, 80 Cruiser Tank A13, 1970, Bellona
The Cromwell Tank, 1983, HMSO
The Churchill Tank, 1983, HMSO
British Military Doctrine: Land Operations, 2006, MoD

Anon, *Cromwell Tank*, 1983, HMSO
Barnett, Correlli, *The Audit of War*, 1986, MacMillan
Beale, Peter, *Death By Design: British Tank Development in the Second World War*,
    1998, Sutton
Ben-Moshe, Tuvia, *Churchill: Strategy & History*, 1992, Lynne Rienner
Birch, David (Ed), *The Rolls Royce Meteor*, 2004, Rolls Royce Heritage Trust
Briggs, Asa, <I>Go To It! Working for Victory on the Home Front 1939–1945,
    2000, Mitchell Beazley,
Broadberry Stephen & Howlett, Peter, *Blood, Sweat, and Tears: British Mobilisation
    for World War II*, 2002, unpublished draft
Brown, Peter *A13*, 2015, Model Centrum
Buckley, John, *British Armour in the Normandy Campaign 1944*, 2004, Cass
Cameron, L.R., *Report No.38: Tank Production in Canada*, 1950, unpublished
Cantwell, John D., *The Second World War: A Guide to Documents in the PRO*, 1992,
    HMSO
Carver, Michael, *Dilemmas of the Desert War*, 1986, Batsford/IWM
Chamberlain, Peter, *Encyclopedia of German Tanks of World War Two*, 1978, Arms
    & Armour Press
Chamberlain, Peter & Ellis, Chris *The Churchill Tank, 1971*, Arms & Armour Press
Chamberlain, Peter & Ellis, Chris *British & American Tanks of World War Two*,
    1972, Cassell
Chamberlain, Peter & Ellis, Chris *Tanks of the World 1915–1945*, 1969 Arms &
    Armour Press
Church, R, *The Rise and Decline of the British Motor Industry* 1995, Cambridge
    University Press
Churchill, Winston, *The Second World War Volume II: Their Finest Hour* 1949,
    Cassell
Copp, Terry (Ed), *Montgomery's Scientists: Operational Research in North-West Europe*
    2000, Ontario, Laurier University
Crisp, Robert, *Brazen Chariots* 2005, Norton
Croucher, Richard, *Engineers at War 1939–1945* 1982, Merlin,
Crow, Duncan (Ed), *British Armoured Fighting Vehicles 1919/1940* 1970, Profile
Crow, Duncan (Ed), *Armoured Fighting Vehicles of the World Vol 3* 1971, Profile
Delaforce, Patrick, *Churchill's Secret Weapons* 1998, Robert Hale
Dewey, Peter, *War and Progress: Britain 1914–1945* 1997, Longman
Dintenfass, Michael, *The Decline of Industrial Britain* 1992, Routledge
Donnelly, Mark, *Britain in the Second World War* 1999, Routledge
Dunstan, Simon, *Centurion* 1980, Ian Allan

Dunstan, Simon, *Centurion* 2017, Haynes

Edgerton, David, *Warfare State: Britain 1920–1970* 2006, Cambridge University Press

Fleming, Peter, *Operation Sealion* 1975, Pan

Fletcher, David, *The Great Tank Scandal: British Armour in the Second World War Part 1* 1989, HMSO

Fletcher, David, *The Universal Tank: British Armour in the Second World War Part 2* 1993, HMSO

Fletcher, David, *Mechanised Force: British Tanks Between the Wars* 1991, HMSO

Fletcher, David, *Mr Churchill's Tank* 1999, Schiffer

Fletcher, David, *Matilda Infantry Tank 1938–1945* 2003, Osprey/New Vanguard

Fletcher, David, *Crusader and Covenanter Tanks 1939–1945* 2005, Osprey/New Vanguard

Fletcher, David, *Cromwell Cruiser Tank 1942–1950* 2006, Osprey/New Vanguard

Fletcher, David, *Sherman Firefly*, 2008, Osprey/New Vanguard

Fletcher, David, *British Light Tanks 1927–45* 2014, Osprey/New Vanguard

Foss, Christopher F. & McKenzie, Peter, *The Vickers Tanks* 1995, Keepdate

Fraser, W. Hamish, *The History of British Trade Unionism 1700–1988* 1999, Palgrave

French, David, *Raising Churchill's Army* 2000, OUP

Gander, Terry, *Anti-Tank Weapons* 2000, Crowood

Gardiner, Juliet, *Wartime Britain 1939–1945* 2005, Review

Gibbs, N.H., *Grand Strategy. History of the Second World War Volume 1: Rearmament Policy* 1976, HMSO

Gilbert, Martin, *Continue to Pester, Nag and Bite: Churchill's War Leadership* 2004, Pimlico

Hall, H. Duncan, *North American Supply* 1955, HMSO

Halstead, Ivor, *The Truth About our Tanks* 1943, Lindsay Drummond

Hancock (Ed), W.K., *History of the Second World War: UK Civil Series: British War Economy* 1949, HMSO

Hancock (Ed), W.K., *History of the Second World War: UK Civil Series: Statistical Digest of the War* 1951, HMSO

Hancock (Ed), W.K., *History of the Second World War: UK Civil Series: The Control of Raw Materials* 1953, HMSO

Hancock (Ed), W.K., *History of the Second World War: UK Civil Series: Design and Development of Weapons* 1964, HMSO

Harris, J.P., *Men, Ideas and Tanks: British Military Thought and Armoured Forces 1903-1939* 1995, Manchester University Press

Harrison (Ed), Mark, *The Economics of World War II* 1998, Cambridge University Press

Horne, Alistair, *The Lonely Leader: Monty 1944–1945* 1995, Pan

Icks, Robert, *Armour in Profile No.16 Carden Loyd Mk VI* 1967, Profile

Inman, P., *History of the Second World War: UK Civil Series: Labour in the Munitions Industries* 1957, HMSO

Jackson, Robert, *The Nuffield Story* 1964, Frederick Muller

Jarymowycz, Roman J., *Tank Tactics* 2001, Lynne Riener

Jentz, Thomas & Doyle, Hilary, *Germany's Panzers in World War II* 2001, Schiffer

Kieser, Egbert, *Operation Sealion* 1997, Cassell

Knight, P.M. *A13 Covenanter* 2014, Black Prince

Law, Clive M., *Making Tracks: Tank Production in Canada* 2001, Service Publications

Levy, James, *Appeasement and Rearmament: Britain 1936–1939* 2006, Rowman & Littlefield

Lewin, Ronald, *Man of Armour – A Study of Lt Gen Vyvyan Pope* 1976, Leo Cooper

Liddell Hart, Basil, *Europe in Arms* 1937, Faber & Faber

Liddell Hart, Basil, *The Tanks Volume 1* 1959, Cassell

Lister, David, *The Dark Age of Tanks* 2020, Pen & Sword

Mackay, Robert, *Test of War: Inside Britain from 1939–1945* 1999, UCL

Macksey, Kenneth, *A History of the Royal Armoured Corps and its Predecessors 1914 to 1975* 1983, Newtown

Macksey, Kenneth, *Tank Force: Allied Armour in the Second World War* 1970, Pan/Ballantyne

Macksey, Kenneth, *The Tank Pioneers* 1981, Jane's

Marr, Andrew, *A History of Modern Britain* 2007, MacMillan

Martel, Giffard, *An Outspoken Soldier* 1949, Sifton Praed

McKenzie, Peter, *The Barnbow Story: A History of Armoured Vehicle Manufacture at Leeds* 2000, Longhirst

Milsom, Peter, Sandars, John & Scarborough, Gerald, *Crusader* 1976, Airfix

Moorhead, Alan, *AfricanTrilogy* 2006, Natraj

Mosier, John, *The Blitzkrieg Myth* 2003, Harper Collins

Ness, Leland, *Jane's World War II Tanks and Fighting Vehicles* 2002, Harper Collins

Ogorkiewicz, R.M., *Design and Development of Fighting Vehicles* 1968, MacDonald

Ogorkiewicz, R.M., *Technology of Tanks* 1991, Jane's

Overy, Richard, *Why The Allies Won*, 1995, Cape

Overy, Richard, *The Bombing War: Europe 1939–1945* 2013, Allen Lane

Parker, H.M.D., *History of the Second World War: UK Civil Series: Manpower* 1957, HMSO

Peden, George C., *British Rearmament and the Treasury 1932–1939* 1979, Scottish Academic Press

Perrett, Bryan, *The Matilda* 1973, Ian Allan

Perrett, Bryan, *The Churchill* 1974, Ian Allan

Perrett, Bryan, *Churchill Infantry Tank 1941–1951* 2005, Osprey/New Vanguard

Plant, John, *Cruiser Tank Warfare* 2014, New Generation

Plant, John, *British Anti-tank Warfare* 2014, New Generation

Postan, M.M., *History of the Second World War: UK Civil Series: British War Production* 1952, HMSO

Price, Christopher, *Britain America and Rearmament in the 1930s: The Cost of Failure* 2001, Palgrave Macmillan

Ritchie, Sebastian, *Industry and Air Power: The Expansion of British Aircraft Production 1935–1941* 1997, Frank Cass

Ross, G. Macleod, *The Business of Tanks* 1976, Stockwell

Scott, J.D., *Vickers: A Story* 1963, Weidenfeld & Nicholson

Scott, J.D. & Hughes, Richard, *History of the Second World War: UK Civil Series: The Administration of War Production* 1955, HMSO

Von Senger und Etterlin, F.M., *German Tanks of World War II* 1969, Arms and Armour Press

Shay, Robert Paul, *British Rearmament in the Thirties: Politics and Profits* 1977, Princeton University Press

Smart, A.R., *The Churchill Tank – Its Development and Manufacture* 1946, Journal of the JIE October 1946

Smithers, A.J., *A New Excalibur – The Development of the Tank 1909–1939* 1986, Grafton

Smithers, A.J., *Rude Mechanicals – An account of Tank Maturity during the Second World War* 1987, Grafton

Spencer, Reginald, *Rolls-Royce at Clan Foundry, Belper* 2000, http://www.rrec.co.uk

Sutton, Anthony C., *The Best Enemy Money Can Buy: Chapter 12: Russian Tank Production* http://www.reformed-theology.org/html/books/best_enemy/

Taylor, Dick, *Into the Vally: The Valentine Tank 1938–1960* 2012, MMP

Taylor, Dick, *Firing Now* 2016, MMP

Taylor, Dick, *Panzer III* 2017, Haynes

Taylor, Dick, *Matilda infantry tank* 2021, Haynes

Taylor, Dick & Hughes, Chris, *Comet Cruiser Tank* 2008, Model Centrum

Tooze, Adam, *The Wages of Destruction: The Making and Breaking of the Nazi Economy* 2006, Allen Lane

Tucker, Spencer C., *Weapons and Warfare: Tanks* 2004, Library of Congress

Turner, H.A., *Labour Relations in the Motor Industry* 1967, George Allen & Unwin

Wardlaw-Milne, Sir John, *Command paper 6856 War-Time Tank Production: Report by the Select Committee on National Expenditure* 1946, HMSO

Winton, Harold R. (Ed), *Challenge of Change: Military Institutions and New Realities 1919–1941* 2000, University of Nebraska Press

Index

AFVs
  A1 Independent 20, 21, 79, 94
  A6 Sixteen Tonner 20, 21, 26, 80, 81, 83, 95
  A7 Ten Tonner 19, 27, 68, 81–3, 92, 95
  A9 10–12, 14, 59, 61, 62, 64, 65, 78, 80, 97–100, 102, 136, 140
  A10 11, 14, 59, 65, 69, 89–91, 100, 102, 136, 140
  A11 3, 3, 27, 59, 65, 69, 89–91, 100, 140, 145, 196
  A12 Matilda 5, 8, 15, 51, 589, 65, 72, 78, 91–7, 100, 109–111, 120, 121, 124, 126, 129, 131, 145, 151, 152, 159, 163, 164
  A13 5, 14, 15, 44, 59, 65, 67, 97, 100, 101, 102, 113, 129, 136
  A13 Covenanter 5, 14, 44, 59, 67, 74, 113, 120, 121, 126, 129–34, 136, 159, 163, 193, 194
  A15 Crusader 4, 5, 8, 14, 15, 44, 50, 58, 59, 61, 80, 89, 113, 120, 121, 125, 130, 135–8, 151–4, 159, 163, 164, 167, 176
  A22 Churchill 4, 5, 8, 15, 47, 48, 59, 60, 78, 108, 114, 120, 121, 124–7, 131, 139, 142–9, 151, 155, 159–61, 163, 165, 171, 196, 198
  A24 Cavalier 5, 44, 61, 113, 136, 138, 139, 155, 159, 175, 176, 178
  A27L Centaur 4, 5, 44, 63, 113, 139, 159, 175, 178–83, 194, 195
  A27M Cromwell 4, 14, 15, 59, 113, 125, 126, 139, 153, 159, 161, 163, 164, 167, 168, 175, 177–83, 185, 195, 198, 211
  A30 Challenger 14, 181, 182
  A34 Comet 14, 15, 97, 113, 153, 164, 166, 167, 183, 186, 195, 197, 199, 211
  A41 Centurion 4, 15, 19, 55, 56, 164, 166, 167, 185–9, 199, 200, 211
  Carriers 2, 36, 63
  Close Support tanks 78, 99, 100, 133, 145, 178

Cruiser tanks 3, 5, 7, 23, 26, 34, 59, 60, 63, 64, 69, 97, 105, 108, 109, 111, 113, 119, 121, 122, 141, 163, 195, 196, 203, 204
French tanks 8, 35, 69, 78, 84, 109
German tanks 4, 8, 14, 15, 18, 27, 35, 69, 70–2, 109, 122, 136, 155, 168–72, 179, 185, 188, 193, 203
Heavy tanks 1, 63, 75
Infantry tanks 2, 3, 5, 7, 8, 25, 26, 59, 60, 63, 68, 69, 90, 108, 109, 119, 121, 122, 141, 163, 195, 196, 203, 204
Light tanks & Tankettes 1, 2, 17, 22, 25, 36, 63, 69, 75, 84, 87, 88, 94, 105, 108, 109, 116, 121, 131, 140, 203, 204
Medium tanks 1–3, 7, 17, 21, 35, 46, 51, 63, 75, 79–81, 83, 109
Medium I 16, 75, 76, 82
Medium II 8, 16, 64, 76–9
Medium III 20, 21, 80–3, 92
Russian tanks 14, 22, 27, 35, 100, 122, 142, 193, 203
Specialist tanks 14, 70, 76, 79, 85, 138, 139, 142, 147, 195, 197, 202
TOG 111
US tanks 14, 15, 22, 35, 122, 123, 164, 182, 192, 193, 198, 199, 203, 210
Valentine 4, 5, 14, 15, 44, 59, 60, 63, 89, 111, 120, 121, 126, 140–2, 151, 159, 160, 163, 164, 201
Air raids 115, 116, 123, 170
Armour 3, 7, 8, 60, 64–6, 70, 79, 81, 83, 90, 94, 99, 100–102, 108, 113, 124, 129, 131, 133, 135, 138–41, 160–2, 170, 178, 182, 185, 186, 188
Armour piercing ammunition 7, 78, 117, 170, 181, 184, 197

Canada 63, 69, 142, 164, 201
Capital & Universal tank 4, 122, 164, 195–8
Classification of tanks 4, 5
Communications 17, 78, 79, 81, 82, 90, 185

Construction methods 54
Contracts 58, 59, 61, 63, 75, 96, 130, 142, 144, 146, 147, 176, 185, 189

Doctrine & Policy 3, 6, 11, 26, 39, 50, 68, 69, 79, 90, 100, 109, 117, 145, 160
Drawing Board orders 113, 114, 130, 134, 139, 143, 151, 156

Egypt 64, 75, 95, 110, 133, 134, 137
Engines 9, 10, 34, 47, 64–7, 70, 73, 74, 77, 80, 82, 83, 90, 94, 95, 98, 101, 113, 130–2, 135, 136, 139, 140, 143, 145, 161, 167, 168, 175–80, 183, 186, 188, 195, 199, 211

Finance 18, 21, 24, 29, 30, 32–7, 40, 41, 45, 53, 58, 60, 62, 67, 75, 80, 90, 97, 101, 141, 177, 194
Formations and Units
    Mobile Division 3
    Armoured Divisions 3, 40, 41, 105, 110, 183, 189, 196
    Armoured & Tank Brigades 26, 122, 196, 197, 199
    Cavalry 121
    RAC 121, 122, 152, 158, 160, 163, 184, 196
    RAOC 149
    RTC 2, 6, 11, 12, 16, 17, 21, 25, 36, 77, 152, 172, 189, 195, 208
    RTR 121
    Tank Corps 16, 24, 25, 75
    5DG 189
    15/19H 185
    3RTR 98, 99
    5RTR 102, 189
    6RTR 136
    8RTR 110
    9RTR 147
    3/4CLY 198

Gunnery 69, 77, 80, 83, 95, 178, 187

High explosive ammunition 7, 21, 25, 78, 162, 180, 184, 197

India 17, 24, 25
Industry 18–20, 22, 30, 32, 43, 48, 51, 53, 58, 65, 89, 96, 112, 113, 115, 118, 123, 125, 129–31, 142, 143, 146, 151, 162, 166, 177, 178, 180, 185, 188, 189, 193–5, 206, 210, 211

Lend-Lease 122
Lulworth (Gunnery School) 58, 95

Manpower 11, 23, 45, 46, 48, 49, 51, 52, 54, 60, 74, 92, 107, 108, 124, 126–8
Mock-ups 54, 130, 141, 143, 188

Names 4, 5, 144, 201
Nomenclature 4, 5, 182, 201
North Africa 44, 67, 72, 91, 98, 100, 110, 111, 122, 123, 150, 153, 156, 157, 161, 196, 198
Norway 105

Optical instruments 60, 99, 171, 172
Organisations
    Carden-Loyd 22, 85, 86
    CIGS 24, 25, 53, 141, 156
    DTD 17, 50, 51, 55, 56, 162, 166, 168, 186, 188, 199, 200, 211, 212
    HM Treasury 18, 29, 31–3, 58, 59
    MGO 8, 17–19, 22, 27, 53, 56, 66, 91, 111, 112
    MoS 37, 43, 44, 47, 48, 52, 56–61, 108, 111, 112, 114, 116, 117, 119, 122, 123, 125, 126, 139, 145, 146, 154–8, 160, 162, 165, 167, 173–5, 177, 210, 212
    ROF 17, 19, 81, 89, 102, 189, 211
    Tank Board 8,
    Vickers-Armstrong 4, 11, 17, 19–22, 32, 42, 50–4, 60, 62, 73, 75, 80, 85, 89, 91, 97, 99, 100, 140, 160, 184, 189, 206, 210, 211

Paint 116
Parent companies 43, 50, 60, 91, 96, 138, 143, 148, 185, 189
Personalities
    Broad, Charles 6, 27
    Carden, John 11, 21, 22, 64, 85, 90, 97, 140, 212
    Christie, Walter 67, 100, 101, 129, 135, 183, 188
    Churchill, Winston 30, 75, 107, 108, 110, 111, 113–115, 117, 122, 124, 127, 143, 144, 156, 161, 191, 192, 212
    Elles, Hugh 8, 22, 25, 26, 66, 67, 91, 96, 111
    Fuller, JFC 24, 195
    Gibb, Claude 186, 199, 200, 212
    Hobart, Percy 2
    Liddell Hart, Basil 8, 24, 39

Lindsay, George 6, 2
Little, Leslie 22, 140
Martel, Giffard 2, 8, 22, 66, 84, 85, 100, 101, 130, 156, 167, 212
Nuffield, Lord (William Morris) 44, 61, 101, 135, 139, 152, 153, 178
Pope, Vyvyan 108, 109, 212
Robotham, WA 175–83, 212
Stokes, Richard 191, 212
Tilly, Justice 12, 36, 98, 133
Production
Capacity 23, 32, 153
Delays 62, 112, 120, 123–8
Figures 62, 63, 67, 86, 91, 96, 99, 100, 102, 104, 106, 107, 110, 114, 117, 120, 122, 125, 134, 141–4, 159, 163, 182, 192, 195, 201–206
Forecasts 119–21, 164
Methods 45–54, 65, 66, 76, 77, 96, 112, 131, 149, 165, 210
Organisation 56, 57, 68, 112, 190, 191
Priorities 39, 112, 116
Prototypes & Pilots 36, 57, 58, 91, 101, 113, 130, 132, 143, 144, 147, 151, 163, 185

Quality control 137, 138, 153–5, 179

RAF & MAP 18, 32, 37–42, 49, 54, 55, 67, 68, 72–4, 116, 117, 123–5, 152, 165, 172–7, 194, 208, 210
Railway gauge 12, 13, 186
Raw materials 11, 108, 124
Rearmament 18, 23, 29, 32, 33 63, 208
Re-work programmes 114, 125, 133, 146, 164, 201
Royal Navy & Admiralty 18, 32, 37, 49, 117, 124

Shadow scheme 42, 52, 209
Smoke ammunition 78, 151
Spare parts 126, 156–8, 195
Suspension 11, 60, 67, 77, 81, 82, 92, 97, 98, 100, 101, 102, 129, 135, 140, 178, 179, 183, 188

Tank Armament
2-Pounder 7, 14, 15, 72, 89, 99, 102, 108, 113, 117, 135, 141, 151, 153, 212
3-Pounder 7, 78
6-Pounder 7, 14, 15, 78, 96, 112, 113, 117, 137–9, 142, 145, 146, 166, 170, 178, 180, 211, 212
17-Pounder 14, 15, 147, 181, 182, 187, 197, 212
75mm 15, 142, 180, 181, 184
77mm 14, 181, 183, 184, 185
95mm 78, 145, 178
3" 144
3.7" 78, 99, 100
MG turrets 21, 58, 79, 80, 91, 93, 98, 100, 138
Browning MG 187
BESA MG 100, 102, 132, 135, 144, 187
Polsten Cannon 187
Vickers MG 79–81, 85, 90, 100, 102
Tank testing & trials 25, 58, 131, 133, 134, 136, 149, 163, 176, 180, 189, 194
Ten-Year Rule 29–31, 37, 75, 208
Tracks 11, 99, 102, 131, 134, 182
Turret design 14, 16, 65, 78, 80, 81, 89, 94, 96, 99, 135, 139, 141, 142, 149, 166, 181, 183, 185, 186
Turret rings 13, 14, 71, 101, 136, 148, 149, 181, 185, 186

Universal tank – see Capital tank
Vision cupolas 78, 81, 136, 141, 182, 183, 188

Welding 66, 131, 144, 147, 165, 166, 170, 171, 182, 183, 185, 193–5
Woolwich 17, 19, 46, 53, 76, 165, 189
WW1 3, 6–8, 16, 20, 23–5, 28, 31, 35, 37, 39, 43, 61, 65, 75, 77, 83, 94, 127, 142, 172, 195